CONTEMPORARY'S

Economics

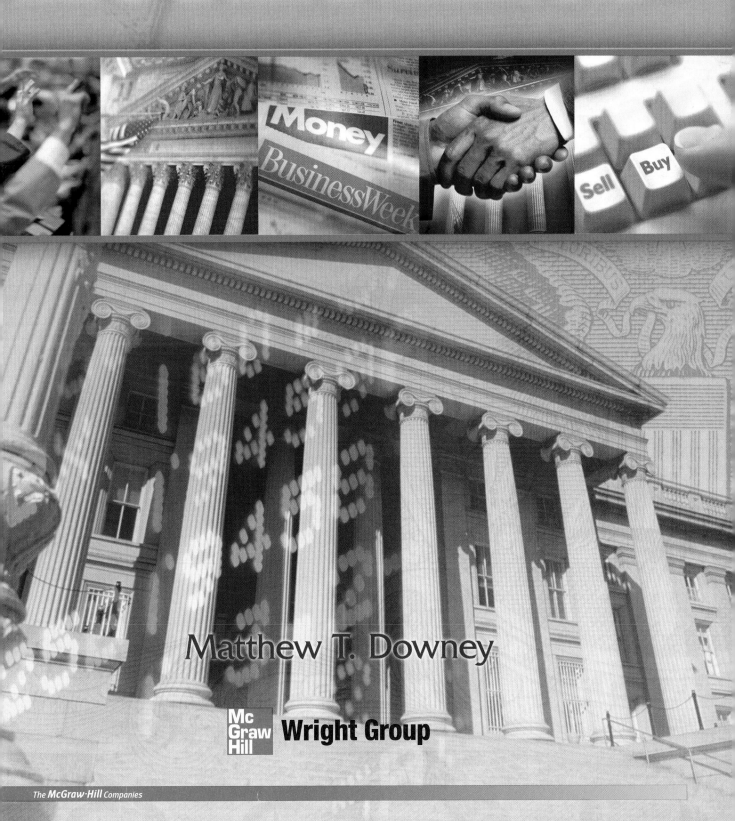

Matthew T. Downey

Mc Graw Hill **Wright Group**

Author

Matthew T. Downey received his Ph.D. in American History from Princeton University. He served as Director of the Clio Project in History-Social Science Education in the Graduate School of Education at the University of California, Berkeley. He also directed the U.C. Berkeley site of the California History-Social Science Project. He has taught at the University of Colorado, the University of California at Los Angeles, and at Louisiana State University. Currently, he directs the Social Science Program and the William E. Hewitt Institute for History and Social Science Education at the University of Northern Colorado.

Contributors

BusinessWeek

BusinessWeek is the most widely read business publication in the world and is the only weekly business news publication in existence. *BusinessWeek* provides incisive and comprehensive interpretation of events by evaluating the news and its implications for the United States, regional, and world economies.

STANDARD
&POOR'S

Standard and Poor's is a leading source of data, news, and analyses on regional, national, and global economic developments. Standard and Poor's information is used by industrial firms, financial institutions, and government agencies for setting policy, managing financial positions, planning production, formulating marketing strategies, and a range of similar activities. Standard and Poor's data services represent the single most sophisticated source of information for organizations that need to understand the impact of the path of economic growth and of government fiscal and monetary policies on their activities.

Senior Editor: Mitch Rosin

Executive Editor: Linda Kwil

Reviewers

Jeanette Bennett
  Economic Education Specialist
  Memphis Branch, Federal Reserve Bank of St. Louis

Jill DeLuccia
  Economics Instructor
  Atlanta, Georgia

Austin Kim
  Financial Analyst
  Los Angeles, California

Bill Lickiss
  Program Manager, National History Day
  College Park, Maryland

Brian Silva
  Social Studies Instructor and Technology Coordinator
  Long Beach, California

Susan Spaulding
  Director, Professional Development
  Florida Council for Economic Education

Consultants

Kimberly Johns
University of Illinois at Chicago

Photo credits are on page 380.

Wright Group

ISBN: 0-07-704441-X (Student Softcover Edition)
ISBN: 0-07-704440-1 (Student Softcover Edition with CD)
ISBN: 0-07-704521-1 (Student Hardcover Edition)
ISBN: 0-07-704522-X (Student Hardcover Edition with CD)

Send all inquiries to:
Wright Group/McGraw-Hill
P.O. Box 812960
Chicago, Illinois 60681

Printed in the United States of America.

5 6 7 8 9 10 QWD/QWD 11 10 09 08 07

Contents

To the Student

This textbook provides an introduction to economics in the United States. It also includes sections about political and economic systems around the global community. Economics is part of our daily lives. It includes making a purchase at the local mall and deciding whether or not to see a movie. This book begins with an examination of the basic concepts in economics: scarcity and choice. Because we cannot have everything we want, we continually make choices.

The book next examines the four key elements of a market economy: demand, supply, price, and competition. Supply and demand are two of the basic concepts in economics. These interact with price and competition in a market economy.

The economy functions, in part, because of the various groups it contains. The next section of the book examines the market institutions of business, finance, labor markets, and government. Business, financial institutions, various labor markets, and the multiple levels of government all work together to promote and maintain competition.

The national economy of the United States is complex. Economists use a variety of measures to monitor and predict how the nation's economy is performing. Government spending and taxes also influence the economy. The next section of this book examines the national economy and the challenges it presents. It also investigates the roles of the Federal Reserve System, inflation, unemployment, and government policies.

We live in a world with a constantly changing economic climate. While change brings opportunities, it also causes problems. The last section of this book examines the global economy. International trade and economic development are important topics that are often highlighted on the evening news. The final chapter in this book presents five case studies that relate to globalization. By having an understanding of other nations and systems, you are better prepared to contribute to the world community.

As a member of the world community, it is important to understand the economic factors that influence your life and the decisions made by businesses and government around the world. I hope that this book helps you to better understand the importance of economics.

Matthew T. Downey

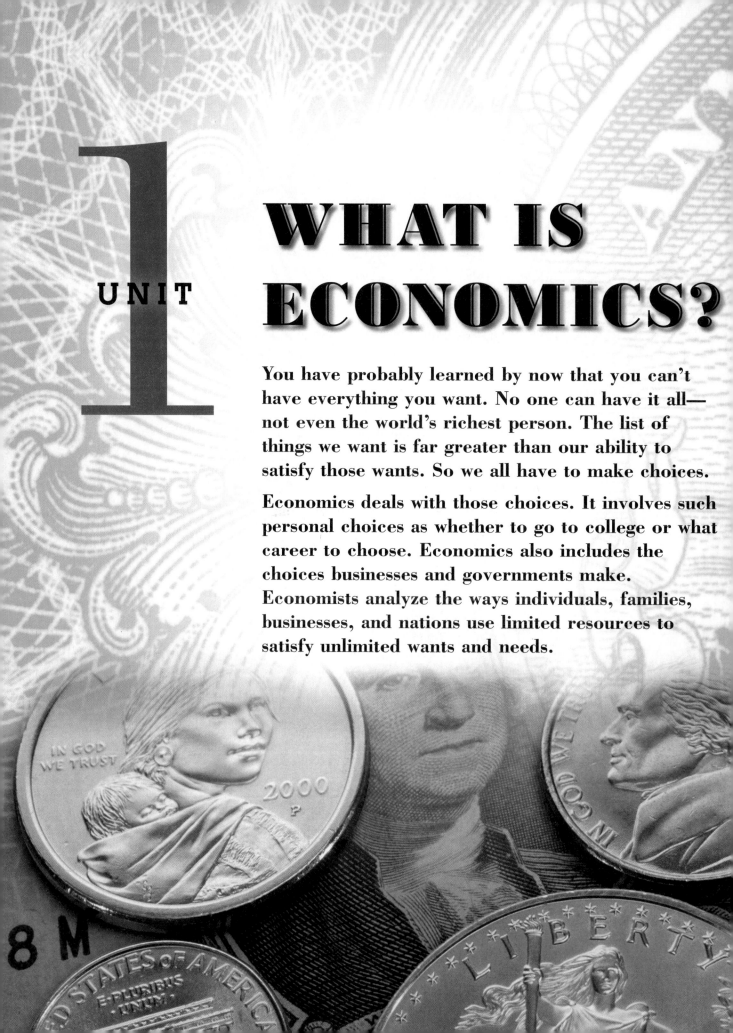

UNIT 1

WHAT IS ECONOMICS?

You have probably learned by now that you can't have everything you want. No one can have it all—not even the world's richest person. The list of things we want is far greater than our ability to satisfy those wants. So we all have to make choices.

Economics deals with those choices. It involves such personal choices as whether to go to college or what career to choose. Economics also includes the choices businesses and governments make. Economists analyze the ways individuals, families, businesses, and nations use limited resources to satisfy unlimited wants and needs.

Chapter

1 SCARCITY AND CHOICE

Getting Focused

Skim this chapter to predict what you will be learning.

- Read the lesson titles and subheadings.
- Look at the illustrations and read the captions.
- Examine the charts and graphs.
- Review the vocabulary words and terms.

Because we cannot have everything we want, we have to make choices. Economics can help us make the most of limited resources. As you read this chapter, turn each heading into a question. As you finish a section, write an answer to that question.

Governments and people must make choices in a world of limited resources. Economics is the study of production, distribution, and consumption of goods and services.

Scarcity: The Basic Economic Problem

Thinking on Your Own

Create a working definition of *scarcity*. A working definition is one that changes and evolves as you read and think about an idea. Write what you know about the term before you begin reading. Then add to that definition as you read and discuss the lesson.

66 "I want that. I need it. I have to have it." Sound familiar? The list of things we want is limitless, but our ability to satisfy those wants is limited. Economics focuses on the ways individuals, businesses, and nations deal with scarcity. How do we decide which wants to satisfy? How can we make the most of our limited ability to acquire the things we want? Without scarcity, we would have no need to choose and no economic problem to solve.

Scarcity means that people do not have enough resources at a given time to satisfy their long list of needs and wants. **Resources** are things people use to produce the things they want or need.

---

focus your reading

What is the economic problem?

What are the characteristics of scarcity?

Explain how trade-offs help people maximize their resources.

vocabulary

scarcity	wants
resources	trade-off
needs	opportunity cost

How many resources can you find in this photograph?

Economists consider the things that keep us alive to be **needs**. Everything else is considered a **want**. Many point out that what starts as a want often becomes a need. To understand why, think about the importance of electricity, indoor plumbing, or a telephone.

Value and Scarcity

Usually people describe something that is rare or in short supply as *scarce*. In economics, scarcity has a slightly different meaning. Scarcity has two important characteristics. To be scarce, an item must have value. It must be useful to someone. Second, an item must be in short supply in comparison to the number of people who would like to own the product.

Gasoline is a good example. In the 1850s, when workers refined oil to make kerosene, they threw out the gasoline they accidentally produced. It was not valued, because no one had a use for it. Forty years later, in 1893, two Americans invented a gasoline-powered car. By 1920, nine million of those cars were on the road in the United States, and gasoline had become a scarce resource.

The supply of gasoline did not change much between 1850 and 1920. The only thing that changed was the value attached to gasoline. Economists refer to this kind of scarcity as *relative scarcity*. The world has a large supply of gasoline, but it is

The price of gasoline has risen dramatically over the years. How does the concept of relative scarcity apply to gasoline prices today?

scarce in comparison to the number of people who want it. People today need gasoline to keep their cars running.

Making Choices

In choosing one thing over another, we make a **trade-off**. We give up one thing in order to have another. You and a friend decide to go to a ball game. That decision has a cost that goes beyond the price of your tickets.

In going to the game, you are also giving up the next best alternative. It is what you would have done if you had not gone to the game. For example, you might have spent the afternoon practicing your jump shot. The **opportunity cost** of watching the game was missing the practice. Whenever you choose one thing over another, you give up the next best option.

As consumers, people make decisions based on opportunity cost every day.

Putting It All Together

Why is scarcity the basic problem in economics? Write a paragraph that answers the question and explains its importance.

The Factors of Production

Thinking on Your Own

As you read about the factors of production, create a three-column chart. In column one, list each factor of production. In column two, write a brief definition of each factor, and in column three, give examples of the factor.

The problem of scarcity affects individuals, families, businesses, and nations, because no one has an unlimited supply of resources. A resource is anything used to produce goods and services. **Goods** are products like motion pictures, soap, cereal, cars, or T-shirts. Goods are things you can touch or see. **Services** are activities that satisfy a want or need. Teachers perform a service. So do clerks, doctors, lawyers, and police officers.

Resources are often divided into four large groups known as the **factors of production**. They are natural resources, human resources, capital resources, and entrepreneurship. Wealth is determined by how much of each factor an individual, business, or nation has.

focus your reading

Describe how each factor of production contributes to the production of goods and services.

How does capital contribute to the production of goods and services?

Explain how entrepreneurs play a unique role in the production of goods and services.

vocabulary

goods

services

factors of production

natural resources

human resources

capital resources

productivity

entrepreneurship

Natural resources include wind power.

Natural Resources

Natural resources refer to anything found in nature that can be used to produce goods or services. Economists sometimes refer to this factor of production as *land* with the understanding that it includes much more than soil.

Human resources are an important factor of production.

Land is a natural resource, as are oil and water. Air, plants, animals, iron ore, and other minerals are all natural resources. Environments like forests, mountains, oceans, and deserts are natural resources as well.

Human Resources

Human effort is needed to change natural resources into finished goods and services. That effort is sometimes called *labor*. Labor means more than physical work. It also includes jobs that involve planning, organizing, managing, and distributing the process of turning raw materials into goods and services.

stop and think

How does a gas station use natural resources to provide a service? How does it use human resources? Compare and contrast the way a gas station uses these two factors of production with the way a grocery store uses those same resources. How are the two uses similar? What differences do you notice?

Capital Resources

Capital resources refer to technology—the tools and other manufactured goods used to make other goods and services. Machines are examples of capital resources. So are buildings.

When capital resources are combined with natural and human resources, the value of all three factors of production increases. Capital boosts **productivity**—the amount of goods and services that result from the input of a certain amount of natural and human resources. The manufacture of cars is a good example. In 1901, a young machinist named Henry Ford started a car company. At first, he struggled to stay in business. In those days cars were so expensive that only a handful of people could afford one. Then Ford came up with an idea. He would find a way to make cars faster, and therefore cheaper, so that more people could purchase a car.

What capital resources can you identify in this photograph of a Ford assembly line?

In 1913, workers needed 12 hours and 28 minutes to build one car. The following year, with new production methods, Ford was able to produce a car every 90 minutes. In 1912, a Ford cost $600—more than a year's salary for most people at the time. By 1916, the cost had dropped to $360. The number of workers did not change, but with the new tools, their productivity increased. By 1916, Ford had sold well over one million cars.

Entrepreneurship

Entrepreneurship is the fourth factor of production. The word describes the work of people who start new businesses, introduce new products and services, or develop new ways of managing the factors of production. Entrepreneurs take risks in order to make money. However, they don't always succeed. Only a few become successful.

Entrepreneurship is important in business, especially with new technology.

Henry Ford was an entrepreneur. He had an idea that by changing the way cars were built, he could produce more cars for less money. He took a chance on his idea, and it made him and his company very rich. His idea also changed the way Americans lived and worked.

Putting It All Together

Use the chart you created in Thinking on Your Own to explain how the four factors of production work together to produce one of the following goods: T-shirts, bread, or a baseball bat. How might the scarcity of one or more factors affect the process of production?

reading for understanding

Explain Samuel Colt's idea.

On which factor of production did his idea focus?

Why did he think it would boost productivity?

With which factor of production do you associate Colt?

Samuel Colt's Idea

In the 1830s, Samuel Colt invented the Colt revolver. This gun could be fired six times without reloading. Many people claim that it helped the United States settle the West. Colt had a plan for manufacturing his guns. He explained his idea in a letter to his father:

"The first workman would receive two or three of the most important parts, and would affix these together and pass them on to the next who would do the same, and so on until the complete [revolver] is put together. It would then be inspected and given the finishing touches by experts and each [gun] would be exactly alike and all of its parts would be the same. The workmen, by constant practice in a single operation, would become highly skilled and at the same time very quick and expert at their particular task. So you have better guns and more of them for less money than if you hire men and have each one make the entire [revolver]."

Quoted in *Yankee Arms Maker: The Incredible Career of Samuel Colt,* by Jack Rohan (Harper & Bros., 1935).

Curriculum Connection

The Digital Hospital

Learn how the four factors of production are helping to save lives in a New Jersey hospital.

Peter A. Gross has been a doctor for 40 years, rising up the ranks to become chairman of internal medicine at Hackensack University Medical Center in Hackensack, N.J. But one day this winter, a homeless man checked into the hospital with HIV [the virus that causes AIDS], and Gross made a decision that could have seriously harmed his patient. He chose to give the patient an HIV drug, tapping a request into a hospital computer and zapping it off to the two-year-old digital drug-order entry system. Moments later he got back a message he never would have received before the system was in place: a warning that the drug would mix dangerously with the antidepressant the patient was already taking. Gross got on the phone to figure out the problem, eventually asking the man's psychiatrist to reduce the dosage of his antidepressant. "There's no way I would have picked that up," Gross says. "It was totally unexpected."

Scenes like this are unfolding across the country, providing a glimpse into the potential of information technology to transform the health-care industry. ■

"The Digital Hospital" by Timothy J. Mullaney and Arlene Weintraub. *BusinessWeek*, March 28, 2005.

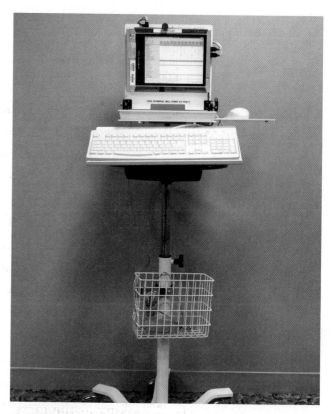

A WIRELESS MOBILE laptop, or "chart on wheels," is used by nurses to input patients' vital signs and other information.

reading for understanding

What decision did the doctor make? Why might that decision have harmed his patient?

Who alerted the doctor that he had made a mistake?

To what factor of production does the warning system belong?

Explain how that factor of production improved productivity. How did it help save lives?

Economic Decision-making

Thinking on Your Own

As you read about economic decision-making, list the steps that can help you make the most of your choices.

Whenever we choose one thing over another, we are making a trade-off. The cost of that trade-off is known as an opportunity cost. In deciding on one thing over another, we lose the opportunity to have the next best alternative. Understanding what will be gained and lost in the choices we make can help us make more informed decisions. The goal is to **maximize**—to get the most from our choices.

focus your reading

Why does knowing the facts help people maximize their choices?

What part do opinions play in making decisions?

Discuss how models help people make better trade-offs.

vocabulary

maximize   subjective

objective   model

Facts and Opinions

How do we get the most from the choices we make? One way to begin is by looking at the facts. What are the benefits of each option? What will be gained by choosing it? Facts are **objective**; that is, they can be measured and their truth tested. For example, you and a friend are debating whether to go to a movie or rent a film to watch at home. You can verify the price of a ticket and the cost of a rental by making two phone calls. That information can help you make an informed choice.

However, money may not be the deciding factor in the choice you make. If you prefer to see films as soon as they are released, you may decide to go to the theater even though the tickets cost more than a rental. A personal preference or a value judgment cannot be measured or tested. It is **subjective**—based on likes and dislikes rather than facts. In maximizing limited resources, we have to take into account both the facts and our values and personal preferences.

As consumers, we weigh costs and benefits each time we shop.

Weighing Costs and Benefits

Making choices also involves identifying the opportunity cost of each option. If we have limited resources (and everyone does), we want to make the most of those resources.

Economists use a model called the production possibilities curve to help them analyze trade-offs. A **model** is a graph, diagram, or other simplified view of the real world. Models focus on certain information and ignore everything else. Because the information in the model is limited, it makes clear the opportunity cost of a trade-off. A production possibilities curve is a model that shows the greatest amount of goods or services that can be produced from a fixed amount of resources in a limited time period.

Graphs are models that are particularly useful for highlighting the relationship between various combinations of two values. As demonstrated on the graph below, one value is shown along the line at the bottom—the horizontal line, or x-axis. The other appears on the line on the left side of the graph—the vertical line, or y-axis.

Figure 1.1 shows a production possibilities curve for a yard work business. Suppose you spend 20 hours a week mowing

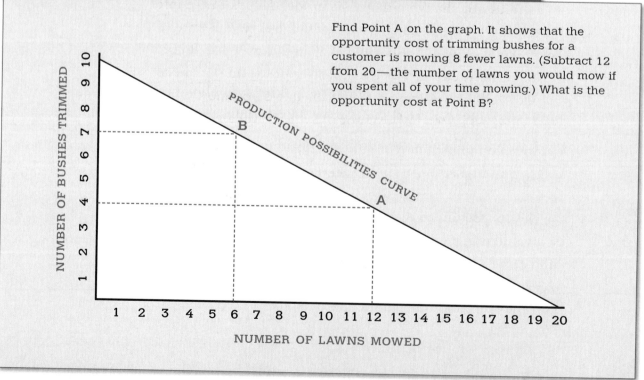

Production Possibilities for Yard Work (based on a 20-hour workweek)   Figure 1.1

Find Point A on the graph. It shows that the opportunity cost of trimming bushes for a customer is mowing 8 fewer lawns. (Subtract 12 from 20—the number of lawns you would mow if you spent all of your time mowing.) What is the opportunity cost at Point B?

PRODUCTION POSSIBILITIES CURVE

NUMBER OF BUSHES TRIMMED

NUMBER OF LAWNS MOWED

lawns with a push mower. It takes you one hour to mow one lawn. Recently, several customers have asked to have their bushes trimmed as well. It is a more time-consuming job. It takes two hours per yard to trim the bushes.

The *x*-axis shows the number of lawns that can be mowed in a 20-hour workweek. The *y*-axis shows the number of bushes trimmed. Notice that if you devote all of your resources to mowing lawns, you can mow 20 lawns a week. If you devote all of your resources to trimming bushes, you will satisfy 10 customers a week. The opportunity cost for trimming bushes for one customer is mowing two fewer lawns each week—18 lawns instead of 20.

The graph shows that the more bushes you trim, the less time you have to mow lawns. Although the model shows that you can trim bushes as well as mow lawns, it also shows that you cannot increase the amount of time spent on one activity without giving up time on the other.

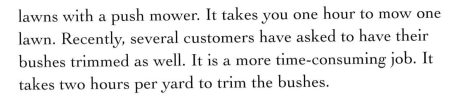

> **stop and think**
>
> Discuss with a partner the section you just read. What is the opportunity cost of each choice? Make a recommendation about lawn mowing. Then make a list of five decisions you made last week and the opportunity costs associated with each.

Applying Models to Real Life

Economic models always assume some factors will not change. For example, the number of hours you are able to work stays the same on the model shown on page 12. Your next best choice does not change either. The model does not take into account unexpected changes—a week of heavy rain or a broken lawn mower. It does not take into account an increase in productivity, either. For example, suppose you borrow a gas-powered mower from a neighbor. It lets you mow a lawn in 30 minutes, instead of one hour. By mowing lawns more quickly, you will have more time to trim bushes.

The graph does not tell you whether you should add trimming bushes to your yard work business. It simply provides a clear picture of the opportunity costs involved in doing so.

Putting It All Together

Use the list you created in Thinking on Your Own to write a letter giving a friend advice on how to use trade-offs and opportunity costs to make a decision.

Chapter Summary

- Economics focuses on the ways individuals, businesses, and governments deal with the problems caused by a long list of **wants** and **needs** and limited **resources**.

- **Scarcity** refers to things that have value and are in short supply in comparison to the number of people who would like to have them.

- In making a **trade-off**, people give up one thing in order to have another.

- An **opportunity cost** is the result of a trade-off; it is the cost of the next best alternative.

- Economic resources are used to produce **goods** and **services**.

- The four **factors of production** are **natural resources**, **human resources**, **capital resources**, and **entrepreneurship**.

- The use of capital increases **productivity**.

- The aim of economic decision-making is to **maximize** scarce resources.

- Taking into account both **objective** and **subjective** information is a part of economic decision-making.

- Economists use **models** in decision-making.

Chapter Review

1 Explain the connection among the following three terms: scarcity, trade-off, and opportunity cost.

2 Draw a diagram that shows how the four factors of production work together to produce goods or services.

3 Choose one of the economic systems studied in this chapter and describe its advantages and disadvantages.

4 In your opinion, which economic system is most beneficial to ordinary people? Write a paragraph stating your opinion. Be sure to include reasons and evidence to support your answer.

Skill Builder

Main Idea and Details

Finding the main idea of a lesson, paragraph, or passage can help you organize information. One way to figure out the main idea is by finding the **topic sentence**. It is the sentence in the paragraph that talks about the big picture. Sometimes it refers to more than one thing.

Details support the main idea. Detail sentences are usually more specific than the topic sentence. They focus on a single idea or a part of an idea. Words or phrases like *for example, that is,* or *first, second,* or *third* often signal a detail sentence. Most detail sentences support, give examples, prove, explain, or point toward the main idea in some way.

How can you be sure that you have found the topic sentence? Turn the sentence into a question. If the other sentences seem to answer the question, then you've found the topic sentence.

Read the following paragraphs, which appear in this chapter. Find the main idea and then answer the questions that follow.

> **Natural resources** refer to anything found in nature that can be used to produce goods or services. Economists sometimes refer to this factor of production as *land* with the understanding that it includes much more than soil.
>
> Land is a natural resource, as are oil and water. Air, plants, animals, iron ore, and other minerals are all natural resources. Environments like forests, mountains, oceans, and deserts are natural resources as well.

1 What is the main idea?

2 Name three details.

3 How does each of the details you named support the main idea?

Chapter

2 ECONOMIC SYSTEMS

Getting Focused

Skim this chapter to predict what you will be learning.

- Read the lesson titles and subheadings.
- Look at the illustrations and read the captions.
- Examine the chart.
- Review the vocabulary words and terms.

Every country has an economic system. It consists of all of the ways that its people have developed to decide what goods and services to provide, how to produce those goods and services, and for whom to do so. As you read this chapter, compare and contrast the various ways those decisions are made.

Much like highway systems, economic systems link multiple components so that they can work together.

The Basic Economic Questions

Thinking on Your Own

As you read, identify the three basic economic questions. Then draw a diagram that explains how those questions are connected to one another.

An **economic system** consists of all of the ways a nation or society uses limited resources to satisfy its people's unlimited wants and needs. Scarcity forces nations and their citizens to make tough choices. As a result, every country has to answer three basic economic questions: *What* goods and services will be produced? *How* will those goods and services be produced? *For whom* will they be produced?

focus your reading

State the questions every economic system has to answer.

Explain how nations decide what goods and services to produce and how to distribute them.

How do you account for differences in the ways the basic economic questions are answered?

vocabulary

economic system

allocate

efficient

What to Produce

In a world where resources are scarce, nations have to decide which needs and wants to satisfy. Should they produce more consumer products like bicycles, clothing, and cell phones, or more capital goods like factories, bulldozers, and robots? What are the trade-offs? What are the opportunity costs?

recall

Scarcity means that people do not have enough resources at a given time to satisfy their needs and wants.

A **trade-off** is giving up one thing in order to have another.

An **opportunity cost** is when you choose one thing over another, giving up the next best option.

In weighing alternatives, a nation is deciding how to **allocate**, or divide, limited resources among hundreds of thousands of possible goods and services. For example, if a nation is facing a possible war, its leaders may choose to produce fewer cars and more tanks and trucks for the military. When the danger passes, fewer tanks will be needed and the production of cars may increase.

Businesses make decisions every day about what, how, and for whom to produce.

How to Produce

Once the decision is made to produce a particular product, someone has to decide how it will be made and with what resources. Which workers will make the bicycles and which will build the computers? What skills will each group need? Will those jobs be done by businesses that are privately owned or government-owned? What role will technology play in the production process?

In a world where resources are scarce, producers seek the most **efficient** method of production. That is, they want to use as few resources as possible to produce as many goods as possible.

For Whom to Produce

Once goods and services have been produced, someone has to decide who will get those goods and services. You may have heard the saying "money talks" and, at some times and in some

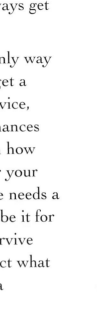

places, it does. If two families want to buy the same house, the one who offers the most money will almost always get the house.

Money is not the only way of deciding who will get a particular good or service, however. If you attend a public school, for example, chances are that your admission to the school was not based on how much money your family has. It was based on whether your family lives in the district the school serves. If someone needs a medicine in short supply, doctors usually try to prescribe it for patients who need it the most and are least likely to survive using other methods of treatment. Such decisions reflect what people in a particular society consider fair and just in a particular case.

Money is one factor in determining who buys or receives a good or service.

Putting It All Together

With a partner, discuss how a nation's response to one of the three basic economic questions affects its responses to the other two. Use the diagram that you began at the start of the lesson.

Kinds of Economic Systems

Thinking on Your Own

As you read about economic systems, create a three-column chart. In column one, explain how each system answers the question of *what* to produce. In column two, write a brief explanation of *how* those goods and services are produced. In column three, explain *for whom* those goods and services are produced.

Every society has to address the three basic economic questions—what to produce, how to produce it, and for whom. In doing so, societies have to make trade-offs. That is, its members have to give up some things in order to get others. Economists have identified three main ways societies respond to scarcity.

Traditional Economies

For much of human history, people looked to the past for answers to the three basic economic questions. In a pure **traditional economy**, each generation lives the way earlier generations did. For example, if you live in a traditional economy and your parents are farmers, some day you, too, will farm for a living. When that day comes, you will prepare your land, plant your seeds, and harvest your crops in much the way your parents, grandparents, and great-grandparents did. The past will also determine whether you sell your harvest in the local market, use it for your family, or give a portion of it to a political or religious leader.

focus your reading

Who controls the factors of production in each economic system?

How do you account for differences in the ways goods and services are produced and distributed in each economic system?

In what ways are the three economic systems alike? What are the major differences?

vocabulary

traditional economy

stable

incentive

command economy

market economy

In many traditional economies, such as in the Peruvian Andes, economic decisions are based on customs.

Traditional economies are **stable**—that is, they change very little from one generation to the next. In fact, change is discouraged. People have no **incentive**, or encouragement, to try new ideas or invent new products. Entrepreneurship has little or no value in a traditional economy.

> **recall**
>
> **Entrepreneurship** is the idea of taking a risk to start a new business.

The other three factors of production—natural resources, human resources, and capital resources—also have limited value, because they cannot be bought or sold. This does not mean that no one owns mines, land, or other property. It does mean that people are not free to buy or sell those resources. Workers are not free either. They cannot improve their lives by finding a new job or acquiring a new skill.

Today, traditional economies can be found only in the most remote communities. No modern country has a traditional economy because it is difficult to avoid the technological and social changes that are part of the modern world.

> **stop and think**
>
> What would your future be like if you lived in a traditional society? What might you gain? What might you lose?

Command Economies

The word *command* means "to have control" or "to direct activities." It is a good name for an economic system in which a central authority or government provides the answers to the questions of *what, how,* and *for whom* to produce goods and services.

In a pure **command economy**, the government makes most of the decisions about production and distribution. It identifies the needs of the economy and then decides not only which goods and services to produce, but also how to create those goods and services. The government can do so because it owns or controls most of the factors of production. It owns the country's natural and capital resources. It also trains and hires most workers. Once goods and services have been created, the government also decides how those products will be distributed.

North Korea still maintains a command economy.

Those who favor a command economy assume that the nation's planners are able to determine what is best for everyone within the system. They also assume that government planners can figure out the opportunity costs of every decision. In the modern world, where even the smallest decision can have a wide variety of consequences, that kind of knowledge may be harder to obtain than many people realize.

For some tasks, a command system works well. For example, in wartime or after a natural disaster, a nation with a strong central economy is quickly able to redirect resources to deal with the emergency. For other tasks, a command system does not work at all—mainly because it provides no incentives for people to do their best or show ingenuity. For example, the government of India used to own many businesses. In 1979, one of those companies employed 1,200 people. For 12 years, those employees showed up for work every day and were paid regularly. The only problem was that they never produced a product that could be sold. The workers had no incentive to produce.

Adam Smith and the "Invisible Hand"

Adam Smith, a Scottish political economist and moral philosopher, is often called the "father of economics." In 1776, he published a book called *The Wealth of Nations*. It describes a market economy and explains how it works. Smith believed that as people in a free society try to better themselves, they find that others have similar goals and that taking care of yourself makes everyone better off.

According to Smith, people determine how many goods and services will be produced. How do they do it? If people prefer DVD players to VCRs, they will buy more DVD players. Their preference for the product will, in turn, encourage manufacturers to produce more.

Smith explained that every individual acts in his or her own self-interest. "He intends only his own gain, and he is in this, as in many other cases, led by an invisible hand to promote an end which was no part of his intention. . . . By pursuing his own interest he frequently promotes that of the society more effectually than when he really intends to promote it."

reading for understanding

What is the "invisible hand" that Adam Smith describes?

Explain how the "invisible hand" influences how a nation answers the basic economic question.

Who plays a similar role in a command economy?

Market Economies

In a **market economy**, ordinary people decide *what, how,* and *for whom* to produce goods and services with little or no government involvement. They make those decisions through the market. In economics, a *market* is more than a place where people buy and sell goods. It is any arrangement that makes buying and selling easier. In many large markets, buyers and sellers never meet.

A market economy answers the three basic economic questions by taking advantage of self-interest. Workers exchange their labor for wages or salaries. They use this income to buy goods and services. Owners of natural and capital resources provide these factors of production in return for rent and other payments. Owners of businesses use their income not only to buy goods and services, but also to purchase new equipment to modernize or expand their businesses.

The question *for whom* is answered through the market. Prices—the cost of goods and services—help to solve the problem of distribution by forcing buyers to make choices.

In a market economy, consumers determine what goods and services are produced.

Economists consider a market economy an efficient approach to production and distribution. It allocates scarce resources according to the supply of those resources and the demand for various goods and services. However, it puts those without the money to pay for the resources at a disadvantage.

Putting It All Together

Use the chart you created in Thinking on Your Own to describe similarities in the way each economic system described in this lesson responds to the three basic economic questions. How do you account for differences?

Economic Systems in the Real World

Thinking on Your Own

As you read about economic systems in the world today, look for reasons that they are all, to some degree, a mixture of traditional, command, and market systems. Write a bulleted list of reasons in your notebook.

In the real world, no country has a pure traditional, command, or market economy. Modern nations combine some elements of all three types. Therefore, to some degree, every economic system today is a **mixed economy**.

On a Continuum

The fact that all economic systems are mixed does not mean they are all alike. Some are closer to a command economy, while others rely on the market for most decisions.

One way to think about the range of economic systems is by creating a **continuum**—a collection of points along a straight line. At one end of the line is a pure command economy, and at the other end is a pure market economy.

focus your reading

Why are all economic systems today mixed economies?

Discuss the purpose of an economic continuum.

How do transitional economies differ from other economic systems?

vocabulary

mixed economy

continuum

transitional economy

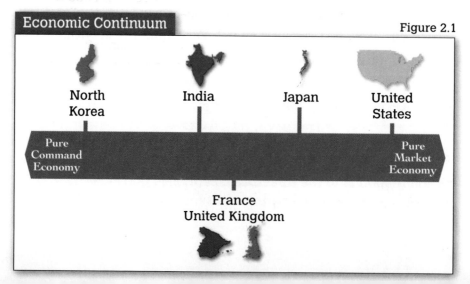

Economic Continuum

Figure 2.1

North Korea   India   Japan   United States

Pure Command Economy   Pure Market Economy

France
United Kingdom

A mixed economy has limited government involvement, such as inspectors to ensure the safety of food.

No economic system today is at either extreme on the continuum. The nations that are closest to the command side are North Korea and Cuba. In both, the government makes most of the decisions about what to produce and how to produce it. Individuals have very little say about what is available in the marketplace. Experts would place China further from a pure command economy than North Korea, but not as close to a pure market economy as France or the United Kingdom. Why? China's government controls much of the nation's economy, even though it allows for some private businesses.

Closest to the market side of the continuum is the United States. It is more market-oriented than other nations and has less government planning. Yet, the United States has laws that protect consumers, outlaw child labor, and require that employers pay their workers a minimum wage. Toward the middle of the continuum are countries like the United Kingdom and France. In both, the government controls more of the economy than is true in the United States, but far less than in North Korea or Cuba.

stop and think

Copy the economic systems continuum in your notebook. Suppose a country has free markets but the government owns all of its airlines and railroads. The government also controls the nation's health-care system. Where on the continuum would you place that country?

Changing Economies

A nation's place on an economic continuum is not fixed. It can change over time. For example, in the 1980s, China's economy was closer to a pure command system than it is today. Over the past 20 years, the Chinese have encouraged some elements of a market economy—including private ownership of some businesses.

China is one of a number of nations today that have **transitional economies**. The word *transition* means "to change or shift." Many of these countries once had command economies. Today they are in the process of shifting to a market economy. Some economists used to think the shift could take place within a few months. Today, many realize that creating a market economy requires more than selling state-owned businesses to private citizens. Attitudes and values also have to change. For example, under a command economy, the manager of a factory had no incentive to improve efficiency or boost productivity. After all, with government support, he or she could not be fired and the company could not go out of business. In a market economy, managers have strong incentives to improve efficiency and productivity.

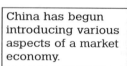
China has begun introducing various aspects of a market economy.

As transitional economies change, their growth affects not only people in their own countries but also those in other nations. They open new markets, develop new ideas, and build new relationships. You will learn more about market economies in the chapters that follow.

Putting It All Together

What are the trade-offs in changing from a traditional economy to a market economy? What are the opportunity costs?

How India Sprang into Action

TSUNAMI SURVIVORS rush for food and clothes donated by volunteer organizations.

In December 2004, a tsunami struck Southeast Asia. The head of *Business Week*'s Bombay bureau traveled to the state of Tamil Nadu to see its effects on people there. In her report, she notes:

After hearing so many stories of . . . the slow pace of the tsunami relief effort, I was surprised to find the East Coast Road south of Madras crowded with trucks carrying grain, water, tents, and clothing. India's record in such catastrophes is dismal: The country has been hit by eight natural calamities since 1989 and has rarely been able to get food, water, and shelter efficiently to the victims. But this time, in the district of Cuddalore, authorities sprang into action, quickly providing relief to local fishermen and their families. In at least this small corner of India, local administration took the steps necessary to care for those in need.

One key to the effort is Gagandeep Singh Bedi. He is Cuddalore's "district collector," the most powerful local official in India's administrative system. The 36-year-old civil servant learned about the tsunami the hard way: He was having breakfast at a waterfront restaurant when the waves struck. . . Within two hours he had mobilized the police,

hospitals, doctors, the phone company, and the state transit authority. Four hours later, Bedi had called a meeting of community leaders and asked individuals and non-government organizations to pool their resources with those of government agencies.

That translated into quick relief. ∎

"How India Is Springing into Action" by Manjeet Kripalani. *BusinessWeek*, January 17, 2005.

reading for understanding

Who decided what, how, and for whom goods and services were produced in Cuddalore after the tsunami?

What kind of economic system does the journalist describe?

What are the advantages of the economy described in the reading after a natural disaster?

Chapter Summary

- An **economic system** is the way a nation or society uses limited resources to satisfy its people's unlimited wants and needs.

- In making decisions, nations choose how to **allocate** limited resources among hundreds of thousands of possible goods and services.

- Producers seek the most **efficient** method of production.

- In a **traditional economy**, each generation answers the basic economic questions in much the same way its parents and grandparents did.

- Traditional economies are **stable** but provide no incentives to try new ideas, invent new products, or increase productivity.

- In a **command economy**, a central authority or government provides the answers to the basic economic questions.

- In a **market economy**, the market provides answers to the three basic questions of economics.

- A **mixed economy** contains elements of traditional, command, and market economies. Most economies can be placed on a **continuum** between command and market systems.

- Economies that are changing are known as **transitional economies**.

Chapter Review

1 Explain how values and beliefs shape the way a nation answers the three basic economic questions.

2 How does a change in one part of an economy affect other parts of the economy?

3 In a paragraph, compare and contrast how the three types of market systems discussed in this chapter each answer the three basic economic questions.

Skill Builder

Comparison and Contrast

When you make a comparison, you study two or more individuals, groups, ideas, events, or objects. Then you look for the ways they are alike (compare) and ways they differ (contrast) from one another.

For example, Chapter 2 compared and contrasted three economic systems. The point of the comparison was how each answered the three basic economic questions. The chart on this page compares a command economy with a market economy. The title of the chart explains the point of the comparison.

Study the chart and then answer the questions that follow.

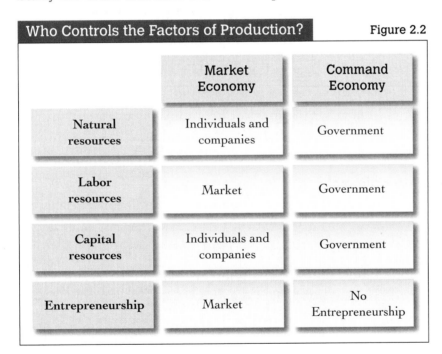

Who Controls the Factors of Production?   Figure 2.2

	Market Economy	Command Economy
Natural resources	Individuals and companies	Government
Labor resources	Market	Government
Capital resources	Individuals and companies	Government
Entrepreneurship	Market	No Entrepreneurship

1 What is the point of comparison—that is, on what idea does the chart focus?

2 In which economic system do ordinary people have the most say?

3 Who decides *how* goods will be produced in a market economy?

4 Who decides *what* natural resources will be used to produce goods and services in a command economy?

Chapter

3 ECONOMIC FACTORS

Getting Focused

Skim this chapter to predict what you will be learning.

- Read the lesson titles and subheadings.
- Look at the illustrations and read the captions.
- Examine the charts and graphs.
- Review the vocabulary words and terms.

In Chapter 2, you learned that a market economy seeks to get the most out of scarce resources. In this chapter, you will learn why a market economy encourages efficiency and the results of that efficiency. As you read this chapter, pay close attention to the causes and effects of the choices people make.

Advances in technology can dramatically improve a country's economic position.

How a Market Economy Works

Thinking on Your Own

As you read, trace the flow of goods and services and factors of production through a market economy. Draw a flowchart in your notebook.

A system is a group or set of parts that work together as a whole. A change in one part of a system affects the other parts. A computer is an example of a system with many parts that work together. So is the human body. An economic system consists of individuals and groups that work together to satisfy unlimited wants and needs with scarce resources. Every economic system provides an organized way of producing and distributing goods and services.

In a market economy, **producers** are the people who transform or change natural resources, labor, and capital resources (three of the four factors of production) into goods and services. Entrepreneurship, the fourth factor of production, is a special form of labor. It describes the work of people who start new businesses and introduce new products and services. They also develop new ways of managing the other factors of production. All four factors are essential to the working of a market economy.

focus your reading

What are the characteristics of a market economy?

Explain what a circular flow model shows about the way a market system works.

What motivates individuals and groups to participate in various markets?

vocabulary

producers

consumers

profit

competition

efficient

circular flow model

factor market

product market

recall

Entrepreneurship describes the work of people who develop new products, services, or ways of managing factors of production.

Resources are things people use to produce the things they want and need.

Economic Factors 31

Characteristics of a Market Economy

No two economies are exactly alike. Every market economy is based on economic freedom, trade, private property, profit, and competition.

There is economic freedom in a market economy. Individuals and groups are free to make choices. Individuals can choose a career, a place to live, and an employer. They can also decide what to do with their earnings. They can save money, buy goods and services, or invest in a business. Businesses also make choices. They are free to decide what kinds of goods or services to offer and how to produce those goods and services.

As its name suggests, a market economy is based on trade. Buyers and sellers are free to enter and leave the market and find exchanges that benefit each. Before **consumers**—people who buy and use goods and services—make a purchase, they have to believe that the product or service they are buying is worth the purchase price. Similarly, sellers must feel that whatever they receive for the item is more valuable than the item itself.

In a market economy, individuals and businesses have the right to own property. They are also able to freely buy and sell land, a business, a car, their skills, or anything else. In the United States, the Constitution guarantees the right to own and use private property. A wide variety of laws protect that right. No city, state, or national government can take away a person's property without payment to the owner. The right to own property gives people an incentive or motive to produce goods and services.

In a market economy, people are willing to risk some wealth in the hopes of making a profit. A **profit** is the extent to which an individual or group is better off after buying or selling a good or service. A person may gain money or satisfaction from the exchange. Profits as an incentive motivate both consumers and producers to participate in various markets.

The right to own private property is an incentive in a market economy.

Yet another characteristic of a market economy is a rivalry among producers or sellers of goods and services. For **competition** to exist, individuals and businesses have to be free to enter or leave a market at any time. Competition encourages the production of products that are innovative, high in quality, and low in price. It also encourages the **efficient** use of resources. Companies have to make the most of their resources if they are going to earn as large a profit as possible.

The Circular Flow of Economic Activity

A **circular flow model** (Figure 3.1) shows how a market economy organizes the production and consumption of goods and services. Individuals and businesses participate in two kinds of markets. One is the **factor market**—a market in which the factors of production are bought and sold. In this market, businesses hire workers for wages and salaries. Anyone who has ever had a job has participated in the factor market. Businesses also purchase natural resources. Additionally, they buy or rent tools and other forms of capital in factor markets.

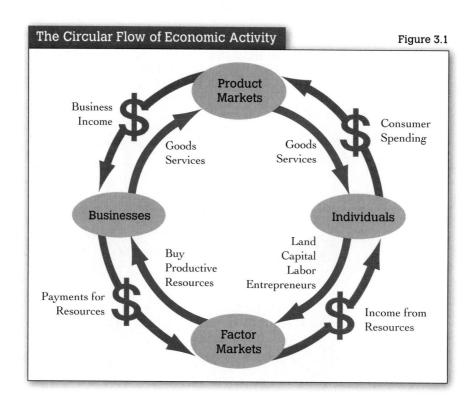

The Circular Flow of Economic Activity   Figure 3.1

Businesses use the factors of production to produce goods and services. Those goods and services are sold in a **product market**. In this market, individuals use the money they received by selling goods and services in the factor markets to make their purchases. It is the market where goods and services are sold. Businesses then use the money they earn to produce more goods and services.

The product markets and the factor markets function as the key links between businesses and individuals. The circular flow model shows this relationship and helps to demonstrate the flow of money through the markets, businesses, and individuals.

Putting It All Together

A feature of any system is that a change in one part of the system affects all of the other parts. Use the circular flow model to explain how a change in a product market might affect the factor markets.

Production Possibilities in a Market Economy

Thinking on Your Own

As you read, make a list of the causes and effects of changes in production possibilities for something you would like to build.

A market economy is based on the idea that the best way to respond to scarcity is by making the most of every resource. Market economies encourage efficiency.

Examining Production Possibilities

A **production possibilities curve** shows the greatest amount of goods or services that can be produced from a fixed amount of resources in a specific time period. It also shows the limits of production—the line between those combinations of goods and services that can be produced and those that cannot.

Figure 3.2 on page 36 is the production possibilities curve you studied in Chapter 1. Notice that it shows what can and cannot be produced in a 20-hour workweek. Moving from one point to another on a production possibilities curve always involves an opportunity cost—giving up the next best option.

According to the graph, a worker cannot mow 12 lawns with a hand mower and trim bushes in five yards in the time available. To produce more, a worker would have to spend more hours on the job or find a way of doing the job faster. On the other hand, if the worker wastes time and other resources—by working slowly, taking time off, or being careless with tools—production will fall.

focus your reading

How do individuals and businesses increase their production possibilities?

Describe the relationship between an expansion of production possibilities and economic growth.

What are the advantages of economic growth? What is the opportunity cost?

vocabulary

production possibilities curve

economic growth

capital accumulation

infrastructure

productivity

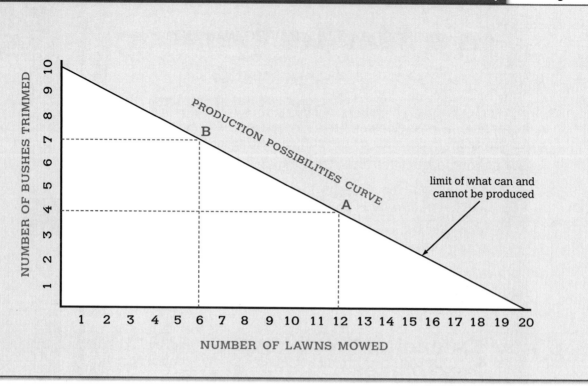

Although the production possibilities at any moment are limited, they are not fixed. If people waste a resource or nature damages it, the production possibilities are reduced. The line on the graph shifts downward. If someone comes up with a great new idea, the production possibilities increase. The line on the graph shifts outward.

> **stop and think**
>
> Work with a partner to list the ways the invention of the computer has expanded production possibilities.

Economic Growth

Over the years, production possibilities in the United States have expanded greatly. The result has been **economic growth**. Although Americans produce more today at a lower cost than they did 50 years ago, production possibilities remain limited. Americans still have to make trade-offs and figure out the costs of each option.

Figure 3.3 shows a production possibilities curve for a nation deciding between purchasing military goods (guns) versus civilian goods (butter). Notice that the purchase of more

civilian goods means giving up some military goods. Whenever individuals, groups, or nations choose one thing over another, they give up the next best option. That option is the opportunity cost. Like other choices, economic growth has an opportunity cost. The opportunity cost of purchasing $7 billion worth of guns is $2 billion worth of civilian goods.

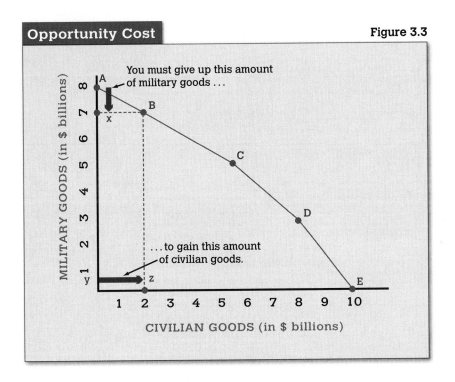

Opportunity Cost   Figure 3.3

One way an individual, nation, or business can expand production possibilities is through **capital accumulation**. To *accumulate* means "to build up or collect." *Capital* refers to the tools and other manufactured goods used to make other goods and services. Spending money to build more roads and airports, expand factory or office space, and purchase new tools and equipment are examples of capital accumulation. The term **infrastructure** is often used to describe a nation's roads, sewers, airports, mass transit, and other public goods that are needed to support a population.

Individuals and businesses invest in capital in the hope of increasing productivity in the future. **Productivity** is the amount of goods and services a worker can produce in a certain amount of time. The opportunity cost of using scarce resources to train workers or purchase new tools and equipment is having less money for producing goods and services today.

People also increase productivity by developing new and better ways of producing goods and services. Many companies spend time and resources on research and development to expand their production possibilities in the future. The opportunity cost is a drop in current production.

Using robotics allows autoworkers today to increase their productivity by producing more cars in less time.

Putting It All Together

Give two examples of the way capital accumulation can expand production possibilities. Give two examples of the way the development of new and better ways of producing goods and services can expand production possibilities. Discuss your ideas with a partner and agree on your examples.

Specialization and Trade

Thinking on Your Own

As you read this lesson, look for the connections between specialization and trade. Also, look for the effects of each on other elements of the economy. Write three examples in your notebook.

Some people are better at some things than others. They may have skills, knowledge, or resources that others lack. The same is true of businesses and nations. Yet even the most talented person, the largest corporation, or the richest nation in the world benefits from trade. By concentrating on a few tasks rather than trying to do everything, they can get more done with fewer resources.

Specialization

Concentrating on the production of a few goods and services is called **specialization**. You specialize when you focus on making a few goods or performing a few services rather than trying to produce everything you need. In the early 1700s, most Americans grew their own food, wove wool into cloth, tanned leather, and built furniture. People then tried to be self-sufficient. That is, they tried to produce all of the goods and services their families needed. People today specialize. They farm, build houses, fix automobiles, teach children, or create music. Few people try to produce everything they need.

The same is true of states and nations. About one-third of all of the potatoes grown in the United States come from Idaho. Potatoes can be grown in other parts of the country as well, but they are especially well suited to Idaho's climate and

focus your reading

How does specialization expand production possibilities?

Explain how trade can benefit those who do not have an absolute advantage.

Summarize the opportunity costs of trade and specialization.

vocabulary

specialization

absolute advantage

comparative advantage

law of comparative advantage

interdependence

soil. Idaho has an **absolute advantage** in growing potatoes. Farmers there are able to grow the crop using fewer resources than other producers require.

Idaho is not well suited to growing oranges. The climate is too cold. The only way Idaho farmers could grow the crop is by planting the orange trees in large greenhouses that they could heat during the cold winter months. Idaho does not have an absolute advantage in growing oranges. The opportunity costs are too high. Farmers in places like Florida and Southern California can produce oranges more efficiently, and their opportunity costs are far less. Florida and California have an absolute advantage in producing oranges. They can produce oranges using fewer resources than other producers require.

> **stop and think**
>
> List examples of absolute advantage in your school. How does it affect which teachers teach which subjects? How does it affect sports and other after-school activities?

Specialization and Comparative Advantage

Specialization allows individuals and businesses to focus on what they do best rather than trying to produce everything they need. What determines which goods or services an individual or business produces? You may think they should produce only those for which they have an absolute advantage. In fact, they should produce only those for which they have a comparative advantage. Those with a **comparative advantage** specialize in producing only the goods or services they can make at a relatively low opportunity cost. The key word is *relatively*. It means "in comparison to others." They do not have to have an absolute advantage—that is, they do not have to produce goods or services more efficiently than anyone else. According to the **law of comparative advantage**, those with the lower opportunity cost should specialize in that product or service even if they do not have an absolute advantage.

To understand how the law of comparative advantage works, imagine two people, Tim (A) and Juanita (B). They

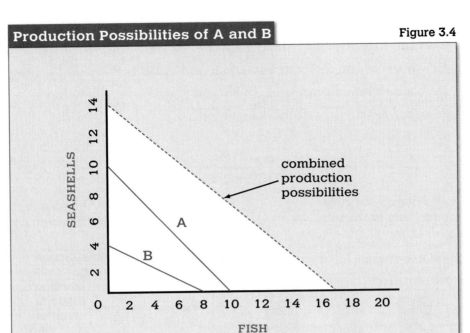

Production Possibilities of A and B   Figure 3.4

combined production possibilities

live on an island, and they both produce seashells and fish. Figure 3.4 shows that Tim (A) has an absolute advantage over Juanita (B) in both collecting shells and catching fish. Tim (A) can produce more fish and shells more efficiently than Juanita (B) in one day's time. This means that Tim (A) is more efficient than Juanita (B).

Notice that if Tim (A) decides to gather 10 seashells a day, he will not be able to catch any fish. Similarly, if Juanita (B) decides to catch 8 fish, she will not be able to collect seashells. Since both Tim (A) and Juanita (B) make trade-offs, they also have opportunity costs. Tim (A) has to give up 1 fish for every shell he collects. Juanita (B) gives up 2 fish for each seashell she gathers and one-half of a seashell for each fish. If each spends half of his or her time collecting shells and the other half fishing, the output for Tim (A) would be 5 shells and 5 fish, and the output for Juanita (B) would be 2 shells and 4 fish. Their combined total would be 7 shells and 9 fish.

Suppose they decide to specialize. Because the opportunity cost of catching fish is lower for Juanita (B) than it is for Tim (A), Juanita (B) has the comparative advantage in producing fish, even though Tim (A) has the absolute advantage. If Tim (A) collects shells and Juanita (B) catches fish, then their combined output will be 10 shells and 8 fish. By working together, they have gained 3 seashells and lost 1 fish. However, if Tim (A) catches 1 fish and collects 9 seashells, they have a combined output of 9 fish and 9 seashells. They have gained 2 seashells with no loss of fish.

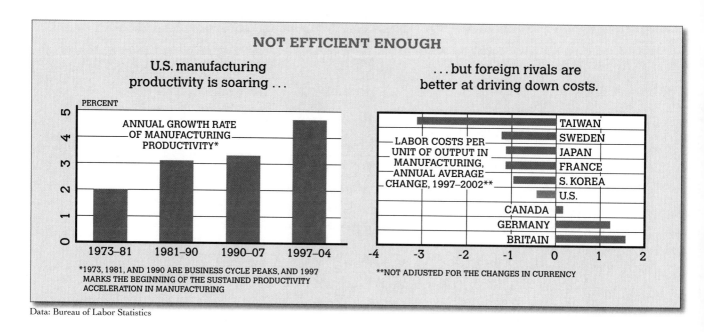

NOT EFFICIENT ENOUGH

U.S. manufacturing productivity is soaring . . .

PERCENT

ANNUAL GROWTH RATE OF MANUFACTURING PRODUCTIVITY*

1973–81   1981–90   1990–07   1997–04

*1973, 1981, AND 1990 ARE BUSINESS CYCLE PEAKS, AND 1997 MARKS THE BEGINNING OF THE SUSTAINED PRODUCTIVITY ACCELERATION IN MANUFACTURING

. . .but foreign rivals are better at driving down costs.

LABOR COSTS PER UNIT OF OUTPUT IN MANUFACTURING, ANNUAL AVERAGE CHANGE, 1997–2002**

TAIWAN
SWEDEN
JAPAN
FRANCE
S. KOREA
U.S.
CANADA
GERMANY
BRITAIN

-4   -3   -2   -1   0   1   2

**NOT ADJUSTED FOR THE CHANGES IN CURRENCY

Data: Bureau of Labor Statistics

Comparing Graphs

U.S. Productivity in Manufacturing

Graphs help people make comparisons. They can also help us understand why comparisons are important to understanding an idea like productivity—the amount a worker or business can produce in a given amount of time.

Graph 1 looks at the percent of growth in the productivity of American factories over a period of 30 years. Graph 2 also looks at productivity. It shows the cost of labor for each unit of factory output by country for the years 1997–2002. In this case, the lower the percent of cost, the higher the productivity. So a negative number is better than a positive number.

reading for understanding

Based on Graph 1, what was the annual growth rate of manufacturing productivity between 1973 and 1981? What was the growth rate between 1997 and 2004?

How do your answers explain the title of Graph 1?

Based on Graph 2, which country did the best job of lowering its labor costs for each unit of output in manufacturing? Which country did the poorest job?

By specializing, they have expanded their individual production possibilities. Even though Tim (A) has an absolute advantage over Juanita (B) for both fish and seashells, both benefit from specialization. The opportunity cost of specializing for both Tim (A) and Juanita (B) is a loss of independence. By working together, Tim (A) and Juanita (B) become more interdependent. They rely on one another. If Tim (A) is ill and unable to work for a few days, Juanita (B) is affected. The opposite is also true.

Interdependence

Tim (A) and Juanita (B) choose to trade because each is better off as a result of their exchange. Individuals and businesses in a market economy tend to make choices that improve their lives. In this case, specialization boosted the production possibilities for both Tim (A) and Juanita (B).

Businesses and nations make similar choices. The U.S. economy is linked to those of dozens of other nations around the world. **Interdependence** is an important part of modern life. Nations rely on one another for information, resources, goods, and services.

Businesses are also interdependent. An automobile company is a good example. The design, natural resources, parts, and much of the labor that goes into producing automobiles involve workers and businesses in countries around the world. That interdependence has made cars more affordable than ever before.

Most automobiles that are imported to the United States consist of parts made in many countries.

Interdependence can seem like a bad idea when an event in another country has a negative effect on businesses close to home. But gains in productivity as a result of increases in specialization usually offset those losses.

Putting It All Together

How does comparative advantage affect the hiring of players for a professional sports team? Write a paragraph explaining how comparative advantage might benefit both players who have no absolute advantage and those with many absolute advantages.

U.S. Factories: Falling Behind

In May 2004, *BusinessWeek* used the two graphs on page 42 to discuss why many American factories are losing business to factories in other countries.

In many ways, the last few years should have been a golden era for American manufacturers. Since 1997, the productivity of American factories has soared, rising at a 4.6% annual average rate. That's the fastest sustained rise in manufacturing productivity in at least 40 years. . . .

Yet despite these gains, . . . domestic factory output is still down 2% from its 2000 peak, while . . . goods [purchased from other countries] are up 8%. Some 3 million factory jobs—one in every six—have been lost since the last peak in mid-2000. And while the manufacturing sector is finally expanding and hiring again—up 37,000 jobs since January—no one expects domestic manufacturers to ever recover the ground lost to overseas competitors.

Economists, business leaders, and politicians give all sorts of reasons for the [terrible] state of U.S. manufacturing. . . . Fact is, as fast as American factories have improved productivity and cut costs, foreign competitors in Asia and Europe have charged ahead even faster.

Consider Banta Corp., a $1.4-billion printing company in Menasha, Wis. In 2000, 70 employees produced by hand 360,000 page plates a year at its book-printing plant. By 2003, all the input material was received in digital form and assembled on Macintosh G3 computers, enabling 50 employees to produce 454,000 plates. That's an 80% increase in output per worker, or about 25% per year.

Yet when it comes to the all-important, capital-intensive step of actually printing the book, Banta has been able to boost productivity by 5% a year by installing new faster and wider presses. The rub? Chinese printers are buying the same $12-million machines, blunting any competitive edge Banta had hoped to achieve. ∎

"U.S. Factories: Falling Behind" by Michael Arndt and Adam Aston. *BusinessWeek*, May 24, 2004.

reading for understanding

How does the author of the article link improvements in productivity to economic growth?

What role does competition play in efforts to improve productivity?

Describe how competition among nations affects the opportunities open to ordinary workers in the United States or any other nation.

Chapter Summary

- A market economy is an economic system in which **producers** and **consumers** interact to satisfy unlimited wants and needs using scarce resources.

- Every market economy is based on economic freedom, trade, property rights, **profit**, and **competition**.

- A **circular flow model** shows how a market economy organizes the production and consumption of goods and services. It includes both **factor markets** and **product markets**.

- A **production possibilities curve** shows the limits of production at a given time. Moving from one point to another on a production possibilities curve always involves an opportunity cost.

- Expansion of production possibilities results in **economic growth**.

- **Infrastructure** refers to highways, mass transit, power, water, and other goods needed to support a population.

- **Productivity** can be increased through **capital accumulation** or by developing new ways of producing goods and services.

- **Specialization** allows individuals and businesses to use both **absolute** and **comparative advantages** to increase productivity.

- As a result of specialization, most individuals, businesses, and nations in the world today are **interdependent**.

Chapter Review

1 In your opinion, which of the following—economic freedom, trade, property rights, profit, or competition—is most essential to the working of a market economy? Write a paragraph stating your opinion. Be sure to include reasons and evidence in support of your opinion.

2 Identify two causes and two effects of each of the following: capital accumulation, specialization, and trade.

Skill Builder

Understand Cause and Effect

A *cause* is any event or condition that makes something happen. For example, in 1913 Henry Ford asked his engineers to find a faster way to build a car. What happened as a result of his request is known as an *effect*.

To identify cause-and-effect relationships as you read:

- Look for *what happened* (the effect).

- Look for *why it happened* (the cause).

Clue words are words or phrases that can alert you to a cause-and-effect relationship. Words such as *because, led to, resulted in, produced,* or *therefore* signal cause-and-effect relationships.

As you read the excerpt that follows, look for cause-and-effect relationships. Then answer the questions.

Productivity is the efficiency with which we convert inputs into outputs. In other words, how good are we at making things? Does it take 2,000 hours for a Detroit automaker to make a car or 210 hours? Can an Iowa corn farmer grow thirty bushels of corn on an acre of land or 210 bushels? The more productive we are, the richer we are. The reason is simple: The day will always be twenty-four hours long; the more we produce in those twenty-four hours, the more we consume. Productivity is determined in part by natural resources—it is easier to grow wheat in Kansas than it is in Vermont—but in a modern economy, productivity is more affected by technology, specialization, and skills, all of which are a function of human capital.

America is rich because Americans are productive. We are better off today than at any other point in the history of civilization because we are better at producing goods and services than we have ever been. . . . In 1870, the typical household required 1,800 hours of work just to acquire its annual food supply; today it takes 260 hours of work.

From *Naked Economics* by Charles Wheelan. W. W. Norton, 2002, page 107.

---

1 In the author's view, what causes an increase in productivity?

2 In a paragraph, describe the effects of an increase in productivity.

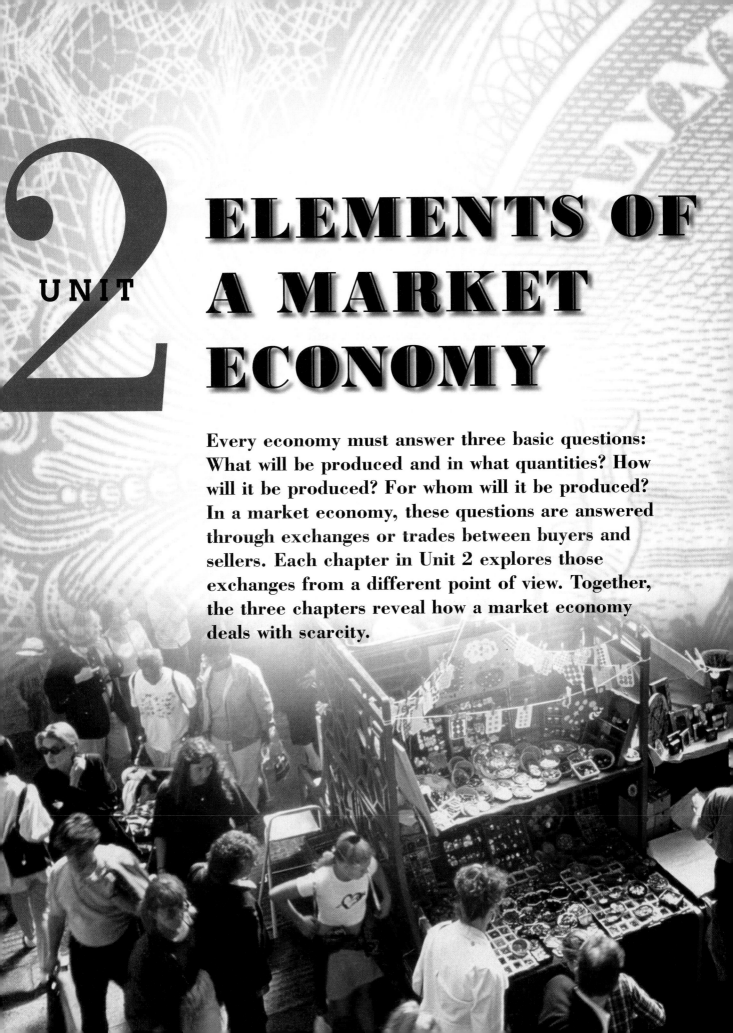

UNIT 2

ELEMENTS OF A MARKET ECONOMY

Every economy must answer three basic questions: What will be produced and in what quantities? How will it be produced? For whom will it be produced? In a market economy, these questions are answered through exchanges or trades between buyers and sellers. Each chapter in Unit 2 explores those exchanges from a different point of view. Together, the three chapters reveal how a market economy deals with scarcity.

Chapter

4 DEMAND

Getting Focused

Skim this chapter to predict what you will be learning.

- Read the lesson titles and subheadings.
- Look at the illustrations and read the captions.
- Examine the charts and graphs.
- Review the vocabulary words and terms.

In economics, many everyday words, such as the word *demand*, have a special meaning. Make a two-column chart in your notebook. Write an everyday definition of the word *demand* in one column. As you read the chapter, write an economist's definition of this word in the second column. Add other words to your chart as you read.

Consumer demand for goods and services is an important factor in a market economy.

Defining Demand

Thinking on Your Own

Write the three Focus Your Reading questions on a page in your notebook. Leave three lines between each question. As you read, answer each question in two or three sentences.

In economics, the word **market** has a special meaning. It describes the exchanges between buyers and sellers of goods and services. It does not refer to a specific location. The questions faced by sellers in those exchanges are related to **supply**—how much to sell and at what price. The questions faced by buyers are related to demand—how much to purchase and at what price. **Demand** is the amount of goods and services consumers are willing to buy at various prices at a particular time and place.

focus your reading

Explain the law of demand.

Why does the quantity demanded change?

How does the law of diminishing marginal utility affect the law of demand?

vocabulary

market	demand schedule
supply	demand curve
demand	real income effect
law of demand	substitution effect
law of diminishing marginal utility	

The Law of Demand

According to the **law of demand**, if all other things are equal, the higher the price of a product or service, the less of it people are willing to buy. The lower the price, the more people will buy. In economics, laws like this one are descriptions of what is likely to happen—if all other things are equal. In this case, most people will buy more goods and services when prices are low. They will buy fewer goods and services when prices are high.

The law of demand is based on the connection between the price of a good or service and the quantity demanded. As the price increases, the quantity demanded of the good or service falls. The relationship is a negative one—that is, if one variable (price) rises, the other variable (the quantity demanded) drops. The opposite is also true. If the price goes down, the quantity demanded goes up. You see the law of demand in action every time you go to a big sale at the mall.

When the price goes down, the demand rises.

Items on sale are often ones for which the supply was greater than the demand.

Graphing the Law of Demand

One way to show the relationship between price and the quantity demanded is by studying a **demand schedule**. This is a list that shows the quantities demanded of a product at various prices during a particular time period. The demand schedule shown in Figure 4.1A shows the demand for CDs at several different prices. At $30, no one is willing to buy a CD. At $20, just one will be sold. At $5, the number jumps to eight.

Figure 4.1B is another way to look at the information in a demand schedule. Each point on the graph shows the quantity purchased at a particular price. The line formed by connecting the points is called a **demand curve**. Notice that it slopes downward. A downward slope shows a negative relationship—as one variable increases, the other decreases.

Why Demand Rises and Falls

Why does the quantity demanded for a product or service fall when the price goes up? One reason is the **real income effect**. Real income is what people can actually buy with their money.

The Demand for CDs Figure 4.1A

DEMAND SCHEDULE

Price	Quantity Demanded
$30	0
25	0
20	1
15	3
10	5
5	8

The Demand for CDs Figure 4.1B

DEMAND CURVE

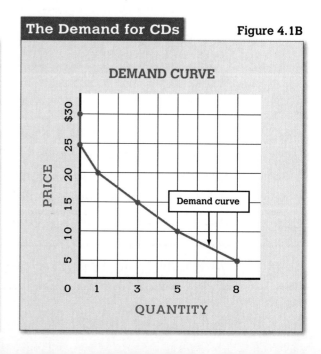

If prices rise and your income stays the same, you are no longer able to buy as much as you once did. Your real income has dropped.

stop and think

In previous chapters, you learned that improvements in technology lowered the price of automobiles. In your notebook, write two or three sentences explaining how the drop in the price of automobiles affected the quantity demanded. Then explain how your answer helps to demonstrate the real income effect.

Similarly, a drop in price increases the demand for goods and services. People can now buy more goods and services for their money. Their real income has grown.

The second reason demand falls when prices rise is the **substitution effect**. When prices increase, people tend to choose a similar product that can be used in place of the now higher-priced good or service. How does the substitution effect work? Suppose you decide to go out for pizza. When you get to your favorite restaurant, you discover that the price of a pizza has gone up. If you order a hamburger instead, or head for a different restaurant, you are substituting a lower-priced product for the now higher-priced pizza.

There is yet another factor that explains why the quantity demanded drops as prices rise. It is called the **law of diminishing marginal utility**. It is sometimes called the law of diminishing marginal returns. To *diminish* means to grow smaller. The usefulness of a product or the amount of satisfaction it provides is called its *utility*. *Marginal utility* is the extra usefulness or satisfaction people get from buying or using more of a product or service. According to the law of diminishing marginal utility, as people use more of a product or service, the satisfaction they get from their additional purchases declines.

What does the law mean? Suppose you purchase a glass of lemonade on a hot day. The first glass tastes so good that you buy a second glass and maybe even a third. The second and third glasses represent marginal utility—the extra usefulness or satisfaction gained from additional purchases. According to the law of diminishing marginal utility, however, the amount of satisfaction you get from those two extra glasses is less than you got from the first. The more you consume, the less pleasure you gain from each new purchase.

Because of diminishing marginal utility, people are not willing to pay as much for the third, fourth, or fifth glass as they were for the first. Their unwillingness to pay as much is one reason a demand curve slopes downward. When an individual reaches the point where the marginal utility—the extra usefulness gained from an additional purchase—is less than the price of the item, he or she stops buying.

Putting It All Together

How and why will each of the following affect the quantity of DVD players demanded?

- a sale on DVDs

- a drop in the price of VCRs

- a rise in the price of tickets to the movies

What factors influenced each of your answers? How would the law of diminishing marginal utility affect the demand for DVD players?

reading for understanding

What change in demand does Gonzales describe?

What does her story suggest about the way a fad grows and develops?

Has the fad ended? How did you decide?

Primary Source

The Little Rubber Band

Roberta Gonzales, a reporter for the local CBS station in San Francisco, writes about the popularity of rubber band bracelets:

❝Sometime last spring, after making a charitable donation to the Lance Armstrong Foundation, I received a yellow rubber bracelet with the word 'Livestrong' stamped on it. I would have never, ever imagined how popular and in demand this yellow band would become.

"Watching the Summer Olympics on television, I saw athletes wearing the bracelet. On the presidential campaign trail, John Kerry sported his yellow bracelet.... Soon, I was being offered sums of money for my sought-after rubber bracelet....

"My son Michael gave me a camouflage bracelet to 'Support Our Troops.'... My other son, Randall, gave me a white one stamped 'Hope.' ... Another white bracelet I received is to fight ovarian cancer, of which my best friend, Donna Hanson, died.

"I noticed the other day the rubber bands are now being auctioned on eBay.❞

"The Little Rubber Band" by Roberta Gonzales, April 22, 2005.

Changes in Demand

Thinking on Your Own

Write the three vocabulary words in your notebook. Leave space between each word. As you read, define each word in a sentence or two.

A demand curve, like the one in Figure 4.1B, on page 50, shows that the quantity demanded changes as prices rise or fall. The demand curve itself, however, does not seem to change. In fact, it changes constantly. What does the demand curve represent, and what causes it to change?

Analyzing Market Demand

A demand curve begins with the preferences of individual buyers—you, friends, and neighbors. The points along the curve show your willingness and ability to buy a good or service at a particular price. Economists add up all of those individual demands to determine **market demand**—the total of all of the individual demands within a market.

Just as graphs show changes in the quantity demanded at various prices, they can also show changes in the demand curve. The two demand curves in Figure 4.2, on page 54, show changes in the demand for CDs. Notice that when the demand curve shifts to the right, it is showing an increase in demand. When the demand curve shifts to the left, it is showing a decrease in demand, indicating that fewer CDs will be purchased at the same set of prices.

Causes of Shifts in Demand

What causes the market demand to increase or decrease? Price is an important factor. But you can probably name at least a dozen products or services you would not buy at any price.

Figure 4.2

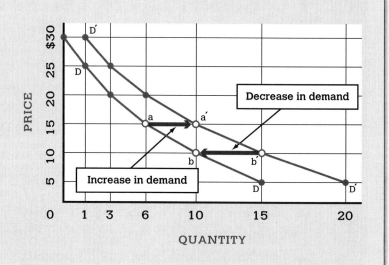

Price	Old (DD)	New (D'D')
$30	0	1
25	1	3
20	3	6
15	6	10
10	10	15
5	15	20

The average income of consumers also affects market demand. (To figure out the *average* income, divide the combined income by the number of consumers.) As income rises, people tend to buy more of almost everything.

Changes in population—the number of people in a market—can also make a difference. The bigger the market, the larger the demand tends to be. California is home to more than 35 million people. Californians buy many more goods and services than do the 500,000 people who make their homes in Wyoming.

A shift in market demand may also occur as the result of a change in complementary products. **Complements** are products or services that are used together. For example, computers and software are complements. So are pens and paper. An increase in the use of one increases the use of the other. Their relationship is positive. If the demand for one drops, the demand for the other is also likely to drop.

Changes may also result from a change in the market demand for **substitutes**, but the effect is different. Pens and pencils can be substituted for each other. They have similar uses. One can be used in place of the other. If the price of one rises sharply, people are likely to buy more of the other. If the price of both is about the same, which one a person buys is likely to be a matter of personal preference.

> **recall**
>
> **Consumers** are people who buy goods and services.

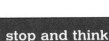

Personal preferences are likes and dislikes. Changes in personal preference can also affect demand. For example, over 90 percent of the people in the United States eat turkey on Thanksgiving. As a result, 15 percent of all the turkeys produced in the United States in a year are eaten on Thanksgiving Day. The demand curve for turkey shifts to the right in November just before the holiday begins and shifts to the left in January after New Year's Day.

Special influences also shape demand. If you have ever tried to buy an umbrella during a rainstorm or a pair of boots just before a big snowstorm, you understand how a sudden change in the weather can influence market demand.

Fads—short-lived fashions—are yet another special influence that can affect demand. These products or services are very popular for a brief period of time. Then no one seems to want them at any price. For example, in 1975, a California man named Gary Dahl came up with the idea of selling rocks as pets. He even wrote a manual on how to care for a pet rock. Within a few months, he had sold over one million pet rocks at $3.95 each. A year later, the fad was over and the demand for pet rocks vanished as quickly as it had appeared.

Expectations about the future can have a similar effect. If people are worried about their jobs or their futures, they are less likely to make major purchases. They also are likely to stockpile goods if they think the price will soon rise, or they may delay purchases if they think the price is about to fall.

stop and think

Suppose large numbers of Americans decided to eat fish or beef on Thanksgiving. How would their choice affect the market demand for turkey? What complementary products that people serve with turkey dinners would also be affected?

Putting It All Together

Work with a partner to list the brand names of ten goods you use. Next, try to identify a complementary product and a substitute for each. Then predict what would happen to the demand for your favorite item or brand and its complementary products if the item doubled in price.

The weather often impacts the supply and demand for products and services.

Demand Elasticity

Thinking on Your Own

As you read about elasticity, list the ways the law of demand affects both elastic and inelastic demand.

According to the law of demand, the quantity demanded tends to change in response to a change in price. If the price rises, the quantity demanded is likely to drop. If the price drops, the quantity demanded is likely to rise. How much will the quantity demanded fall or rise? The answer can vary greatly. Consumers are more responsive to changes in the prices of some goods and services than others. Economists refer to this kind of responsiveness as **elasticity**. They measure the **price elasticity of demand** by how sensitive consumers are to a change in price.

focus your reading

Name two items that are elastic in demand.

Name two items that are inelastic in demand.

What effect do substitutes have on the elasticity of demand?

vocabulary

elasticity   elastic

price elasticity   inelastic
of demand

Elastic and Inelastic Demand

Economists say the quantity demanded is **elastic** when a specific change in price causes a relatively large change in the quantity demanded. They consider the quantity demanded **inelastic** if a change in price does not bring much of a change in the quantity demanded.

The vertical line in Figure 4.3 shows a perfectly inelastic demand—one in which the quantity demanded does not respond in any way to a change in price. The horizontal line shows a perfectly elastic demand—one in which a tiny

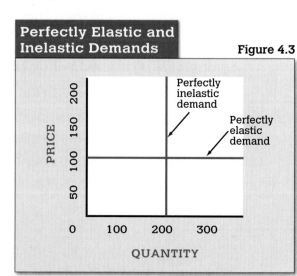

Perfectly Elastic and Inelastic Demands

Figure 4.3

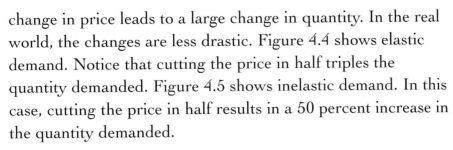

change in price leads to a large change in quantity. In the real world, the changes are less drastic. Figure 4.4 shows elastic demand. Notice that cutting the price in half triples the quantity demanded. Figure 4.5 shows inelastic demand. In this case, cutting the price in half results in a 50 percent increase in the quantity demanded.

Why does elasticity matter? Economists have found that when demand is inelastic, a drop in price *decreases* the seller's earnings. When demand is *elastic*, a drop in price increases earnings.

Effects of Elasticity

Why is the demand for some products more elastic than it is for others? One reason is that some products have more substitutes than others. Vegetables are a good example. They can be purchased fresh, frozen, canned, or even freeze-dried. During the growing season, the price of vegetables is relatively low. Consumers buy lots of fresh corn, peas, beans, and tomatoes. When the price of fresh vegetables goes up during the cold winter months, many people substitute canned or frozen vegetables for fresh ones.

Products that have few substitutes tend to be inelastic. For many people with diabetes, insulin is essential to their health. It is used to control their blood sugar. Insulin is a medication that converts blood sugar into usable energy. The market demand for insulin is inelastic. It has no substitutes. Therefore, the quantity demanded is unlikely to rise or fall because of a change in price.

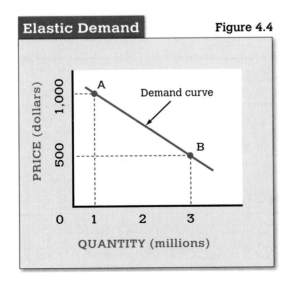

Elastic Demand   Figure 4.4

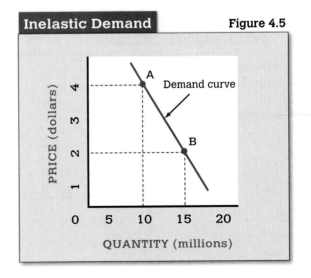

Inelastic Demand   Figure 4.5

Clothing is an example of a good with elastic demand.

If the cost of an item represents a large percentage of a consumer's real income, a change in the price of that item will have a large effect on demand. Such items have an elastic demand. New cars are a good example of this. The demand goes up as the prices go down.

Laundry detergent has an inelastic demand, but for a different reason from medicine. If the cost of an item represents a small percentage of a consumer's budget, a change in price may have little or no effect on demand. The price of a box of detergent is not a significant percentage of a family's purchases. So the quantity demanded is unlikely to be affected much by a rise in price.

stop and think

How does the elasticity of demand affect the price of a product that your family purchases? How does it affect buyers and sellers? In your notebook, list one item that your family would buy less of or switch to a substitute if the price increased sharply. What products would your family continue to buy about the same amount of even if the price changed significantly? Explain in economic terms why your family would act differently in these two instances. Try to add other explanations as you continue to read.

Medicine is an example of a good with inelastic demand.

Time can also affect the elasticity of demand. Some items are inelastic in the short run, but elastic in the long run. The oil used to heat houses is a good example. If the price goes up and you live in a cold climate, there is little that you can do immediately to reduce the quantity demanded. However, over time, you can insulate your house to reduce your heating bills or switch to gas or electric heat. Gasoline is another example. Over time, people and industries will find ways to substitute for gasoline if prices rise. However, in the short term, people still pay higher gasoline prices.

recall

Competition encourages the production of products that are innovative, high in quality, and low in price.

Elasticity is also closely linked to competition. That is, the more choices buyers have in a market, the more competitive that market will be. The next chapter examines the choices sellers make in the market.

Putting It All Together

List some items that you purchase regularly. Which are elastic in demand? Which are inelastic? Write a paragraph explaining how you decided which was which.

Tapping a Market That Is Hot, Hot, Hot

Brian Grow, a reporter for *BusinessWeek*, described the effects of an increase in the number of Hispanics, or Latinos, in the United States population on banks and bankers in 2005:

By now, the growing economic clout of the Hispanic community is well known. So what's driving the banking push? For starters, it's the fact that relatively few Latinos have any kind of banking accounts. Fully 56% of the nation's 40 million Hispanics have never held a bank account, according to market researcher Simmons Inc.

That's a rich vein for banks to tap. With Hispanics' wealth and population rising three times faster than the U.S. average, the FDIC predicts that they will account for more than . . . $200 billion in new business . . . over the decade. . . .

Those numbers have banks both big and small rapidly reshaping their marketing to get in on the boom. In California, Wells Fargo & Co. is redecorating its branches with Mexican themes. . . . At Bank of America, Spanish-language advertising brought in 1 million new checking accounts from Hispanics last year — fully 25% of the new accounts opened. And Banco Popular, a fast-growing bank based in

BANCO POPULAR targets Hispanics through Spanish-language services.

Puerto Rico, now sends trucks that are outfitted with teller booths to U.S. construction sites so Latino laborers can deposit their checks directly into banking accounts. Wherever Latinos live and work, banks are not far behind. ■

"Tapping a Market That Is Hot, Hot, Hot" by Brian Grow. *BusinessWeek*, January 17, 2005.

reading for understanding

How has the rising Hispanic population in the United States affected the shift in demand described in the article?

What other factors may be contributing to the shift in demand?

What does the author suggest about how consumers can influence what goods and services are produced and in what quantities?

Chapter Summary

- In the **market**, sellers face questions related to **supply** and buyers face questions related to **demand**.

- According to the **law of demand**, if all other things are equal, the higher the price of a product or service, the less people are willing to buy. The lower the price, the more people will buy.

- A **demand schedule** shows the relationship between price and the quantity demanded.

- A **demand curve** shows a negative relationship between price and the quantity demanded.

- The **real income effect**, the **substitution effect**, and the **law of diminishing marginal utility** help explain why the quantity demanded for a product or service falls when the price goes up.

- **Market demand** is the sum of all of the individual demands within a market.

- Shifts in demand are caused by changes in average income, population, demand for **complements**, demand for **substitutes**, personal preferences, special influences, and expectations about the future.

- Economists measure the **price elasticity of demand** by how sensitive consumers are to a change in price.

- The quantity demanded is **elastic** when a small change in price causes a relatively large change in the quantity demanded. The quantity demanded is **inelastic** if a large change in price causes only a small change in the quantity demanded.

Chapter Review

1 In a paragraph, explain the connections between price, quantity demanded, and market demand.

2 Draw demand curves reflecting the elasticity of demand for the following items: milk, denim jeans, and washing machines.

Skill Builder

Make Predictions

Economists are often asked to predict what will happen next. Predicting the future can be difficult and sometimes risky. The more information a person has, the more accurate the prediction is likely to be.

You can learn to make predictions, too. To be sure that your predictions are as accurate as possible, you should

- gather as much information as you can about the decision or action.

- use economic laws like the law of demand and what you know about history and human behavior to identify possible consequences.

- analyze each consequence by considering how likely it is to occur.

Study the following situation and then use what you learned in this chapter to answer the questions that follow.

Suppose that the cost of the lowest-priced new car available in your state is $30,000. What effect do you think this price will have on the demand for each of the products and services listed below? Be sure to give reasons for your answers.

1 motorcycles

2 walking shoes

3 used cars

4 public transportation

5 auto mechanics

Economic laws are true *if all other things are equal.* Suppose they are not. How might your answers change if

6 you lived in a place that had long, cold, snowy winters?

7 you lived in a place that had a warm climate all year long?

8 a large percentage of the population of your state was over the age of sixty-five?

Chapter
5 SUPPLY

Getting Focused

Skim this chapter to predict what you will be learning.

- Read the lesson titles and subheadings.
- Look at the illustrations and read the captions.
- Examine the charts and graphs.
- Review the vocabulary words and terms.

In Chapter 4, you learned how the demands of consumers shape a market economy. In this chapter, you will learn how the supply of goods and services affects a market economy. Think about what you already know about the supply of goods and services. For example, what seems to happen when stores have more goods than they can sell? What seems to happen when the supply of a product is very low? Discuss your experiences with a partner.

Hundreds of thousands of products are supplied daily from businesses in the United States.

Defining Supply

Thinking on Your Own

Economists often give an everyday term, like *supply,* a special meaning. Make a T-chart in your notebook for the word *supply.* On one side of the chart, write an everyday definition of the word. Look up the word in a dictionary if you need to. As you read, find an economist's definition of the word. Copy it on the other side of the chart. Then, as you read about the law of supply in this lesson, draw a graph in your notebook that shows how it works.

In a market economy, the word *market* refers to exchanges between buyers and sellers. Chapter 4 focused on the questions faced by buyers in the market. Those questions deal with demand. Sellers also face questions: how much to sell and at what price? These questions are related to supply.

The Law of Supply

According to the **law of supply,** if all other things are equal, the higher the price of a product or service, the more of it suppliers will offer for sale. As the price falls, so will the quantity supplied.

The law of supply is based on the **profit motive**—the desire of individuals and businesses to make money. Therefore, the relationship between the price of a good or service and the quantity supplied is a positive one. That is, if one variable (price) rises, the other variable (the quantity supplied) also rises. If the price goes down, the quantity supplied goes down as well.

One way to show the relationship between price and the quantity supplied is by examining a supply schedule.

Figure 5.1A

SUPPLY OF COMPACT DISCS

SUPPLY SCHEDULE

Price	Quantity Supplied
$30	8
25	7
20	6
15	4
10	2
5	0

A **supply schedule** is a list that shows the quantities supplied of a product at various prices during a particular time period. Figure 5.1A shows the supply for CDs at several different prices. At $30, suppliers will provide eight CDs; at $20, six will be offered; and at $5, they do not provide any CDs.

Figure 5.1B is another way to look at the information in a supply schedule. Each point on the graph shows the quantity supplied at a particular price. The line formed by connecting the points is called a **supply curve**. Notice that unlike a demand curve, it slopes upward. An upward slope shows a positive relationship—as one variable increases, the other also increases. A downward curve shows a negative relationship—as one variable increases, the other decreases.

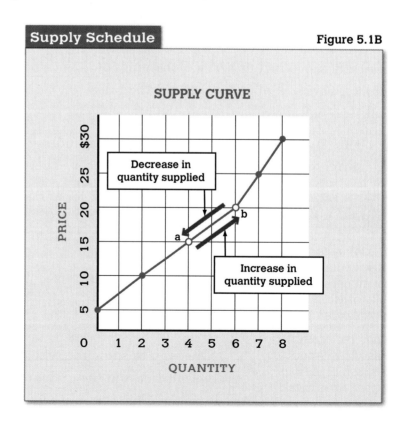

Supply Schedule — Figure 5.1B

SUPPLY CURVE

Analyzing Market Supply

A supply curve begins with the preferences of individual sellers. The points along the curve show the sellers' willingness to provide a good or service at a particular price. Sellers can be individuals or companies. Economists add up all of these individual supply curves to determine market supply. The **market supply** is the total output of all of the individual companies within a market.

stop and think

How does Figure 5.2 illustrate the law of supply? Explain your answer in a sentence or two.

Supply Schedule

Figure 5.2

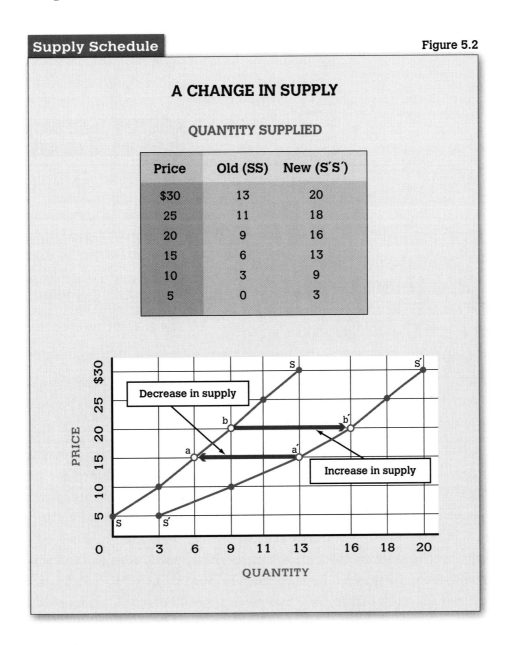

A CHANGE IN SUPPLY

QUANTITY SUPPLIED

Price	Old (SS)	New (S′S′)
$30	13	20
25	11	18
20	9	16
15	6	13
10	3	9
5	0	3

Just as graphs show changes in the quantity supplied at various prices, they can also show changes in the market supply. The two supply curves in Figure 5.2, on page 65, show changes in the supply of CDs. Notice that when the supply curve shifts to the right, it is showing an increase in supply. When the curve shifts to the left, it is showing a decrease in supply, indicating that fewer CDs will be sold at the same set of prices.

Putting It All Together

Make a Venn diagram to compare a supply curve with a demand curve. Then write a paragraph comparing and contrasting a supply curve to a demand curve. Be sure to explain how the two are similar as well how they differ from each other.

reading for understanding

What does the report suggest about the way shoemakers in the 1870s increased the quantity supplied?

Was their response long-term or short-term? How did you decide?

Explain why the market supply of shoes in the U.S. decreased during the Civil War. Why did it increase in the 1870s, after the Union was restored?

"Wonderful Progress Has Been Made"

An 1870s look at the effect the U.S. Civil War (1861–1865) had on the shoe industry:

❝The shoe business is in a most thriving condition. The war reduced a part of the country to bare feet, and as the existing shoe factories had during the war only been able to supply the northern states, the extension of their market makes them very busy.

"Wonderful progress has been made in the shoe business within a few years. A machine is had for everything, and girls to tend machines, and men to finish when the machines stop. There is a machine to roll the leather, which was formerly hammered; a machine to split the leather, which was done slowly by hand in other times; . . . machines to stitch the upper leathers or cloths, and bind the edges; and finally, a more important machine that sews the upper to the sole; and then there are machines for putting on the heels and forming them. By these means, from five to ten times the work can be done by a given number of hands than could have been accomplished twenty years ago under the old system.❞

"Report" in *Mechanics Magazine and Register of Inventions and Improvements*, 1876.

Production and Supply

Thinking on Your Own

Select three of the terms from the vocabulary list. Write them in your notebook. Under each, write what you think the term means. As you encounter the word when you read, correct or add to your definition.

Suppliers use the factors of production—natural resources; labor; and capital resources, like tools and other technology—to produce a product or service. A change in the amount of any one of these production resources can affect supply in the long run. In the short run, only a change in labor is likely to impact production.

To understand why only labor can be increased in the short run, think about a company that produces the most popular running shoe on the market. To keep up with the demand, the company has to produce more shoes. The fastest way to increase production is by hiring extra workers. Building a new factory, developing a new manufacturing process, or adding machines requires more time and expense.

focus your reading

What is the relationship among the factors of production and the supply of a good or service?

What happens to the marginal product at each of the three stages of production?

At what point does adding resources have a negative rather than a positive effect?

vocabulary

law of variable proportions

production schedule

marginal product

stages of production

diminishing returns

The Law of Variable Proportions

The **law of variable proportions** states that in the short run, output or supply will change as one resource is varied, even though other resources do not change. This law highlights the relationship between the input of a production resource and the supply of a good or service.

THE LAW OF VARIABLE PROPORTIONS

A THE PRODUCTION SCHEDULE

Number of Workers	Total Products	Marginal Product*	Stages of Production
0	0	0	Stage I
1	7	7	
2	20	13	
3	38	18	
4	62	24	
5	90	28	
6	110	20	Stage II
7	129	19	
8	138	9	
9	144	6	
10	148	4	
11	145	-3	Stage III
12	135	-10	

* All figures in terms of output per day

B THE PRODUCTION FUNCTION

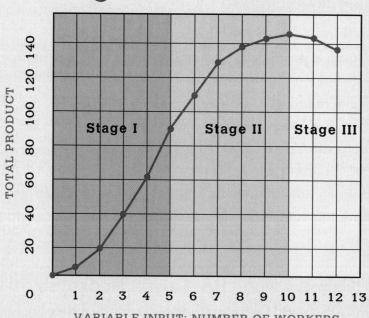

Stage I   Stage II   Stage III

TOTAL PRODUCT

VARIABLE INPUT: NUMBER OF WORKERS

To understand how more or less of a resource affects output, think about a garden. When you add water (a production resource) to the garden, the plants perk up. Water keeps the plants healthy. Suppose every time you water the garden, you increase the amount of water you add. At some point, the soil becomes waterlogged and the plants die. As the amount of input—in this case, water—varies, so does the output—in this case, the crop.

Figure 5.3 shows how the law of variable proportions works. The **production schedule** lists how the quantity supplied changes as the number of workers is increased. The first column lists the number of workers from zero to 12. The second column shows the total number of goods produced by the company. For example, with one worker, the company produces only seven products each day. If a second worker is added, the output increases to 20. Additional workers are able to use resources more efficiently than a single worker can.

The third column in the table shows **marginal product**—the extra output or change in the total product caused by adding a worker. Notice that after six workers have been added, the rise in the marginal product begins to slow. Although adding the fifth worker increases the marginal product by 28, adding the sixth worker increases it by just 20.

Why does adding a sixth worker increase the marginal product less? The answer lies in the fact that only the number of workers changes in the example. The size of the factory does not change, nor does the number of machines the workers use. At some point—in this case, beginning with the addition of a sixth worker—the factory becomes crowded, machines are overworked, and the jobs workers do become less important. You may have experienced the same thing if you have ever had too much help with a task. At some point, you and your helpers are just getting in one another's way.

stop and think

What happens to both the product total and the marginal product after an eleventh worker is added? Before reading further, work with a partner to explain these two numbers. Write your explanation in your notebook. As you read, check to see if your explanation is correct. Discuss your answer with a partner.

Stages of Production

Producers use marginal product to help them figure out when extra helpers hinder rather than help the production process. Notice that the fourth column in Figure 5.3, on page 68, shows the three **stages of production**. Each is based on changes in marginal product.

In the first stage, the supply increases as extra workers are added. In this stage, adding more workers results in a more efficient use of tools and other resources. As long as each new worker contributes more to the total product than the worker before, the total product rises at an increasingly faster rate. Stage I is known as the stage of increasing returns, or gains, on the company's investment in the production process.

In Stage II, the total product keeps growing, but by smaller and smaller amounts. This stage shows the principle of **diminishing returns**. The amount of output is still growing but not as quickly as it did in Stage I. Notice that the stage begins when the marginal product has begun to decrease.

Stage III shows negative returns. It begins when so many workers have been added that each extra worker results in a decrease in total output. Most companies do not add workers when the production schedule reaches Stage III. By the end of Stage II, it is clear each new worker is contributing less to the marginal product. The factory is becoming overcrowded and the machines are so overused that they are beginning to break down. Workers are now getting in one another's way. Adding workers only increases the problem.

Putting It All Together

You have been asked to hire workers for the project shown in Figure 5.3. Based on the information in the table and the graph, at what point should you stop hiring extra workers? In one or two sentences, explain how your answer reflects the law of variable proportions.

Changes in Supply

Thinking on Your Own

Find out what the word *elastic* means. With a partner, discuss how the supply of any item that you buy might be elastic. Write your answer in your notebook.

Changes in supply—decreases as well as increases—occur for a variety of reasons. One reason is a change in price. According to the law of supply, suppliers will offer more for sale at high prices and less at low prices. Supply changes for other reasons as well.

Why Supply Rises and Falls

A cold snap brings freezing temperatures to Florida and destroys the orange crop. The Great Plains suffers from a lack of rain, which wipes out corn and wheat crops. A war interferes with shipments of rubber, oil, and other resources. These dramatic changes in supply are the result of events beyond the control of any one business. Most changes in supply are far less dramatic. They are often the result of an increase in the costs of buying or renting the various factors of production.

focus your reading

What factors affect supply?

Name two items that are elastic in supply.

Name two items that are inelastic in supply.

vocabulary

productivity

tax

subsidy

regulation

elasticity of supply

Production costs affect supply. Any change in the cost of producing a good or service will affect the quantity supplied. If the cost of one or more of the factors of production decreases, the quantity supplied is likely to increase. Sellers are now able to offer more goods at the same set of prices. On the other hand, if production costs rise, the quantity supplied is likely to decrease. Sellers will now supply fewer products at the same set of prices.

Productivity—the amount of output for each unit of productive input—also affects production costs. Productivity increases if the same quantity of input (work, for example) produces more output (quantity supplied). When Henry Ford and his engineers reorganized the way cars were made in the early 1900s, workers were able to turn out more cars (output) in the same amount of time (input). Productivity decreases if the same quantity of input produces less output. If the company shown in Figure 5.3 hires an eleventh worker, the result will be a decrease in productivity.

Government plays a role in the rise and fall of supply. Governments at all levels can change supply. Taxes are a good example. A **tax** is a required payment made by an individual or business to support government programs and services. Businesses view taxes as costs. If a tax goes up, the cost of producing a good or service is also likely to rise.

On the other hand, a **subsidy** is a government payment to an individual or business to encourage or protect a particular economic activity. In the 1860s, for example, the United States government gave subsidies to companies willing to help build railroads that would stretch across the United States and link states along the Atlantic Coast with those that bordered the Pacific Ocean.

The government can also cause a change in supply by issuing regulations. A **regulation** is a rule that controls or directs a business or industry in order to protect consumers or the nation as a whole. In 1906, for example, Congress passed the Pure Food and Drug Act. It created an agency that tested all foods and medicines. It also required that patients have a prescription from a physician before buying certain drugs. Producers also had to put warning labels on habit-forming drugs.

The law had a variety of effects. It increased the demand for physicians. People had to see a doctor in order to buy certain medicines. The law also made many foods and drugs safer but more expensive. Why did prices tend to rise?

U.S. government subsidies were given to railroad developers who built the transcontinental railroad.

The new regulations required companies to add steps to their production process, which in turn increased costs. In general, increased or tighter government regulations tend to limit supply by raising costs. Relaxed or looser regulations lower the cost of production and increase supply.

Opinions—particularly opinions about the future price of a product—can also affect supply. If producers think the price of their product will go up in a few months or even a year, they may withhold some of the supply. If they expect lower prices in the future, they may try to produce and sell as much as possible immediately.

The factors described so far affect individual supply curves as well as the market supply or total supply within a market. The number of sellers in the market affects only market supply.

As more companies enter a market, the supply increases. If some sellers leave the market, fewer products are offered for sale at all prices. Therefore, the supply decreases.

Customer opinion often plays a key role in supplying products to the marketplace.

Supply Elasticity

According to the law of supply, the quantity supplied changes in the same direction as a change in price. If the price rises, the quantity supplied rises. How much will the quantity supplied rise or fall in response to a change in price? The answer depends on how quickly producers are able to respond to the change. Economists refer to the speed with which producers respond to price changes as elasticity. The **elasticity of supply** is measured by how quickly the quantity supplied changes as a result of a change in price.

A painting is unique. It is a one-of-a-kind piece of work. The quantity supplied is inelastic. Therefore, the supply curve for an original painting is vertical. (See Figure 5.4, on page 74.) No matter how high the price rises, the quantity supplied remains the same. On the other hand, Earth's supply of sand is almost limitless.

recall

Inelasticity in economics means that a change in price does not cause much of a change in the quantity demanded.

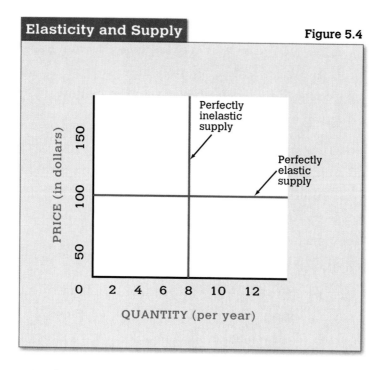

Elasticity and Supply   Figure 5.4

It is also easy to mine. So the quantity supplied can change quickly in response to changes in price. The supply of sand is elastic, and its supply curve is therefore nearly horizontal.

Supply elasticity is based solely on production capabilities. If a company can respond quickly to a change in price, then supply is considered elastic. If a company needs time to react to a change in price, the supply is likely to be inelastic.

Putting It All Together

How will each of the following factors affect the market supply of pineapples?

- a tax on fruits and vegetables

- a storm that destroys part of the crop

- the invention of a machine that speeds up the process of harvesting the pineapple crop

- more growers in the pineapple market

- a popular diet that requires a glass of pineapple juice with every meal

How elastic is the supply of pineapples? Be sure to give reasons for each of your answers.

Policy That Rewards Productivity

Greg Blonder, a partner in an investment firm, expressed his opinions on how government can help increase productivity in *BusinessWeek*. He writes:

GOVERNMENT SUBSIDIES do not always benefit the consumer.

Real wealth emerges only when we discover ways to produce something vital for less. That means, for example, selling higher-performance computers, which once cost $3,000, for $300. Or it could entail using half as much coal to refine the same ton of steel.

Such transformations work almost magically as they free scarce resources and raise the average standard of living. . . .

Unfortunately, most of America's current governmental incentives don't encourage wealth creation. They confuse spending money with creating value. Not all jobs are equally productive, and not all subsidies are equally vital. . . .

. . . A crop subsidy keeps the family farm alive, but reduces the incentive to raise the yield per acre, thus increasing the price of food for everyone. . . . A mortgage deduction encourages home ownership, but does nothing to make housing more affordable or reduce onerous real-estate fees.

These kinds of subsidies only encourage what I call "phantom productivity."

But what if the government were to institute genuine productivity-enhancing incentives? . . .

. . . Instead of taxing the increased profitability that often flows from better productivity, we would be reinforcing success—giving creative innovators a double boost of profits, plus subsidy. Companies that boost productivity significantly could grow faster. . . . Overall, real wealth would expand, and our society would become more vibrant. ∎

"Policy That Rewards Productivity" by Greg Blonder. *BusinessWeek*, May 31, 2005.

reading for understanding

How does the writer seem to define the word *productivity*?

A policy is a course of action to achieve a long-term goal. What is the writer's goal? What actions does he believe will result in achieving that goal?

Why does the writer believe that improving the productivity of individual businesses benefits the nation as a whole?

Chapter Summary

- According to the **law of supply**, if all other things are equal, as the price of a product or service rises, so will the quantity supplied. The lower the price, the lower the supply.

- The **profit motive**—the desire of individuals and businesses to make money—is demonstrated in the law of supply.

- A **supply schedule** shows the relationship between price and the quantity supplied.

- Economists add up all of these individual **supply curves** to determine **market supply**.

- The **law of variable proportions** highlights the relationship between the input of a factor of production and the supply of a good or service.

- A **production schedule** shows how the quantity supplied changes as the number of workers increases.

- Each of the three **stages of production** is based on a change in **marginal product**, including **diminishing returns**.

- **Productivity** increases if the same quantity of input produces more output, and decreases if the same quantity of input produces less output.

- The government affects supply through **taxes**, **subsidies**, and **regulations**.

- Economists measure the **elasticity of supply** by how quickly producers can respond to a change in price.

Chapter Review

1 Explain the connections between price, quantity supplied, and market supply.

2 Draw a diagram showing the relationship between supply elasticity and the production process.

Skill Builder

Make Comparisons

This chapter focuses on supply. Chapter 4 examined demand. Both affect the price of a good or service. Comparing the two can help you understand the effects of each. When you make a comparison, you look for similarities and differences between two or more individuals, groups, ideas, events, or objects.

In comparing and contrasting ideas, you should

- identify the point of comparison.

- pay attention to words that signal a comparison or contrast. Among these words are *like, unlike, similar,* and *different.*

- use economic laws, like the law of demand, and what you know about history and human behavior to identify possible consequences.

- analyze each consequence by considering how likely it is to occur.

One way to make comparisons is by studying the diagrams you created as you read the two chapters. What similarities do you notice between the two ideas? What differences seem most striking?

Use your diagrams to answer the following questions.

1 How is the law of supply similar to the law of demand? What is the most important difference between the two?

2 How is the law of diminishing marginal utility similar to the principle of diminishing returns? What is the main difference?

3 Both the quantities supplied and demanded are affected by factors other than price. How do those factors differ? In what ways are they alike?

4 How does elasticity affect both market supply and demand? What is the most striking difference between the way it affects each?

Chapter

6 PRICE

Getting Focused

Skim this chapter to predict what you will be learning.

- Read the lesson titles and subheadings.
- Look at the illustrations and read the captions.
- Examine the charts and graphs.
- Review the vocabulary words and terms.

In a market economy, supply and demand determine the price of almost everything. Based on your own experience, write a one-paragraph explanation of how supply and demand determine price. Be prepared to revise your explanation as you read the chapter. For ideas about how the system works, look at the major headings, charts, and graphs in this chapter.

What factors do you consider when deciding whether to purchase an item? Price is probably one of the factors you think about. Low prices may attract buyers, but they also impact sellers. In a market economy, prices are determined by supply and demand.

Why Price Matters

Thinking on Your Own

List in your notebook what you already know about price and how it works in a market economy. Then, describe how a change in the price of an item can change your decision to purchase the item. Compare your notes with those of a partner.

You deal with prices every time you go to the store, eat in a restaurant, see a movie, shop online, or buy from a catalog. If you have ever tried to scrape together enough money to buy something you really want, you have a good idea of why price matters. **Price** is the value in money of a good or service. In Chapters 4 and 5, you learned that in a market economy, price is established by the interaction of supply and demand. In this lesson, you will learn how each affects the other.

focus your reading

Discuss how prices act as signals.

How do buyers and sellers differ in the ways they respond to changes in prices?

What is the advantage of using prices to answer the three basic economic questions—what to produce, for whom, and in what amounts?

vocabulary

price	surplus
shortage	equilibrium price
rationing	

Market Signals

In a market economy, prices send signals to both producers and consumers. A rise in prices is a signal to producers that it is time to increase production. It has a different meaning for consumers. To consumers, it is a signal to buy fewer goods. Falling prices also have meaning. They let sellers know it is time to cut back on production or make something else. They let buyers know it is time to stock up on an item.

In Chapter 4, you learned that the quantity demanded is the amount of a good or service that consumers plan to buy in a given period of time at a particular price. The quantity demanded may vary with

- the price of the good or service
- the price of related goods or services (substitutes and complements)

- consumers' incomes

- expectations about future prices

- the number of consumers in the market

- personal preferences

According to the law of demand, the higher the price, the smaller the quantity demanded. If the quantity demanded is greater than the quantity supplied, a **shortage** occurs. An example is when ticket scalpers raise prices outside a concert or sports event. When demand is greater than supply, rising prices act as a way of **rationing**, or limiting, the demand for that product. The higher the price of a ticket, the shorter the lines will be to purchase it.

In Chapter 5, you learned that quantity supplied is the amount of a good or service that producers plan to sell in a given period of time at a particular price. The quantity supplied depends on

- the price of the product

- the prices of the factors of production used to make that product

- the prices of related goods

- the number of suppliers in the market

Price plays such an important factor in the economy that sellers may have to explain an unusually high price.

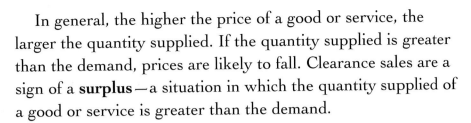

In general, the higher the price of a good or service, the larger the quantity supplied. If the quantity supplied is greater than the demand, prices are likely to fall. Clearance sales are a sign of a **surplus**—a situation in which the quantity supplied of a good or service is greater than the demand.

The aim of the market is to eliminate both shortages and surpluses. There is only one price at which the quantity demanded is exactly equal to the quantity supplied. It is called the **equilibrium price**. At that price, buyers have no incentive, or motive, to offer more money for a product and sellers have no incentive to reduce the price.

Figure 6.1 shows a market for CDs. Notice that the demand curve (D) on the graph reflects the law of demand. As the price goes down, demand rises and the demand curve slopes downward. Notice too that the supply curve (S) reflects the law of supply. As the price drops, the supply curve slopes downward. The place where the two curves cross one another is

stop and think

Why do you think the equilibrium price is also known as the price that "clears the market"? Write down your ideas and share them with a partner.

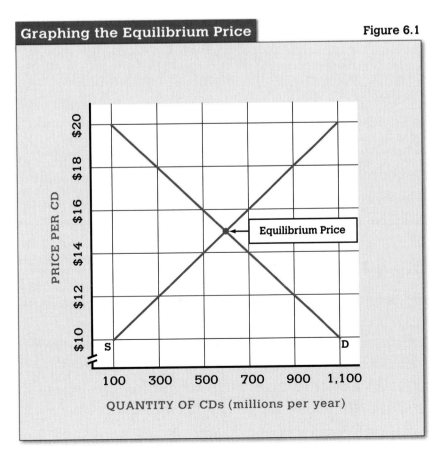

Graphing the Equilibrium Price

Figure 6.1

PRICE PER CD — $10, $12, $14, $16, $18, $20

Equilibrium Price

S   D

QUANTITY OF CDs (millions per year) — 100 300 500 700 900 1,100

the equilibrium price. At $15 per CD, suppliers will produce 600 million CDs and buyers will purchase the entire supply. At the equilibrium price, there is no shortage or surplus.

Market Forces

Prices in a market economy seek to eliminate both shortages and surpluses. Eventually, a market surplus forces prices down, which clears the market. Likewise, a market shortage forces prices up. This continues until the market reaches equilibrium. How does the system work? Suppose disease wipes out a portion of the nation's cattle. With beef supplies limited, consumers can expect the price of beef to rise. As the price goes up, some consumers will buy less beef. Others may turn to substitutes, such as chicken or pork. As the price of beef rises, producers also make choices. Some may take advantage of the high prices by importing healthy cattle. Others may decide to raise chicken or pigs to meet the new market demand. As the cattle become healthy, the price of beef will drop, the supply increase, and the demand decrease.

The market deals with surpluses in a similar way. Suppose great weather results in a huge increase in the size of the nation's wheat crop. As the supply increases, the price of wheat drops. Consumers respond to the low prices by buying more bread. Producers, on the other hand, decide to plant less wheat. Slowly, the price of wheat rises as the supply decreases and the demand increases.

No one developed a special plan to balance supply and demand in either example. In both, buyers and sellers simply acted in their own best interest. By doing so, the supply gradually balanced the demand.

Putting It All Together

You and your classmates have decided to wash cars to help raise money for a class field trip. How much should you charge? At $10 per car, you will not be able to compete with the commercial car wash down the street that charges only $8. Charging $2 per car will bring in more customers than you can handle. Explain how you and your friends will be able to balance supply and demand to arrive at an equilibrium price.

Supply, Demand, and Price

Thinking on Your Own

Draw a diagram in your notebook that shows what you already know about how supply and demand interact to establish price. As you read, add to your diagram.

In this lesson you will use a model to see how supply and demand work together to determine the price of almost everything. Keep in mind that a model focuses on some information and ignores everything else.

Establishing a Price

How do supply and demand work together to establish price? One way to find out is by combining the demand schedule and graph you used in Chapter 4 with the supply schedule and graph in Chapter 5.

Together they show how, in a competitive market, the interaction between buyers and sellers results in a price that satisfies both groups.

Figure 6.2A shows that at a price of $25, there is one buyer and 11 CDs available for purchase. Therefore, at a price of $25, sellers have a surplus—too many CDs and too few buyers. To attract more buyers, sellers will have to lower the price.

As the price goes down, the quantity demanded rises. At $10 for each CD (Figure 6.2B), sellers have a shortage—too few CDs and too many buyers. Whenever there is a shortage, producers wish they had more CDs to offer customers or that they had charged higher prices for the ones they had on hand. Shortages usually result in a rise in price as buyers compete with each other for a limited supply. Figure 6.2C shows that producers respond to the shortage by raising the price to $20, and a surplus causes the price to drop again.

The equilibrium price is $15. The **equilibrium amount** is six. At that point, the quantity supplied equals the quantity demanded, and buyers and sellers have reached the equilibrium price. Notice the sound of the word *equal* in the word *equilibrium*. An equilibrium price is one in which the quantity supplied and the quantity demanded are identical. At the end of the day, both sellers and buyers are satisfied. In the example shown in Figure 6.2D, everyone who is willing to pay

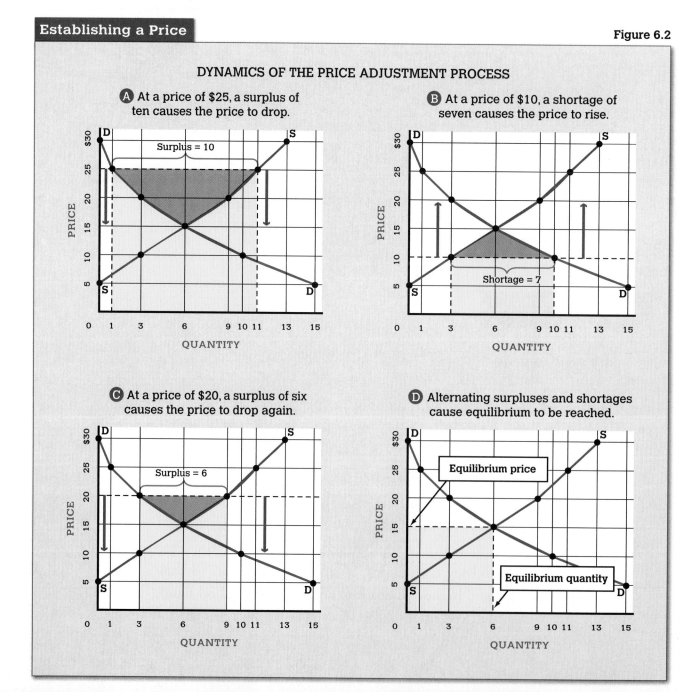

Establishing a Price

Figure 6.2

DYNAMICS OF THE PRICE ADJUSTMENT PROCESS

Ⓐ At a price of $25, a surplus of ten causes the price to drop.

Ⓑ At a price of $10, a shortage of seven causes the price to rise.

Ⓒ At a price of $20, a surplus of six causes the price to drop again.

Ⓓ Alternating surpluses and shortages cause equilibrium to be reached.

a CD is able to purchase one. Everyone who is willing to sell a CD for $15 has sold all of the CDs supplied.

Explaining Shifts in Equilibrium Price

Once the equilibrium price for a good or service is reached, the price will change only if there is a change in demand or supply. Such changes take place all the time. Regardless of whether the change is in supply, demand, or both, the equilibrium price will be affected. The elasticity of the supply and the demand also makes a difference.

Figure 6.3 shows what happens when the quantity supplied changes. Notice that as the demand curve shifts to the right, the new equilibrium price is higher than the old one. The new equilibrium quantity is also higher. If the reverse happened, and the quantity demanded decreased, the new equilibrium price and quantity would be lower than the old one. If nothing else changes, the graph suggests that a change in demand would have the following effects:

- If demand increases, both the equilibrium price and the quantity supplied increase.

- If demand decreases, both the equilibrium price and the quantity supplied decrease.

What happens if there is a change in supply? If nothing else changes, the graph suggests the following:

- If supply increases, the quantity supplied increases and the price falls.

- If supply decreases, the quantity supplied decreases and the price rises.

As long as only one curve shifts, it is fairly easy to determine what will happen to the equilibrium price and the quantity supplied. If both demand and supply change in the same direction, the equilibrium price will shift in that

Figure 6.3

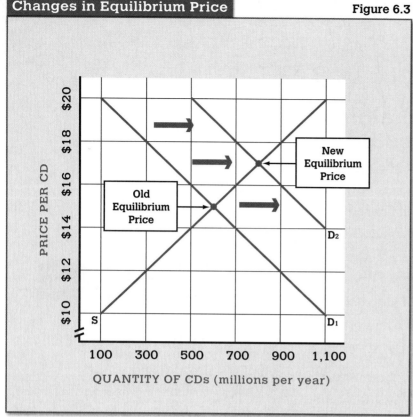

PRICE PER CD

$20 $18 $16 $14 $12 $10

New Equilibrium Price

Old Equilibrium Price

S

D₂

D₁

100   300   500   700   900   1,100

QUANTITY OF CDs (millions per year)

direction. What will happen to the price? If the demand curve increases more than the supply curve, the equilibrium price will increase. For example, in the 1990s, the demand for new houses increased more than the supply, so both the price and the equilibrium amount increased.

If the supply curve increases more than the demand curve, the equilibrium price will decrease. That is exactly what has happened to the market for personal computers. The supply increased more than the demand did, so the price decreased even though the equilibrium amount increased.

If both the demand and supply curves decrease, the equilibrium amount also decreases. If demand decreases more than supply does, the price will drop. If the supply drops more than the demand does, the price will rise.

What happens if the demand and supply shift in opposite directions? The equilibrium price will increase if demand increases and supply decreases. The equilibrium price will decrease if demand decreases and supply increases.

Does this sign represent a surplus or a shortage of a good?

Putting It All Together

Write a paragraph explaining what is likely to happen to milk prices if 1) there is a surplus of milk, 2) the milk producers launch an ad campaign to increase the demand for milk, and 3) at the same time, they increase milk production in anticipation of an even greater increase in demand.

The Machine of a New Sole

In March 2005, Adidas announced the development of a new running shoe. *BusinessWeek* reported:

Three years ago, a trio of engineers for Adidas-Salomon began toiling away in a windowless boiler-room-turned-secret-workshop beneath downtown Portland, Ore. Their goal: to create the first intelligent running shoe, one that would have an in-sole computer to adjust its heel cushioning in real time according to changes in the running surface. "We knew we would have to rewrite the rules," says Christian DiBenedetto, chief shoe engineer at the North American headquarters of Adidas. "But we knew it would be massive if we could pull it off."

Well, maybe. Even if Adidas can make a reliable computerized shoe, the unknown is whether enough customers will value the breakthrough. The Adidas I, a $250 high-tech wonder, hits store shelves this month. . . . Inside the heel of the aerodynamic shoe are a wafer-thin sensor and magnet that monitors the amount of shock applied to the foot and adjusts the footbed 1,000 times per second. Adidas executives believe the shoe . . . can be adapted to the company's basketball and soccer shoes and eventually enter the profitable league of "gotta-have" sneakers among urban youth. ■

"The Machine of a New Sole" by Stanley Holmes. *BusinessWeek*, March 14, 2005.

THE ADIDAS computerized shoe

reading for understanding

What is the advantage of the Adidas I?

What question do people have about the price of the shoes? Who will answer the question?

What do you think the answer will be?

Controlling Prices

Thinking on Your Own

Turn the headings in this lesson into questions and write an answer to each using what you already know. Try to use the vocabulary words in your answers.

In a market economy, prices determine the **allocation** of limited resources. That means that the market decides what will be produced, how much will be produced, and who will get those products. Although in the long run, prices are the most efficient way of answering the basic economic questions, in the short run, they can cause hardships for both producers and consumers. From time to time, governments try to protect one or the other from market forces by controlling prices.

focus your reading

Give at least one example of a price ceiling. Give one example of a price floor.

What effect does rationing have on the price of goods and services?

What effect do price floors have on shortages and surpluses?

vocabulary

allocation

price ceiling

rent control

rationing

black market

price floor

minimum wage

price support

Price Ceilings

A **price ceiling** is a maximum price that the government sets for a product or service. Prices can be lower than the maximum but not higher. For example, if a city has a housing shortage, landlords are likely to respond by raising rents. To protect consumers, city officials may vote to limit how much landlords can charge for an apartment. Such a limit is known as **rent control**. Figure 6.4 shows what happens when a city tries to control rents by establishing a price ceiling.

Without the ceiling, the equilibrium price of an apartment is $900 a month. With rent control, the maximum price is $600 a month. At $600 a month, the demand for apartments increases from 2 million at the equilibrium price to 2.4 million. The supply, however, drops to 1.6 million. What happened to the other 400,000 apartments available at $900 a month? Some landlords may have converted their apartment buildings to other uses—offices, for example. Others may have decided to sell individual apartments as condominiums rather than rent them.

What the graph does not show are some of the other effects of a price ceiling. Rent control freezes the income of landlords and threatens their profits. Landlords, in turn, may decide to make up for their losses by spending less on the upkeep of their apartments or delaying needed repairs. The price ceiling also discourages other businesspeople from entering the market. They have no incentive to increase the number of apartments by building additional units.

Price ceilings also have intended and unintended outcomes. The intended outcome (what lawmakers expected to happen) is to make existing housing more affordable. The unintended outcomes (what lawmakers did not expect) include an increase in the shortage of apartments and a decreasing supply of existing apartments.

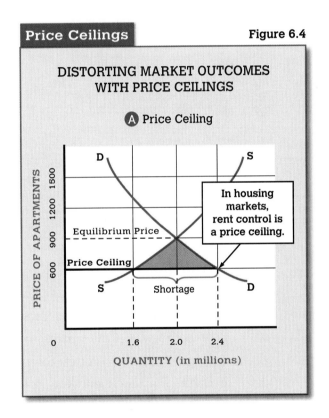

Price Ceilings

Figure 6.4

DISTORTING MARKET OUTCOMES WITH PRICE CEILINGS

Ⓐ Price Ceiling

In housing markets, rent control is a price ceiling.

PRICE OF APARTMENTS

Equilibrium Price

Price Ceiling

Shortage

QUANTITY (in millions)

Rationing

Rationing—limiting purchases—can also lead to shortages. During World War II, for example, the United States rationed purchases of goods that were needed for the war effort. The government created a shortage of consumer products by limiting what people could buy. How did rationing work? Every person in the nation had to apply for a ration book. It contained a limited number of coupons. The number of coupons in the book determined the amount of canned goods, coffee, sugar, or other rationed items a person could buy.

Ration books were used during World War II to ensure that the armed forces had needed supplies.

Like rent control, rationing had both intended and unintended consequences. The intended consequence was to provide the armed forces with enough food and other supplies to win the war. One unintended consequence was an expensive new government agency to enforce rationing. Another was the growth of a black market. A **black market** is one in which illegal goods are bought and sold or goods are traded at prices above the ceiling price.

Are price ceilings and rationing bad ideas? Most economists think they are. Yet rationing helped the United States win World War II by ensuring that troops received a steady supply of food and other necessities.

stop and think

How would an excess in demand for tickets to a championship game affect the price of those tickets? How might high demand encourage a black market? Work with a partner to write a paragraph to explain your answer.

Price Floors

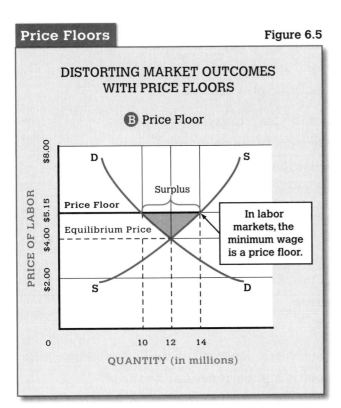

DISTORTING MARKET OUTCOMES WITH PRICE FLOORS

B Price Floor

PRICE OF LABOR

$8.00
$5.15
$4.00
$2.00

D — S
Surplus
Price Floor
Equilibrium Price
S — D

In labor markets, the minimum wage is a price floor.

0   10   12   14

QUANTITY (in millions)

A **price floor** is a minimum price that the government sets for a product or service. Prices can be higher than the minimum, but not lower. Price ceilings seek to protect consumers. Price floors try to protect sellers of a product or service.

A **minimum wage** is an example of a price floor. It is the lowest legal wage that can be paid to most workers. Figure 6.5 shows the effects of a price floor for wages. At a minimum wage of $5.15 per hour, 14 million people would be willing to work. According to the demand curve, however, only 10 million would find a job—a surplus of 4 million workers.

Notice that price ceilings lead to shortages and price floors result in surpluses. Producers—in this case workers—respond

Minimum-wage jobs are an example of a price floor.

to high minimum wages by increasing the supply—in this example, more workers enter the job market. Consumers—in this example, employers—respond to high prices by hiring fewer workers. The result is a surplus of workers.

Is a minimum wage, then, a bad idea? Economists agree that it is not as efficient as a wage set by supply and demand, but some maintain that not all economic decisions should be based on efficiency. They favor a minimum wage because it raises the incomes of poor people. Others believe that a minimum wage actually increases the number of unemployed people because employers do not hire as many workers. Still other economists believe that a minimum wage has little meaning in the real world, because it is often lower than the lowest wage paid in many parts of the country.

Another kind of price floor is a price support for the nation's farmers. A **price support** is a government action to increase the price of a product, usually by buying it. Suppose farmers produce a record crop of wheat. They grow so much wheat that the nation has a surplus. As you might expect, the

Read a Primary Source

Rationing at a Glance

COFFEE AND SUGAR—Stamp 24 in Book 1 is good for one pound of coffee through June 30. Stamp 13 is good for five pounds of sugar through Aug. 5. Stamps 15 and 16 are good for five pounds of sugar apiece, for use in home canning, through Oct. 31. If more is needed for canning, an additional allotment may be granted on application to local rationing board.

reading for understanding

Give examples of the way rationing affected everyday life in the United States in 1943.

What do the rules suggest about the amount of work ordinary citizens had to do in order to get the various products they needed?

SHOES—Stamp 18 in Book 1 is good for one pair of shoes through Oct. 31. Families may pool the coupons of all members living in the same household.

GASOLINE—All non-essential driving is banned to holders of A, B, and C books. All A coupons are valued at three gallons, B and C unit coupons are valued at 2 and one half gallons. Coupon 5 in A book is valid through July 21.

New York Times, June 20, 1943

price of wheat will fall. That price may even drop to the point that farmers do not earn enough to pay their bills. To avoid that possibility, the government may set a price floor for wheat to keep the price from dropping below a certain level. That's a good thing for farmers. Or is it? Economists point out that if farmers know they will get at least a certain amount for their wheat, they have no incentive to reduce the supply. As a result, they continue to produce surpluses as long as they can make a profit.

Communication in the Market

Markets bring buyers and sellers together. Although they may not talk in a literal sense, they communicate through changes in price. Whenever governments try to interfere in that communication, the result is a loss of efficiency.

A government can also influence markets through its actions. When a government announces a change in personal or corporate taxes or other financial policies, the market will respond positively or negatively. For instance, suppose that the federal government announces it will raise personal and corporate income taxes to pay off some of its debt. If investors do not agree with this decision, they might sell some stock and reinvest their money in other assets, such as gold and silver. This will cause stock prices to fall and the prices of gold and silver to rise. Through their actions, investors send a message to the government that they do not like the new tax policy.

Putting It All Together

How will each of the following events affect the price of beef?

- an increase in the number of ranchers

- beef rationing

- beef price supports

- a popular new high-protein diet

- unusually low prices for chicken and turkey

Write a sentence for each event. Be sure to give reasons for each of your answers.

Chapter Summary

- In a market economy, **prices** send signals to both producers and consumers.

- If the quantity demanded is greater than the quantity supplied, a **shortage** occurs.

- When demand is greater than supply, price acts as a way of **rationing**, or limiting, the demand for that product.

- When quantity supplied is greater than the quantity demanded, a **surplus** occurs.

- At the **equilibrium price**, the quantity demanded is equal to the quantity supplied. The point at which the two meet is known as the **equilibrium amount**.

- Prices determine the **allocation** of limited resources.

- A **price ceiling** is a maximum price that the government sets for a product or service. **Rent control** is an example of a price ceiling.

- **Rationing**, or limiting purchases, can lead to shortages and the growth of a **black market**, in which illegal goods are bought and sold or traded above the price ceiling.

- A **price floor** is a minimum price that the government sets for a product or service. A **minimum wage** (the lowest legal wage that can be paid to workers) and **price supports** (government actions that increase the price of a product) are examples of a price floor.

Chapter Review

1 Use a diagram to explain how supply and demand work together to reach the equilibrium price.

2 Explain how price adjustments act to reduce surpluses and shortages.

3 Write a paragraph stating your opinion on whether or not the government should control prices through rationing, price floors and ceilings, and/or price supports. Be sure to give reasons to support your opinion.

Skill Builder

Make Predictions

Predicting future events can be difficult and sometimes risky. The more information you have, however, the more accurate your predictions will be.

In making a prediction, you should

- gather information about the decision or action.

- apply economic laws like the law of demand and the law of supply as well as what you know about history and human behavior to identify possible consequences.

- analyze each consequence by asking how likely it is to occur.

ABC Bike Company has been in business for 50 years. The company specializes in road bikes and sells their products in all parts of the country. For the past ten years, demand for ABC products has been steady, with an equilibrium price of $125 for a bike and an equilibrium quantity of 30,000 bikes.

A year ago, ABC was faced with competition from several new companies. The result has been an increase in the supply of bikes. That change is shown in Figure 6.6 below. Quantity Supplied (1) is the original quantity supplied. Quantity Supplied (2) reflects the increase in the quantity supplied.

Use the chart to answer these questions.

1 What is the new equilibrium price? How does it differ from the old equilibrium price? What is the reason for the change?

2 If everything else remains the same, what long-run effect do you think the decline in price will have on the bike industry?

3 What advice would you give the ABC Bike Company on how to deal with the drop in price?

Figure 6.6

Price	Quantity Demanded	Quantity Supplied (1)	Quantity Supplied (2)
$200	2,000	100,000	200,000
175	5,000	50,000	100,000
150	10,000	40,000	80,000
125	30,000	30,000	60,000
100	50,000	25,000	50,000
75	80,000	10,000	20,000
50	150,000	3,000	6,000

Chapter 7 COMPETITION

Getting Focused

Skim this chapter to predict what you will be learning.

- Read the lesson titles and subheadings.
- Look at the illustrations and read the captions.
- Examine the charts and graphs.
- Review the vocabulary words and terms.

Competition is central to a market economy. Only with competition will supply and demand work together to determine which goods and services will be offered for sale and at what price. What do you know about competition? How does it work? Have you ever benefited from competition? If so, how? Discuss your ideas with a partner.

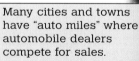

Many cities and towns have "auto miles" where automobile dealers compete for sales.

Market Structures and Perfect Competition

Thinking on Your Own

Think about an item that you bought recently. Were other competing products available? If so, how do you think the competing products affected the price that you paid for it?

If you are like most people, you think of competition as a contest—a race, a rivalry, perhaps even a battle. In economics, the word **competition** means freedom to choose from several alternatives. Sellers cannot raise prices whenever they want if buyers have alternative products from which to choose. Competition forces sellers to be efficient in their use of resources and respond to consumer demands.

focus your reading

What elements or characteristics define a market structure?

How does perfect competition affect the equilibrium price?

Why are perfectly competitive markets so rare?

vocabulary

competition

market structure

perfect competition

Market Structures

Economists categorize industries by their **market structure**—by the amount of competition that exists in an industry. Economists have identified six conditions that determine how competitive a market is:

- number of buyers and sellers in the industry
- type of product produced (identical or unique)
- degree to which individual firms in the industry control price
- amount of information available to producers and consumers
- ease of entry and exit from the industry
- role of government

Perfect Competition

The most competitive market structure is perfect competition. **Perfect competition** is a market structure in which thousands of firms, acting independently, turn out identical products for consumers. Supply and demand work together to decide which goods and services will be produced and at what price.

Perfect competition rarely exists anywhere in the world. It is most useful as an economic model—a simplified view of the real world that is useful in comparing and contrasting various market structures. The industry that most closely resembles perfect competition is farming.

Thousands of buyers and sellers Imagine a 5,000-acre farm in Iowa. It is one of thousands of farms that produce corn

Corn is an example of an identical product.

in the United States. While 5,000 acres is a large farm, it is just a tiny portion of the nation's 73 million acres of farmland devoted to growing corn. If the farm produces 125 bushels per acre, its total output is 625,000 bushels. That sounds like a lot of corn, but it is only a small percentage of the over 9 *trillion* bushels of corn American farmers harvest each year.

Identical products The corn produced on that 5,000-acre farm is identical to the corn produced by other farms, not only in Iowa, but also in Kansas, Nebraska, and elsewhere. Because there is little or no difference between the corn produced on one farm and that grown on other farms, buyers have no reason to prefer corn from one farm to that of another. That means that buyers will expect to pay the same price for corn, regardless of who produced it.

No control over price In a perfectly competitive market, neither buyers nor sellers can individually influence the price of a product. The price is determined by the interaction of supply and demand. If the owners of the Iowa farm stopped

planting corn tomorrow, their action would have no effect on the nation's overall supply of corn or its price.

Complete information Perfect competition requires that both buyers and sellers have access to information, or common knowledge, about the market and the product. Farmers have easy access to information that can improve the size of their crop and its quality as well the most up-to-date information about price. They can gather this information from a variety of sources—including trade journals, manufacturers of farm equipment, government bulletins, and the Internet. Buyers have access to the same information.

Easy entry and exit In a perfectly competitive industry, sellers and buyers can enter or leave the market whenever they wish to do so. If the price of corn rises, the number of farmers eager to plant the crop will increase. If the price falls, some farmers may decide to grow something else. One of the main features of perfect competition is that there are no barriers to entering or leaving the market.

Small role of government The government plays a very small role in a perfectly competitive industry. Usually governments try to keep firms from organizing to set prices or limit supplies of a product. With thousands of independent firms in a competitive industry, there is little chance of one firm or a combination of businesses dominating the industry.

stop and think

Why is access to information about a product and its price important for both buyers and sellers? Think of an example from your own experience, such as information on computers, jeans, or sneakers. Write a paragraph describing the product, where you found the information, and how it influenced your choice of purchase.

Putting It All Together

Fruits, vegetables, table salt, concrete, and safety pins are all examples of products that are identical or almost identical. What other items do you or your family purchase that are so nearly identical as to make perfect competition possible?

Farmers can decide which crops to plant based on having complete market information.

Imperfect Competition

Thinking on Your Own

As you read about examples of imperfect competition, compare and contrast imperfect competition to perfect competition. Draw a Venn diagram in your notebook and use that to organize your facts. In what respects are they alike? How do you account for differences?

Perfect competition is rare in the world today, but it is important. Economists use it to evaluate other market structures. **Imperfect competition** is the name given to market structures that lack one or more of the conditions for perfect competition. Most industries today are considered examples of imperfect competition. They fall into one of two main categories—monopolistic competition and oligopoly.

Monopolistic Competition

Monopolistic competition is a market that has a large number of sellers who produce goods and services that are essentially alike but not identical. By making their products a little different, sellers in an industry marked by monopolistic competition try to attract more customers. This is the largest market structure in the United States. The goal of producers is to monopolize, or control, a small portion of the market. The word *monopolize* refers to a **monopoly**—a market structure in which a single seller controls an entire industry. However, in monopolistic competition, there are many companies competing.

---

focus your reading

What is monopolistic competition? How is it similar to perfect competition? How is it similar to a monopoly?

Describe the single most important feature of an oligopoly.

Explain how monopolistic competition and oligopolies differ from each other.

vocabulary

imperfect competition

monopolistic competition

monopoly

differentiate

oligopoly

patent

collusion

cartel

Many sellers and buyers In a monopolistically competitive industry, there are many sellers and buyers. The restaurant industry is an example of an industry with monopolistic competition. A small city may have 50 restaurants; a large city may have several thousand.

Differentiated products Sellers in a monopolistically competitive industry try to attract buyers by making their product a little different from anyone else's. When people **differentiate** products, they distinguish one from another. *Product differentiation* refers to real or imagined differences among competing products in the same industry. Those differences rarely involve price.

The market for toothpaste is an example of monopolistic competition. One tube of toothpaste is essentially like another, regardless of the brand name. However, sellers use brands and advertising to persuade buyers that their toothpaste is not only different but also better. So buyers are willing to seek out the brand that promises the whitest teeth or freshest breath.

Limited control over price Buyers are willing to pay a little more for differentiated products. However, because most brands of toothpaste are very similar, sellers cannot raise prices too high, or buyers will switch. So, on the whole, sellers in a market made up of monopolistic competition have limited control over the price they can charge for a product. If your favorite Italian restaurant charges more than you are willing to pay for a pizza, you have other choices. If the price of a popular brand of toothpaste is considerably higher than other brands, you may decide to switch to another brand.

Companies strive to differentiate their products from those of their competition.

Good access to information Buyers and sellers have access to considerable information about the market. Sellers have a good idea about the costs of production for rival products and the prices charged for those products. They also gather information about competitors' special offers, discount coupons, and other selling points from their advertisements. They use this information to adjust their own products or prices. Buyers also have access to this information.

Relatively easy entry and exit In a monopolistically competitive industry, it is relatively easy to enter or leave the industry. Individual firms face few barriers to entry. New restaurants open regularly, and older ones close. The investment in natural, capital, and human resources is small compared with the investment in much larger businesses.

Restaurants are an example of an industry with monopolistic competition.

Small role of government The government plays a very small role in monopolistically competitive industries, because neither buyers nor sellers can control prices or limit competition. Although sellers can raise their own prices, they have little or no influence on those of rival companies. If a price is too high, buyers will go elsewhere.

Oligopoly

An **oligopoly** is a market structure dominated by a small number of sellers. Because there are relatively few companies in the market, a single firm can cause a change in supply and price. In the United States, many markets are oligopolies.

Few firms Economists define oligopolies as having from three to 12 firms that produce more than 50 percent of the industry's output. In the auto industry, for example, five firms dominate the industry worldwide — General Motors, Ford, Toyota, DaimlerChrysler, and Volkswagen.

stop and think

Read an ad in a magazine or your local newspaper. Draw a three-column chart in your notebook. In the first column, list the information the ad provides about the product and its price. In the second column, write what other information you would like to have before buying the product. In the third column, write where you can find that information.

Differentiated or identical products Some oligopolies produce products that are identical, and others produce differentiated products. Oligopolies that produce identical products are known as *pure oligopolies*. These include the aluminum, steel, and glass industries. Oligopolies that produce products that differ from one another and often carry distinctive brand names are known as *differentiated oligopolies*. These include carmakers, cereal manufacturers, and fast-food restaurants.

Fast-food restaurants are an example of an oligopoly.

Greater influence on price

Rival companies in an oligopoly have considerable influence over price. Each has to respond to the prices of rivals or changes in those prices. If one carmaker announces its new luxury car will sell for $50,000, the others may follow suit or they may reduce the price of their luxury cars slightly. The reduction is likely to force the first carmaker to reduce prices or offer customers rebates (cash-back offers).

Limited information The major firms in an oligopoly try to withhold information from competitors. Rivals are secretive about many aspects of their production. Secrecy is important because there are just a few producers and the competition among them is fierce. Gaining even a small advantage over rivals can make a huge difference in a company's share of the market.

Difficult entry or exit It is difficult for a new company to enter an oligopoly. The barriers to entry include high costs for capital resources, research and product development, and a skilled workforce. Another barrier is the number of patents held by companies in a market characterized by oligopoly. The importance of research and development to the industry encourages companies to protect innovations with patents. A **patent** is a legal procedure to protect an invention or other innovation from being copied for a period of 20 years.

Entry into some markets, such as cereal manufacturing, is difficult.

It is also difficult for a firm to leave an oligopoly and produce a different product for many of the same reasons: the cost of converting plants and equipment, retraining workers, developing new technologies, and applying for new patents.

Larger role of government The role of government increases in an oligopoly. Governments try to encourage competition and protect consumers. So the federal government has outlawed activities that seek to reduce competition. One of those behaviors is collusion. **Collusion** takes place when rival companies within an oligopoly cooperate for their mutual benefit. Because the number of firms in the industry is limited, the decision of even a few firms to work together can significantly impact the market as a whole. They can affect both supply and price.

Some collusion among oligopolies is beyond the reach of any government. A **cartel** is a special case of collusion. It is an organization of sellers who wish to decrease or eliminate competition by limiting its output. By limiting supply, they are able to raise prices. One of the best-known examples of a cartel is OPEC (Organization of Petroleum Exporting Countries). OPEC does not control the oil market. Its 11 member countries produce about 40 percent of the world's crude oil and 16 percent of its natural gas. However, OPEC's oil exports represent about 55 percent of the oil traded internationally. Therefore, OPEC can have a strong influence on the oil market, especially if it decides to change its level of production.

Putting It All Together

Many economists believe that the Internet has made the U.S. economy more competitive. List at least three ways the Internet may have increased competition in each market structure described in this lesson. For example, how does it affect the number of firms in a market? How does it affect the degree to which individuals can control prices? Use the Venn diagram and the chart you developed to answer these questions in a paragraph.

Who's Got Game Now?

Microsoft expects its newest version of Xbox to take business away from its competitors. Sony and Nintendo have similar plans for the newest version of their game consoles. Reporters Cliff Edwards and Jay Greene describe what is at stake for all three companies:

The company that captures the lead will not only sell the most hardware, it will likely collect the biggest slice of revenues from sales of game software and fees from game makers whose titles run on their consoles. They're battling to rule a $24 billion industry that's expected to grow to $27 billion by 2007. . . .

Microsoft did little more than establish a beachhead with its first console, but this time it could do much better. For starters, Xbox 360 will hit stores ahead of PlayStation 3—rather than being 20 months behind, as the first Xbox was when it debuted. . . .

Right now Sony has a 69% market share worldwide, vs. 16% for Microsoft and 15% for Nintendo. . . . By the time the next generation [of game consoles] peaks, [an analyst] predicts, Microsoft will have 25% market share, Sony 65%, and Nintendo 10%.

That's despite the fact that PlayStation 3 is expected to boast hotter technology. . . .

Nintendo is a wild card. Executives there say they'll launch their new console,

MICROSOFT'S Halo 2

code-named Revolution, around the same time as Sony. But they haven't provided any information so far about its capabilities—and little has leaked out. ∎

"Who's Got Game Now?" by Cliff Edwards and Jay Greene.
BusinessWeek, May 15, 2005.

reading for understanding

How competitive is the game console industry?

How many companies are in the industry? What percentage of the market do they hold?

What is the market structure of this industry? How did you decide? What specific characteristics did you take into account?

No Competition

Thinking on Your Own

A monopoly is control of a market by a single firm. Use your knowledge of history to list three industries in the United States that have tried to establish monopolies. Discuss your answers with a partner. Write the names of the industries in your notebook. As you read, look for ways a monopoly differs from other market structures. Create a bulleted list in your notebook.

The exact opposite of perfect competition is monopoly. A *monopoly* is a market structure in which one firm produces virtually all of an industry's output. Like perfect competition, monopoly is an extreme.

Characteristics of a Monopoly

Although a monopoly has some things in common with other market structures, in many ways it is unique. Monopolies share the following characteristics:

One firm The most striking feature of a monopoly is that a single company produces all or nearly all of the industry's output. There are no alternatives for buyers and no competitor can enter the market.

Unique product A monopoly produces a product for which there is no easy substitute. Electricity from your local power company is a good example. It is more than likely the only source of electric power available to consumers in your area.

Control over price A monopoly has considerable control over price, because it does not have to worry about what rivals are charging. The only limits on its ability to raise prices are

focus your reading
Identify the four main types of monopoly.
What is the main difference between a monopoly and other market structures?
Why do governments regulate monopolies?

vocabulary
antitrust law
merger
horizontal merger
vertical merger
conglomerate
regulate
natural monopoly
economies of scale
government monopoly
monopoly franchise
deregulate
technological monopoly
geographic monopoly

legal barriers and the ability of consumers to reduce their demand for a particular product or service.

Complete information A monopoly has complete information about the market, because it is the only company in the market. Monopolies rarely share that information with consumers. Many do not advertise because there are no competing firms or easy substitutes.

Extreme difficulty of entry or exit Whenever a monopoly exists, it is nearly impossible for a competitor to enter the industry or for the company holding a monopoly to leave. The barriers to entry are similar to those found in oligopolies, but may also include control of the raw materials necessary to produce a good or service. In the early 1900s, U.S. Steel Corporation controlled the steel industry because it owned its own coal and iron mines. Coal and iron are essential ingredients in steelmaking.

The Standard Oil Company

The Standard Oil Company was one of the nation's first monopolies. By 1878, it controlled about 90 percent of the nation's oil refineries. Its business practices led to passage of the Sherman Antitrust Act, which forbids contracts, schemes, deals, or conspiracies to limit trade. At the turn of the twentieth century, Americans had strong opinions about Standard Oil and other monopolies or trusts. Some of those opinions appeared in editorial cartoons like the one on this page. An editorial cartoon is rarely a simple statement of a point of view and nothing more. It often uses images, not only to offer an opinion, but also to suggest reasons for that opinion. The cartoon on this page appeared in a magazine in 1904. Its title is "Next!"

reading for understanding

Describe exactly what you see in the cartoon.

Pay attention to scale. What object is very large in the cartoon? What objects are much smaller in size?

What symbol does the cartoonist use to show Standard Oil?

What is the cartoonist's opinion of monopolies like Standard Oil? How does cartoonist Udo Keppler support that opinion?

Curriculum Connection

Federal Law	Function
Sherman Antitrust Act (1890)	Outlawed agreements and conspiracies that restrain interstate trade. Made it illegal to monopolize, or even attempt to monopolize, any part of interstate commerce.
Clayton Act (1914)	Restricted price discrimination, or the practice of selling the same good to different buyers at different prices. Prohibited sellers from requiring that a buyer not deal with a competitor. Outlawed interlocking directorates between competitors.* Outlawed mergers that lessen competition substantially.
Federal Trade Commission Act (1914)	Established the Federal Trade Commission (FTC) as an independent antitrust agency. Gave the FTC power to bring court cases against private businesses engaging in unfair trade practices.
Robinson-Patman Act (1936)	Strengthened the law against charging different prices for the same product to different buyers. An amendment to the Clayton Act of 1914.
Celler-Kefauver Antimerger Act (1950)	Strengthened the law against firms joining together to control too large a part of the market. An amendment to the Clayton Act of 1914.
Hart-Scott-Rodino Antitrust Improvements Act (1976)	Restricted mergers that would lessen competition. Required big corporations planning to merge to notify the FTC and the Department of Justice. A decision would then be made whether to challenge the merger under the terms of the Clayton Act of 1914.

*Interlocking directorate: Two competing companies have interlocking directorates when a majority of the directors of one company also serve on the board of the competing company. Why do you think the government objected to the practice?

Significant role of government Another barrier to entry is government. Governments encourage competition and outlaw actions that limit or abolish competition. When prices are controlled by the actions of a single company, the market works less efficiently. Buyers and sellers are no longer free to choose in their own self-interest.

Antitrust laws, like the Sherman Antitrust Act of 1890 and the Clayton Antitrust Act of 1914, are examples of government action to keep competition alive. A *trust* is another name for a monopoly, and an **antitrust law** tries to prevent new monopolies from forming and break up those that already exist. Figure 7.1 lists these and other laws the federal government has

passed to deal with the problems posed by monopolies. Among the business practices these laws deal with are those that try to bully buyers and force out potential competitors.

A number of antitrust laws deal with mergers. Not all mergers are attempts to create a monopoly or even an oligopoly, but they often limit competition. A **merger** is the combination of two or more companies. There are three kinds of mergers: horizontal, vertical, and conglomerate. (See Figure 7.2)

When two or more companies in the same business join forces, the merger is horizontal. The purchase of two gas stations by the owners of a single station is an example of a **horizontal merger**. When a company tries to control the supply chain, or all of the businesses it depends on, **vertical mergers** take place. In Figure 7.2, notice that as a result of a vertical merger, one company owns oil wells, oil refineries, and gas stations.

Another type of merger is a conglomerate merger. A **conglomerate** is a huge corporation involved in four or more unrelated businesses. Sony is one of the largest conglomerates in the world with sales of more $63.2 billion and 161,000 employees. Sony owns not only PlayStation, a television manufacturing company, and one that makes DVD players, but also motion picture, television production, and music studios. The conglomerate also owns a life insurance company and a wireless service group, among many other companies.

In addition to antitrust laws, the federal government also **regulates**, or controls, a number of industries and services. State and local governments also do some regulation—that is, they control industry through rules that protect consumers, promote efficiency, and encourage competition.

stop and think

Review the elements of perfect competition on pages 98–99. What effect might a merger have on each element? Write one sentence for each element.

Types of Monopoly

Not every monopoly is the result of mergers or efforts to force out competitors. There are four main types of monopolies: natural, government, technological, and geographic.

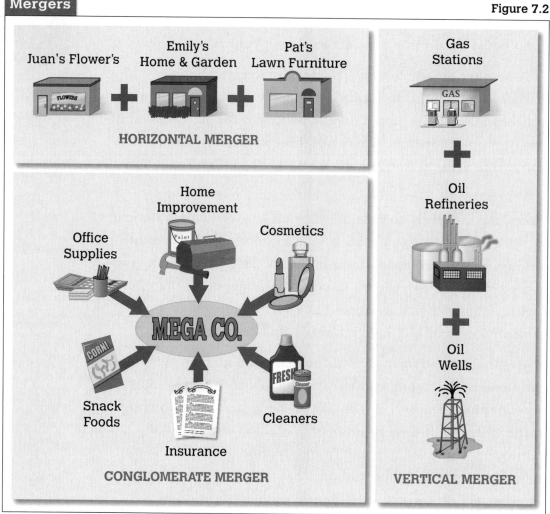

Juan's Flower's + Emily's Home & Garden + Pat's Lawn Furniture

HORIZONTAL MERGER

Office Supplies, Home Improvement, Cosmetics, Snack Foods, Insurance, Cleaners → MEGA CO.

CONGLOMERATE MERGER

Gas Stations + Oil Refineries + Oil Wells

VERTICAL MERGER

A **natural monopoly** exists when a single firm can produce a good or service more efficiently than a number of competing firms could. In certain industries, efficient operation demands that firms be large enough to take advantage of **economies of scale**—the idea that some economic activities become more efficient as production increases. Companies that provide water, gas, and electric power are examples of natural monopolies. A single company can deliver electric power to every customer in the community more efficiently than three or more competing companies, each with its own transmission lines.

Many governments recognize the value of a natural monopoly by giving production of a product or service to a single company exclusively. Such a monopoly is called a **government monopoly**. The best-known government monopoly is the U.S. Postal Service's control over first class

mail delivery. Many cities and towns have government monopolies that provide water and sewer services and garbage collection to local residents. Other local governments award a monopoly franchise to a single company. A **monopoly franchise** is the exclusive right to do business in a given geographical area. The idea is that with such a franchise, a business is able to take advantage of economies of scale. Electric and cable television companies have such franchises in many communities.

When a local government issues such a franchise, it regulates the company to protect consumers. That is, government

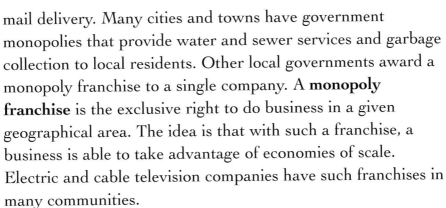

Federal Regulatory Agencies		Figure 7.3

Federal Agency	Function
Federal Trade Commission (FTC) (1914)	Regulates product warranties, unfair methods of competition in interstate commerce, and fraud in advertising.
Food and Drug Administration (FDA) (1927)	Regulates purity and safety of foods, drugs, and cosmetics.
Federal Communications Commission (FCC) (1934)	Regulates television, radio, telegraph, and telephone; grants licenses, creates and enforces rules of behavior for broadcasting; partly regulates satellite transmissions and cable television.
Securities and Exchange Commission (SEC) (1934)	Regulates the sale of stocks, bonds, and other investments.
Equal Employment Opportunity Commission (EEOC) (1964)	Responsible for working to reduce discrimination based on religion, gender, race, national origin, or age.
Occupational Safety and Health Administration (OSHA) (1970)	Regulates the workplace environment; ensures that businesses provide workers with safe and healthful working conditions.
Environmental Protection Agency (EPA) (1970)	Develops and enforces environmental standards for air, water, and toxic waste.
Nuclear Regulatory Commission (NRC) (1974)	Regulates the nuclear power industry; licenses and oversees design, construction, and operation of nuclear power plants.

officials ensure that the price set by a single seller is fair to both consumers and the owners of the business. Although it serves in place of competition to achieve the objectives of a market economy, government regulation is not without problems. Figure 7.3 shows a few of the many agencies in the federal government that regulate businesses.

In the 1980s and 1990s, governments in the United States began to **deregulate**, or remove government restrictions, to restore competition. Economists have different ideas about the effects of deregulation. Some believe that prices would rise if regulations and control were reduced or eliminated. However, deregulation might also increase the number of sellers, which would increase competition and also the supply of goods and services. This would cause prices to drop, which would benefit consumers.

The most famous example is the airline industry. With deregulation, prices have dropped dramatically. With the decline in the price of fares has come a decline in the profitability of many airlines. Some have gone out of business.

An electric company is an example of a local monopoly.

A **technological monopoly** is the result of a firm developing new technology that is used to produce a new product. To protect that product, the firm applies for patents. In the drug industry, for example, companies spend huge sums of money on research. They then obtain a patent on those drugs, giving them the exclusive right to sell that medication for 20 years. Similarly, copyright law protects works of art, literature, songs, and other creative material. The author or artist keeps the rights to the work for his or her lifetime plus 50 years.

The computer industry also has a number of technological monopolies. One of the best known is Microsoft, which developed the operating system used on most computers. Other firms with technological monopolies in the computer industry are Cisco (which dominates the market for Internet routers), Intel (microprocessors), and Intuit (personal-finance software).

Monopolies in the computer industry differ from other technological monopolies in that they are able to keep control of a market because it is in the interest of other high-tech companies to let them do so. Monopolies in the computer industry tend to sell products that allow the entire industry to expand. With these products, a computer gadget developed by one company works with gadgets developed by other firms. So in many ways, they strengthen the computer industry as a whole.

A **geographic monopoly** occurs when a firm is the sole provider of a good or service in a city, town, or other region. If a town is too small to support more than one grocery store, that one store would have a geographic monopoly. Today, such monopolies are rare. Consumers, even in remote areas, are linked to sellers all over the world through the Internet.

Putting It All Together

Economists sometimes define a monopoly as the exact opposite of perfect competition. Write a paragraph explaining the difference between these two market structures. Use terms like *differentiated product, entry, exit,* and *role of government* to highlight differences between the two market structures.

Chapter Summary

- Economists use the degree of **competition** in a market to categorize various **market structures**.

- The opposite of **perfect competition** is **monopoly**.

- **Monopolistic competition** and **oligopolies** are examples of **imperfect competition**.

- **Differentiation** of products is important in monopolistic competition and oligopolies.

- A barrier to entry in some markets is the fact that many products and techniques have **patents**.

- A **cartel** is a form of **collusion**.

- **Antitrust laws** try to maintain competition in the economy.

- Types of **mergers** include **horizontal, vertical**, and **conglomerate mergers**.

- Some industries that required **regulation** in the early 1900s were **deregulated** at the end of the twentieth century.

- A **natural monopoly** may develop as a result of the need for **economies of scale**.

- A **government monopoly** may involve a **monopoly franchise**.

- Two types of monopolies are **technological monopolies** and **geographic monopolies**.

Chapter Review

1 Create a chart that compares perfect competition with monopolistic competition, oligopoly, and monopoly. Column headings should read: "Number of Firms in the Industry," "Type of Product," "Influence Over Price," "Amount of Information," "Ease of Entry and Exit," and "Role of Government." Be sure to include an appropriate title for your chart.

2 Use the information in one of the columns in the chart you created above to write a paragraph that describes similarities and differences among market structures.

Skill Builder

Find the Main Idea

Finding the main idea can help you better understand the information and ideas you encounter as you read.

To find the main idea:

- Ask yourself: What is the purpose of this paragraph, article, section, or chapter?

- Skim the material to identify the general subject. Pay particular attention to the first or last sentence. One of these is often the topic sentence. It gives the main idea of the passage.

- Identify details that support a larger idea or issue.

Read the excerpt below and answer the questions that follow.

"The Internet makes the world simpler. For businesses, the Internet breaks down logistical barriers, offering greater flexibility and power in the way they do business. It shrinks time and distance, simplifies complex business processes, and enables more effective communication and collaboration—a giant corporation can now be as nimble as a tiny startup, while a family firm located in a remote rural village now has the world as its marketplace. Combined with advanced productivity software, the Internet enables individual knowledge workers to use their time more efficiently, and to focus on more productive tasks. And it gives consumers the ability to shop smarter, to find the best products at the right prices. In fact, it empowers them in ways that once were available only to large companies, enabling them to join with others to buy products at lower prices, and bid competitively around the world."

"Shaping the Internet Age" by Bill Gates. *Internet Policy Institute*, December 2000.

1 Who wrote the passage? When was it written?

2 What is the main idea of the passage?

3 What details does the author use to support that main idea?

4 Do you agree with the author's viewpoint? Give details in support of your answer.

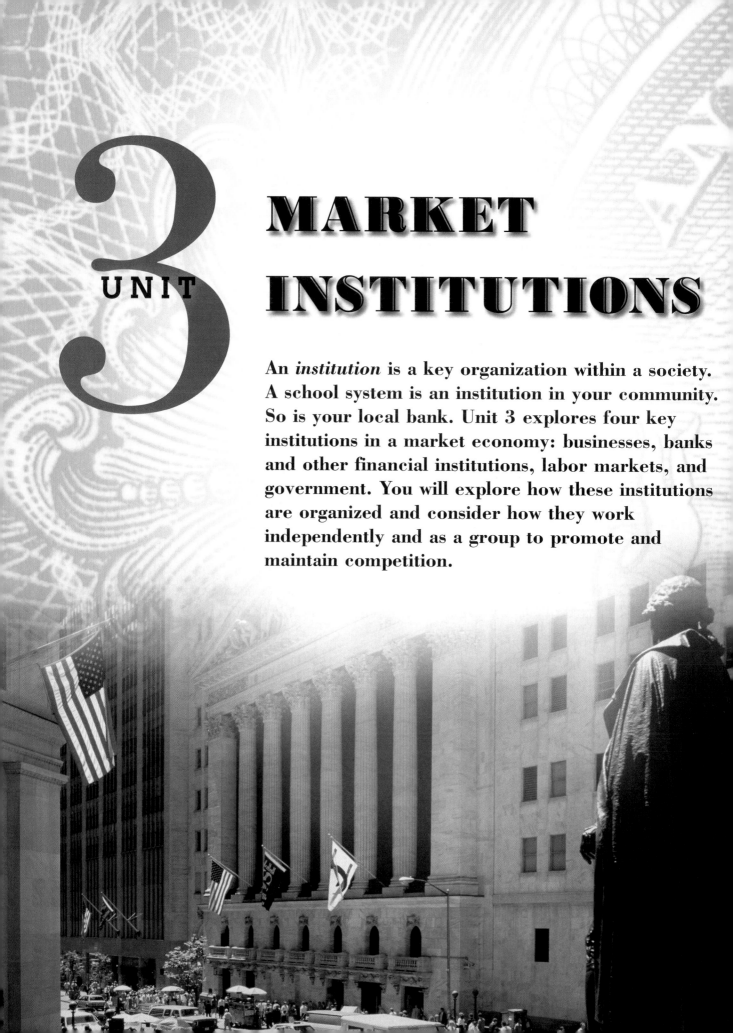

UNIT 3

MARKET INSTITUTIONS

An *institution* is a key organization within a society. A school system is an institution in your community. So is your local bank. Unit 3 explores four key institutions in a market economy: businesses, banks and other financial institutions, labor markets, and government. You will explore how these institutions are organized and consider how they work independently and as a group to promote and maintain competition.

Chapter

8 BUSINESSES

Getting Focused

Skim this chapter to predict what you will be learning.

- Read the lesson titles and subheadings.
- Look at the illustrations and read the captions.
- Examine the charts and graphs.
- Review the vocabulary words and terms.

Businesses play a central role in a market economy. They provide the goods and services you use every day. After you skim this chapter, develop three questions about businesses that you think this chapter will answer. Write the questions in your notebook.

Businesses come in many shapes and sizes. They include everything from the local bookshop to a large international corporation. They may employ one person or tens of thousands. Each business, no matter what its size, plays a role in the economy.

Business Firms

Thinking on Your Own

Select three of the terms from the vocabulary list. Write them in your notebook. Under each, write what you think the term means. As you read the lesson, correct or add to your definition.

A business **firm** is an organization that brings together the factors of production to produce and distribute goods and services. About 21 million firms do business in the United States. They range in size from companies that have no employees (the owner does all of the work) to companies with many thousands of employees.

A firm may have a single place of business or many. Some firms have offices in cities throughout the nation and in countries around the world. Others operate out of the owner's home or car. For example, Apple Computers had its beginnings in the garage of one of its owners. No matter what their size, how they are organized, or where their offices are located, firms in a market economy have much in common.

recall

Goods are products like soap, cereal, cars, or T-shirts.

Services are activities that satisfy a want or need, such as teaching or nursing.

Factors of production consist of natural, human, and capital resources as well as entrepreneurship.

An **entrepreneur** is a person who takes the risk of organizing and operating a business.

The Roles of Firms

Every business firm plays two important roles in an economy. First, it produces a good or service that is in demand. In this role, a firm is a seller of goods and services. When you buy a hot drink on your way to school, shop for shoes at the mall, or buy a movie ticket, you are dealing with business firms as sellers of goods and services.

Firms are also buyers of goods and services. They purchase or rent three factors of production—natural resources, labor (human resources), and capital resources. If you have ever been hired to deliver newspapers, run a cash register, or pump gas, the firm that employed you was acting as a buyer—in this case, of your services (labor).

Risk-Taking and Profit-Making

Every business firm begins with an entrepreneur. Some entrepreneurs are inventors who develop new products or more efficient ways of producing an existing product. Others simply see a need in the community or the nation—for a laundromat, a movie theater, or a less expensive computer—and set out to fill that need. In doing so, entrepreneurs take risks. How risky is a new business? More than 50 percent of all small businesses fail within the first four years.

Entrepreneurs are willing to take risks in the hope that their business will make a profit. A **profit** is the amount of money from sales the firm has after paying its **expenses**—the costs of using the factors of production to produce a product or service.

One way to understand how profits differ from sales is by examining an **income statement**—a report showing a business's sales, expenses, and profit for a certain period of time.

In Figure 8.1, on page 120, the total sales for the first three months of the year (the first quarter) is $1,000. To figure out the firm's **net income**—the amount of money it has left after expenses and taxes have been paid—subtract expenses ($800) and taxes ($80) from total sales. The remainder ($120) is the firm's net income, or profit.

One way companies try to minimize the risk of failure is by controlling their expenses. Every business has expenses. Wages are an ongoing expense. So are **interest** payments, the fees paid to a bank or another lender for borrowing money.

Many small businesses are run from home by an entrepreneur—such as an accountant.

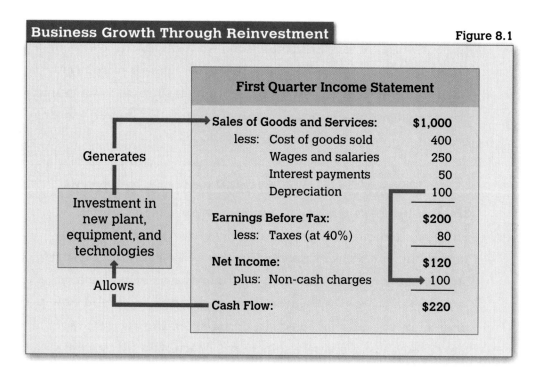

First Quarter Income Statement

Sales of Goods and Services:		$1,000
less: Cost of goods sold		400
Wages and salaries		250
Interest payments		50
Depreciation		100
Earnings Before Tax:		$200
less: Taxes (at 40%)		80
Net Income:		$120
plus: Non-cash charges		100
Cash Flow:		$220

Generates

Investment in new plant, equipment, and technologies

Allows

Other expenses include tools, office supplies, packaging, electricity, heat or air conditioning, telephone service, postage, and transportation costs.

One expense listed under costs on Figure 8.1 does not involve a cash payment. That charge is called depreciation. **Depreciation** is an expense a firm takes to account for wear and tear on its machines and other capital goods. It is later added to the net income to determine the firm's cash flow. **Cash flow** is determined by adding net income plus non-cash charges like depreciation.

Every firm decides how its cash flow will be used. Some of it may be paid back to the owners of the business as their reward for risk-taking. Some of the funds may be reinvested in tools and equipment or marketing in order to produce more products and hopefully generate more sales. As long as a firm is profitable and its reinvested cash flow is larger than depreciation, the firm is likely to grow.

stop and think

Why do you think firms should reinvest cash flow? What do you think the results of not reinvesting cash flow would be?

Financing Growth

A firm can grow by reinvesting some of its profits. It can also grow by offering **franchises**—contracts in which a company sells individuals or other companies the right to use its name and business model and sell its products or services in return for a fee. The parent company is called the *franchiser*, and the person who purchases a franchise is known as the *franchisee*.

In 1851, Isaac Singer developed the first formal franchise contract to solve two problems. Singer had an idea for a sewing machine that people could use at home. He had enough money to build a prototype, or sample, of his sewing machine but not enough to build a factory to produce his machines in large quantities. Singer's second problem was that his machines were not easy to sell. They were expensive, and few people in those days knew how to operate a sewing machine— it was still a new idea. A salesperson would have to teach consumers how to use the machines in order to make a sale. A busy storekeeper did not have the time or knowledge to provide that kind of training.

Singer came up with an idea that solved both of his problems. He offered a limited number of businesspeople the exclusive right to sell his machines within a certain geographical area. In return, the franchisees paid him a licensing fee. Singer used those fees to purchase the capital resources he needed to manufacture his machines. His franchisees had an investment in his company and therefore a financial interest in showing customers not only the benefits of the machine, but also how to use it. Franchising allowed his business to grow without the need to borrow money to buy capital resources or build a distribution network.

Singer's idea was such a success that other companies began to copy and even improve on his idea. At the beginning of the twentieth century, the founders of Coca-Cola divided the country into regions and sold bottling rights to local business-people as a way of reducing their financial risk. In the 1950s and 1960s, fast-food companies, such as McDonald's and Burger King, took franchising to a new level by selling franchises in countries around the world.

Large businesses rely on franchises to expand their market share.

Efficiency and Growth

To remain competitive, firms have to be efficient. A company is efficient if it receives the maximum output from a given amount and combination of resources. Franchises can improve the efficiency of a company by allowing it to focus its limited resources on what the company does best. For example, franchises allowed Singer to concentrate on making sewing machines and leave the selling and training to smaller firms.

A firm can also improve efficiency by purchasing another company or by combining with one or more other companies to form a new company. Mergers can allow the new firm to increase its capabilities without significantly increasing its management costs. In addition, the new company may also take advantage of economies of scale by buying in large quantities or by consolidating manufacturing. The merger may also allow the new firm to make more effective use of advertising.

Diversification is another reason for mergers. Some very large firms believe that their chances for survival are best if they spread their risk by owning several unrelated companies. A change in consumer demand, a downturn in the economy, or even bad weather may affect some of their product lines, but not all of them. Other companies use mergers to eliminate tough competitors.

> **recall**
>
> A **merger** is the combination of two or more companies to form a new company.
>
> **Economies of scale** is the idea that some economic activities become more efficient as production increases.

Putting It All Together

Think of a product that you would like to manufacture and sell. Based on what you learned from this lesson, what steps would you take to increase your chances for success with this product? Share your list with a partner.

Build-A-Bear Workshop

Roger O. Crockett of *BusinessWeek* describes one of the most successful new companies in the nation.

At a Build-A-Bear Workshop in Chicago, little Emily Guisch skips excitedly from one end of the store to the other in search of her mom. "Look, Mommy," she yells, proudly holding up a caramel-colored teddy bear. Not just any ol' bear, mind you. Emily, 7, has stuffed this cub herself, given it a cloth heart, and dressed it with pink panties adorned with one of her favorite characters, Hello Kitty....

Kids all over the world are stuffing millions of these furry creatures.... At an average of $32, the bears, dogs, and other creatures are far from cheap. Every piece of clothing hikes the price.... The 176-store chain boosted sales 41%, to $301.7 million, in 2004, while net income nearly tripled, to $20 million.

Build-A-Bear is the brainchild of Maxine K. Clark.... Clark, who loves children, but doesn't have any of her own, became intrigued with the idea of stuffed animals while taking her neighbor's kids to the mall. During the Internet boom, malls were considered dinosaur destinations. But Clark figured they just needed some imagination. "Ray Kroc didn't invent hamburgers," she says of McDonald's Corp. entrepreneur. "He just invented a way to do it differently"...

Rather than sit on her paws, Clark is rapidly extending the brand. The company is testing a new concept, dubbed Friends 2B

MAXINE K. CLARK poses with a Build-A-Bear.

Made, which lets creative kids build their own humanlike dolls with contemporary clothing and accessories. ∎

"Build-A-Bear Workshop: Retailing gets interactive with toys designed by tots" by Roger O. Crockett. *BusinessWeek*, June 6, 2005.

reading for understanding

What was Build-A-Bear's total sales in 2004?

What was its net income?

How do you explain the difference between the two numbers?

What qualities does the article suggest an entrepreneur needs to build a successful business?

Sole Proprietorships and Partnerships

Thinking on Your Own

If you were to start a business, would you want to be the sole proprietor, or owner, or would you rather form a partnership with a friend or relative? Write a brief explanation of your choice in your notebook.

Firms can be classified in a variety of ways. In Chapter 7, businesses were grouped by how much competition they face. They can also be categorized according to the products they produce or the services they perform. Companies that produce identical or similar products are part of the same industry. Another way of grouping firms is by ownership.

Sole Proprietorships

A **sole proprietorship** is a business owned by one person. It is the oldest form of business organization in the United States and the most common type today. According to the U.S. Census Bureau, sole proprietorships make up more than 70 percent of all businesses in the United States. They range from home-based businesses to manufacturers who sell their goods nationally and even internationally. They include landscapers, architects, software designers, child-care providers, and owners of nail salons, beauty shops, bakeries, and real estate agencies.

Organization The organization of a sole proprietorship is simple. The owner makes all of the decisions, has day-to-day responsibility for running the business, and receives all of the firm's profits. He or she is also responsible for any losses. In the eyes of the law and the public, a sole proprietor and his or her business are one and the same.

---

focus your reading

What are the requirements for starting a sole proprietorship?

What is the advantage of a limited partnership?

What is the main difference between a sole proprietorship and a partnership?

vocabulary

sole proprietorship

liability

partnership

limited partnership

Sole proprietorships make up the majority of businesses in the United States.

Advantages A sole proprietorship is the easiest and least expensive way to start a business. There are no documents or forms to fill out—unless the business operates under a name other than that of its owner, in which case the business needs a fictitious name affidavit. For example, if you started a lawn-mowing business and called it "Lawns Unlimited," you would need to get an affidavit—a sworn written statement—that informs government officials and consumers that your business is operating under the name you chose and that you are the owner of the business.

A sole proprietorship has the following advantages:

- **Control** The owner has complete control over the business and gets all of its profits if the business is successful.

- **Simplicity** A sole proprietorship is easy to start and operate. Few, if any, legal documents are necessary.

- **No double taxation** The business is not taxed separately. Instead, income from the business is on the owner's tax return and is therefore taxed only once.

Disadvantages A sole proprietorship also has several disadvantages.

- **Unlimited liability** The owner is personally liable if anything goes wrong or if the business defaults on its debt. A **liability** is a claim on something that a company or individual owns. *Unlimited liability* means that if the business is a failure, its owner could lose not just the business itself, but—if the debts are large enough—his or her personal possessions, including a house, car, and savings.

stop and think

Think of examples of sole proprietorships in your community. Make a list of at least five. Are there some that are more successful than others? Write a paragraph describing examples of sole proprietorships in your community. Share your paragraph with a partner.

- **Limited fund-raising ability** Banks are often reluctant to loan money to a sole proprietor. Why? A sole proprietor is the only person responsible for the success or failure of a business, and therefore the only person responsible for paying back a business loan.

- **Limited life of the business** A sole proprietorship is a business owned by one person. If that person dies or decides he or she no longer wants to remain in business, the firm will no longer exist. If the sole proprietor wants to bring in another owner, such as a spouse, family member, or friend, the sole proprietorship would have to end and a new business arrangement would have to be created.

Partnerships

A **partnership** is a business organization that is owned by two or more people. Partners jointly make all of the decisions, receive all of the firm's profits, and are responsible for any losses. Partnerships are the least common business organization in the United States.

Organization In a partnership, two or more individuals share both ownership and decision-making. Like a sole proprietorship, a partnership is relatively easy and inexpensive to establish. Unlike a

Partnerships are businesses that are owned by two or more people.

sole proprietorship, a partnership provides opportunities for some specialization in management. For example, one partner might focus on sales, while another handles design or production. A partnership also has better fund-raising abilities than a sole proprietorship, although the ability to borrow money is still limited.

In the eyes of consumers and government officials, partners are equal unless they have a written agreement that states differently. Many partnerships begin with such an agreement. It spells out how

- decisions will be made
- profits will be shared
- disputes will be resolved
- future partners will be admitted to the partnership
- partners can be bought out
- the partnership can be dissolved when needed

Advantages Partnerships have many of the advantages of sole proprietorships. They also have unique benefits.

- **Control** The partners have complete control over their business and receive all of the profits if the business is successful. The business may also benefit from partners who have complementary skills.

- **Simplicity** Partnerships are relatively easy to establish.

- **Greater ability to raise money** With more than one owner, the ability to raise funds may be increased.

- **No double taxation** The profits from the business flow directly through to the partners' personal tax returns, which eliminates being taxed twice.

Disadvantages A partnership has many of the same drawbacks as a sole proprietorship. Partnerships also have a few unique disadvantages.

- **Potential for disagreements** Partners are jointly and individually liable for one another's actions. Since decisions are also shared, the potential for disagreements is great.

- **Limited fund-raising ability** Banks are often only slightly less reluctant to loan money to a partnership than to a sole proprietorship.

- **Limited life of the business** A partnership may have a limited life; it may end with the death of a partner or a partner's decision to leave the business.

- **Unlimited liability** The partners are solely responsible for the success or failure of their business, and therefore solely responsible for paying back business loans. As a result, each partner stands to lose his or her personal wealth because of a decision made by another partner.

The problem of unlimited liability is a particularly difficult one for many partnerships. To understand why, suppose one person invested $90,000 in a partnership and another invested $10,000. The first individual owns 90 percent of the business, and the other, 10 percent. At first glance, it seems like a fair arrangement, particularly if the first individual receives 90 percent of the profits and the second, 10 percent. However, suppose the person who owns 10 percent of the business runs up $100,000 in business debts. If he or she has no other assets, his or her partner could end up liable for the entire $100,000.

One way to avoid the problem of unlimited liability is by forming a **limited partnership**. This is a partnership that consists of two or more persons with at least one general partner and one limited partner. The general partner or partners control the business and have unlimited liability. This includes managing the daily aspects of the business and assuming full responsibility for debts. The limited partners are regarded as investors, and their liability is limited to the amount of money they invest in the company. If the limited partner invests $90,000 in the business, $90,000 is the extent of his or her liability.

Putting It All Together

Think again about the choice you made at the beginning of this lesson. Would you still make the same choice between starting a sole proprietorship or a partnership? In your notebook, explain the advantages of your choice and the disadvantages of the alternative you did not choose.

Corporations

Thinking on Your Own

Some businesses are started as corporations. The vocabulary words below are related to the corporate form of business. After looking over this list, briefly describe in your own words what you think a corporation is. Write your description in your notebook.

A **corporation** is a business owned by many people but treated by the law as if it were one person. A corporation can own property, pay taxes, make contracts, and sue and be sued, just as a person can. Even though corporations make up about 20 percent of all businesses, they account for about 90 percent of all business revenues, or earnings.

Organization Unlike a sole proprietorship or a partnership, a corporation begins with a legal arrangement. People who want to start a corporation need permission from the state to do so. In most states, the founders must register the company and file **articles of incorporation**—a document that lists basic information about the firm. The document includes the name, address, and purpose of the corporation and the names and addresses of the people who will initially manage the corporation. If the articles of incorporation are in agreement with state laws, the state will grant the company a **corporate charter**—a license from that state to set up a business.

To raise the money to start and later expand the business, a corporation can sell stock. As Figure 8.2 on page 130 shows, **stock** is a share in the ownership of a corporation. Each

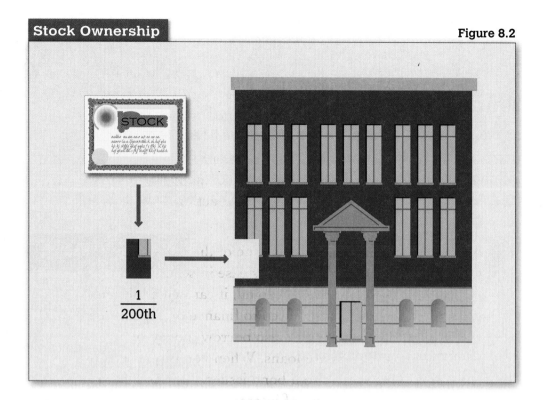

stockholder owns a small percentage of the corporation. There are two kinds of stock: common stock and preferred stock. A share of **common stock** gives an investor voting rights and a portion of future profits. The owner of common stock has one vote for each share of stock he or she owns. Common stockholders elect the corporation's **board of directors**—the group of individuals who supervise and control the corporation. The board, in turn, hires the company's managers—the individuals who run the business on a daily basis.

Owners of **preferred stock** own non-voting shares in the company. They have no say in electing a board of directors, but they do receive dividends before any profits are paid to common stockholders.

Dividends are the portion of a corporation's profits that is paid to each stockholder. How much money a stockholder receives depends upon the amount of stock he or she owns.

> **stop and think**
>
> What is the difference between common stock and preferred stock? Write a sentence or two in your notebook and discuss your answer with a partner.

Advantages Corporations have a number of important advantages over other business firms.

- **Limited liability** If a corporation cannot pay all of its debts, it may go out of business. But because of limited liability, stockholders lose only the money they invested in the company. Even if the firm has debts, the stockholders are not personally responsible for those debts. Officers and directors of the company, however, can be held personally liable for their actions—such as their failure to pay corporate taxes.

- **Great ability to raise money** One of the main advantages of a corporation is its ease in securing money. If a corporation needs more capital, it can sell additional stock. The revenue can be used to finance or expand the business. A corporation can also borrow money by issuing bonds. **Bonds** are loans. When you buy a bond, you are lending money to a bond issuer—in this case, a corporation—at a set rate of interest.

- **Professional management** The directors of a corporation can hire professional managers to run the firm. Figure 8.3 is an organizational chart. It shows how one corporation has divided responsibilities for the firm.

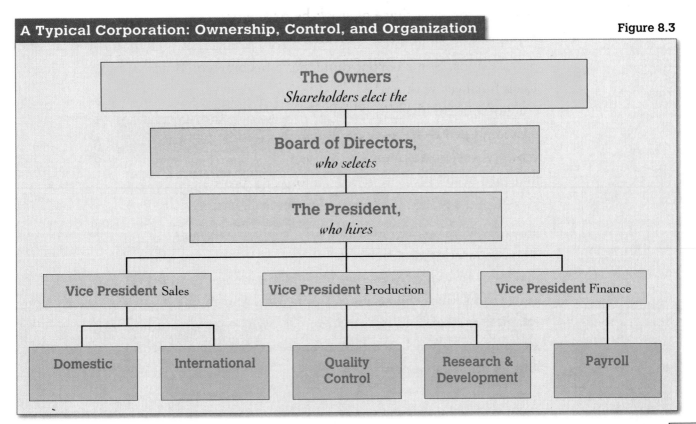

A Typical Corporation: Ownership, Control, and Organization Figure 8.3

The Owners
Shareholders elect the

Board of Directors,
who selects

The President,
who hires

Vice President Sales   Vice President Production   Vice President Finance

Domestic   International   Quality Control   Research & Development   Payroll

- **Unlimited life** A corporation is capable of continuing indefinitely. The death or incapacity of shareholders, directors, or officers of the corporation has no effect on the continued existence of the corporation. Ownership is easily transferred from one person to another.

Disadvantages Like the organization of other business firms, a corporation has a number of disadvantages.

- **Lack of simplicity** The process of incorporation requires more time and money than other types of organization.

- **Government oversight** Corporations are monitored by federal, state, and some local agencies. As a result, more paperwork is needed to conform to government regulations.

- **Double taxation** Incorporating may result in higher overall taxes. Dividends paid to shareholders are not deductible from business income. The corporation pays a tax on this income. The shareholders also pay personal income taxes on it. As a result, this income is taxed twice.

Corporate Growth

Because corporations are able to raise large sums of money by selling stock and issuing bonds, they are able to grow rapidly. Corporations tend to be larger than sole proprietorships or partnerships. Some corporations have become conglomerates. Each business within a conglomerate makes unrelated products, none of which is responsible for a majority of the firm's sales.

> **recall**
>
> A **conglomerate** is a huge corporation involved in four or more unrelated businesses.

General Electric (GE) is an example of a conglomerate. The corporation describes its products and services as ranging "from jet engines to power generation, financial services to plastics, and medical imaging to news and information." It owns a movie studio, a television network, a storage rental service, theme parks, and insurance companies.

Like many large corporations, GE is a **multinational**—a corporation that has manufacturing and service operations in a number of different countries. Multinationals are not only subject to the laws of every country in which they have operations, but also must pay taxes in those countries. Almost every major automobile company is a multinational. The same is true of oil companies.

Some multinationals are conglomerates, but many focus on related products and services. They are welcomed in most countries because they often bring new technology and create new jobs.

Putting It All Together

Make a three-column chart with the headings "Sole Proprietorship," "Partnership," and "Corporation." Divide each column in half. In the top half, explain how that form of business is different from the other two. In the bottom half, explain what it has in common with at least one of the other two.

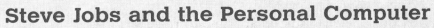

Steve Jobs and the Personal Computer

Steve Jobs and Steve Wozniak founded Apple Computers in 1976. Jobs had dropped out of Reed College after a semester and worked for a while as a technician for video game maker Atari. Jobs started the company working from his parent's garage.

In ten years, with the success of the Apple II personal computer, Apple grew into company with over 4,000 employees. However, the company's growth came at a price. Jobs clashed with the CEO and the board of directors. In 1985, he was fired from the company he had founded.

Jobs believes that being fired from Apple was the best thing that ever happened to him. He went on to start two companies, including Pixar Animation Studios. It has produced some of the most successful animated movies of all time, including *Toy Story*. In 1997, he returned to Apple and was named CEO in 1997. He currently works for a salary of $1, earning him a listing in the Guinness Book of World Records as "Lowest Paid Chief Executive Officer."

reading for understanding

What type of business organization did Apple have when it was founded?

What type of business organization did the company have ten years later?

Explain how getting fired ended up being an advantage to Jobs.

Chapter Summary

- A business **firm** seeks to make a **profit** by bringing together the factors of production to produce and distribute goods and services.

- A firm's **income statement** shows its sales; **expenses**, including **interest** payments and **depreciation**; and **net income** or **profits**.

- **Net income** plus non-cash charges like depreciation are used to determine a company's **cash flow**.

- Some firms minimize expenses by offering **franchises**.

- **Sole proprietorships** and **partnerships** are relatively easy to establish, but raising capital can be difficult.

- One way that partners try to avoid the problems of unlimited **liability** is by forming a **limited partnership**.

- To form a **corporation**, founders must register the company and file **articles of incorporation** in order to secure a **corporate charter**. Some corporations sell **bonds** to raise money.

- **Stockholders** who own **common stock** elect a corporation's **board of directors**; owners of **preferred stock** do not have voting rights, but do receive **dividends**.

- A **multinational** company is subject to the laws of each country in which it operates. It also pays taxes in those countries.

Chapter Review

1 Suppose a friend asked you for advice about starting a new business. What type of business organization would you suggest to your friend? Write a letter that gives your recommendation and explains why you made it.

2 What advice would you give your friend about the best way to minimize the risks of starting a new business? Use examples from the chapter to support your advice.

Skill Builder

Make Generalizations

Generalizations are judgments that are based on the facts at hand. If you say, "Sole proprietorships are important to the U.S. economy," you are making a generalization. If you add that 73 percent of all businesses in the United States are sole proprietorships, you are providing evidence to support your generalization.

In making a generalization, it is important to

- gather related facts and examples.

- identify similarities among those facts and examples.

- use those similarities to form some general ideas about the subject.

Study Figure 8.4 and then answer the questions.

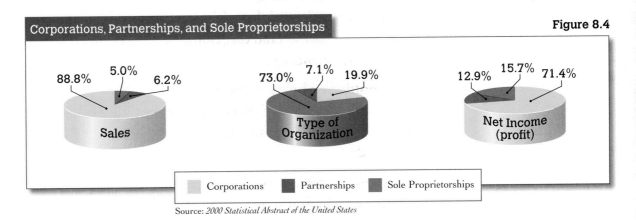

Figure 8.4

Corporations, Partnerships, and Sole Proprietorships

88.8%   5.0%   6.2%   Sales

73.0%   7.1%   19.9%   Type of Organization

12.9%   15.7%   71.4%   Net Income (profit)

Corporations   Partnerships   Sole Proprietorships

Source: *2000 Statistical Abstract of the United States*

1 Rank the three types of business organizations according to the percentage of businesses in each category, from largest to smallest. Then rank each by sales and net income.

2 Based on the information in Figure 8.4, someone could make the following generalization:

Corporations make up a small percentage of businesses in the United States but produce the most sales and profits.

What generalization could you make about sole proprietorships based on these three graphs? What generalization could you make about partnerships?

Chapter

9 FINANCIAL INSTITUTIONS

Getting Focused

Skim this chapter to predict what you will be learning.

- Read the lesson titles and subheadings.
- Look at the illustrations and read the captions.
- Examine the chart and graphs.
- Review the vocabulary words and terms.

This chapter focuses on firms that provide financial services to producers and consumers. A bank is a financial institution. So are credit unions and insurance companies. Look over the major headings, chart, and graphs for clues about the roles that financial institutions play in a market economy and why those roles are so important. List those clues in your notebook.

Financial institutions are an important part of daily life around the world. They include banks, savings and loans, credit unions, and stock exchanges.

Financial Networks

Thinking on Your Own

Select three terms from the vocabulary list. Write them in your notebook. Under each term, write what you think it means. Then use the word in a sentence. As you encounter each term, correct or add to your definitions. If necessary, revise your sentences.

A **financial system** is a network of savers, borrowers, and financial institutions such as banks. They work together to transfer savings to borrowers. In economics, **savings** refers to money set aside for future use. Until it is time to spend that money, savers can choose to **invest** it. That is, they can use their money to make more money—usually with the understanding that there is some risk involved. Those investments are essential to growth in a market economy.

Savings and Growth

To start or expand a business, a firm needs money for capital and other resources. As you learned in Chapter 8, people can use their own money—including their profits—to expand their business. They can also borrow money to build factories, buy machinery and other tools, and hire workers. Where does the money they borrow come from? It comes from savers—people who have a surplus of money and are willing to make an investment.

Suppose you received a sum of money as a birthday gift. If you decided to save it, you would have several choices. You could keep the money hidden in a drawer in your bedroom until you were ready to spend it. Or you could open a **savings account**—an account at a bank on which interest is usually paid and from which withdrawals can be made.

focus your reading

What role do savings play in a market economy?

Give three examples of a financial intermediary.

Describe the main difference between a bank as a financial intermediary and a non-bank financial intermediary.

vocabulary

financial system

savings

invest

savings account

certificate of deposit

financial assets

financial intermediary

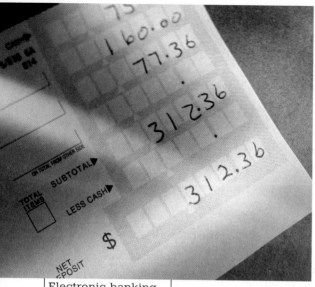

Electronic banking is reducing the amount of paper needed for banking.

When you deposit your money in a bank, the bank makes a promise to return that money to you. It even buys insurance to make sure it can honor that promise. The bank also agrees to pay you interest on your deposit. Why does the bank pay you interest? One reason is to attract more depositors. Another reason is because the bank uses its deposits to make loans to other customers. Interest is your payment for letting them loan your money to someone else.

You could also purchase a certificate of deposit (CD) with your money. A **certificate of deposit** is a document that shows you made a loan to a bank at a certain rate of interest, usually a higher rate than a savings account earns. You generally earn more with a CD because you agree not to cash it in for a certain length of time—one year, 18 months, or more. If you withdraw your money early, you may have to pay a penalty. The opportunity cost of keeping the money in a drawer is the interest the money would have earned in a savings account or by purchasing a certificate of deposit.

Whether you open a savings account or buy a CD, you are given a receipt acknowledging the money you entrusted to the bank. These receipts represent **financial assets**—claims on the property and the income of the borrower. These receipts are assets because they have value. They specify the amount you put into the account and the terms involved in the transaction.

The bank takes the money you deposited and loans it to individuals and firms. Banks do not loan money to everyone who asks for it. Instead, they look for people who are most likely to repay a loan. Although the bank will make money on the deal, it is acting as an intermediary, or go-between. In this case, the bank is the intermediary between you and the borrower. As Figure 9.1 shows, most borrowers and lenders go through a **financial intermediary**.

A Circular Flow

Figure 9.1 is a circular flowchart. It shows what happens when funds are transferred from savers to borrowers. Few savers provide funds directly to the borrower. Most do so indirectly through banks and other financial intermediaries. The borrowers then generate financial assets, which they return to the lender. The result is a circular flow.

Any part of the economy can supply savings, but households and businesses are the most important. Any part of the economy can borrow, but governments and businesses are the largest borrowers. If a corporation or government wishes

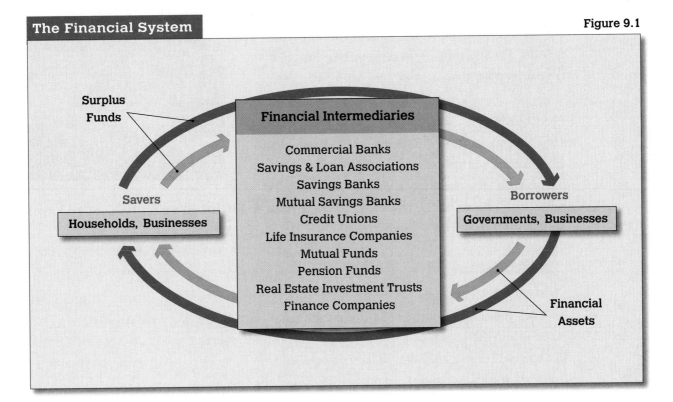

The Financial System
Figure 9.1

Surplus Funds

Financial Intermediaries

Commercial Banks
Savings & Loan Associations
Savings Banks
Mutual Savings Banks
Credit Unions
Life Insurance Companies
Mutual Funds
Pension Funds
Real Estate Investment Trusts
Finance Companies

Savers

Households, Businesses

Borrowers

Governments, Businesses

Financial Assets

to borrow directly from savers, it will usually issue bonds. However, most borrowing takes place indirectly though a financial intermediary.

Almost everyone in a market economy participates in and benefits from this financial system. The smooth flow of funds through the system helps ensure that savers will have an outlet for their savings. Borrowers, in turn, will have a source of financial capital.

Putting It All Together

Suppose a friend gives you an I.O.U. for the $5 he or she borrowed from you. Is the I.O.U a financial asset? Why or why not? What if you deposited that same $5 in a savings account? Write a paragraph in your notebook comparing the two, and discuss it with a partner.

Career Connections

Financial Planner

Do you like numbers? Do you like to analyze trends? Do you enjoy working with people? If so, financial planning may be the career for you.

The Work

U.S. News and World Report listed the position of financial planner as one of the 20 hottest professions for the future. Financial planners help their clients make the most of their money. Financial planners need to have a good understanding of investments, tax law, and estate planning.

Qualifications

Strong analytical skills and experience with computerized data are essential. College courses in business, business law, economics, and psychology are highly recommended. Many in the field urge that those entering the field become Certified Financial Planners (CFPs). To become a CFP, you have to pass an exam that covers over 175 topics on investing and financial planning.

Our Hidden Savings

In his article, Michael J. Mandel comments on the importance of how terms like *savings* and *investment* are defined. He writes:

Americans don't set aside much. But include R&D [research and development] and education spending, and the picture changes.... Over the past year, the household savings rate has averaged a meager 0.8%....

Yet the savings rate is a misleading measure of future economic performance. In today's economy, education and innovation are the main engines of wealth-producing growth, not physical capital. Yet the official statistics count spending on education and research and development as consumption, rather than as an investment.

That's a crucial distinction, since an outlay that is counted as investment ends up increasing savings. For example, if U.S. companies buy new capital equipment, that bolsters the U.S. savings rate. But if those same companies hire more scientists and boost R&D, that spending would not be counted as investment or add to savings, even though it would boost long-run growth....

Spending on education and R&D offers a stronger foundation for solid long-term growth. Having a large pool of college-educated workers is crucial for competing globally, for example, especially in innovative industries.

In the end, what will propel growth is human capital and innovation. It's the hidden savings rate that deserves the attention, not the official one. ∎

"Our Hidden Savings" by Michael J. Mandel. *BusinessWeek*, January 17, 2005.

reading for understanding

According to the author, how do economists define savings?

Describe the relationship between savings and investment.

Why does the author call spending on education and research and development "hidden savings"?

Savings in America

Figure 9.2

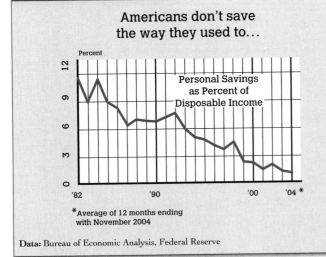

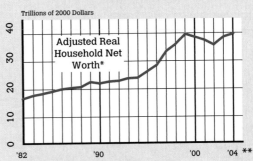

Americans don't save the way they used to...

Percent

Personal Savings as Percent of Disposable Income

'82   '90   '00   '04 *

*Average of 12 months ending with November 2004

...but their wealth is near a record high.

Trillions of 2000 Dollars

Adjusted Real Household Net Worth*

'82   '90   '00   '04 **

*Household net worth minus outstanding federal government debt, adjusted for inflation

** Third quarter

Data: Bureau of Economic Analysis, Federal Reserve

Financial Intermediaries

Thinking on Your Own

List the names of three banks or other financial institutions in your community. Do they offer similar services? How are they different? Discuss your list and answers with a partner.

Financial intermediaries provide a variety of services that aid producers and consumers in their roles as borrowers and savers. Most financial intermediaries are banks, but other firms may play a similar role.

Banks and Banking

A **bank** is an institution that deals in money and provides a variety of financial services. Banks accept deposits and make loans. Banks earn a profit by charging more to borrow money than they pay to savers. They also charge fees for various services. Banks provide three basic services.

- **Keeping money safe** A bank provides customers with a safe place to keep their money until they are ready to use it. Banks work on trust. When you deposit money in a bank, the bank promises to return that money. It even advertises that it will buy insurance to make sure it can honor that promise.

- **Transferring funds** Banks provide a way to transfer money from one person or firm to another. Carrying a large amount of cash or sending it through the mail is risky. Writing a check is an easier and safer way to make a payment. It is also possible to transfer funds by phone,

focus your reading

Name three services banks provide.

In what respect are all banking institutions similar?

What do finance companies have in common with life insurance companies and pensions? How is each unique?

vocabulary

bank

reserve

commercial bank

thrift institution

credit union

finance company

life insurance company

premium

pension

by computer, or by authorizing the bank to take a certain amount of money from an account to make a payment, such as rent or for delivery of your local newspaper.

- **Loaning money** Another crucial service banks perform is loaning money to individuals and businesses. Where does that money come from? It comes from depositors. Since all of a bank's depositors are unlikely to want all of their money at the same time, banks hold back only a relatively small portion of cash for future withdrawals. That money is called a **reserve**—it is money set aside to cover future payments. The rest is loaned to individuals and businesses.

Types of Banks

There are several types of banking institutions. At one time, each played a distinctive role in the economy. Today, most of those distinctions are gone. Now most banking institutions offer many of the same services.

At one time, **commercial banks** were banks that served only businesses. Today, most commercial banks offer accounts to everyone. Savings banks, savings and loan associations, cooperative banks, and credit unions are often classified as **thrift institutions**. Each originally concentrated on meeting the needs of people who were not covered by commercial banks. Savings banks provided accounts for workers who wanted to save some of their income. So did savings and loan associations and cooperative banks. These banks also helped workers buy homes.

Increased use of the Internet has made banking easier for consumers.

People with a common concern started credit unions. These people might work for the same company, belong to the same labor union, or live in the same community. A **credit union's** main function was to provide emergency loans for its members, many of whom were unable to get loans from other lenders. Those loans were often used to pay medical bills or for home repairs.

Today, all of these banking institutions offer similar services. Commercial banks offer car and home loans; thrift institutions and credit unions make loans to factories, shops, and other businesses.

Other Financial Intermediaries

When customers or members deposit money in an account, banking institutions use those funds to make loans. Other financial intermediaries get their funds in other ways. Those intermediaries include finance companies, life insurance companies, and pension funds.

- **Finance companies** A **finance company** is a firm that specializes in making loans directly to consumers and in buying installment contracts from merchants who sell goods on credit. Many merchants cannot afford to wait years for their customers to pay off high-cost items on an installment plan. Instead, the merchants sell the customer's contract to a finance company for a lump sum. The agreement allows the merchant to advertise instant credit without having to absorb losses for unpaid accounts or take customers to court if they do not pay.

Finance companies also make loans directly to consumers, particularly to high-risk borrowers. A borrower is considered "high risk" if he or she earns very little money, has few financial assets, is slow to pay bills, or is already deeply in debt.

A person with any one or a combination of these factors is considered less likely to repay a new loan. So finance companies generally charge more for their loans than banks do.

- **Life insurance companies** Another financial institution that does not get its funds through deposits is a **life insurance company**. Although its main purpose is to provide financial protection for survivors of the insured, it also collects a great deal of cash.

When a person buys a life insurance policy, he or she pays a **premium**—the price of the policy usually paid monthly, quarterly, or annually. Because insurance companies collect these premiums on a regular basis, they have a considerable amount of money they can invest.

Life insurance companies offer consumers a variety of services and serve as financial intermediaries.

- **Pension funds** Another institution that channels savings to borrowers is a pension fund. A **pension** is a retirement plan that provides a fixed amount of income for life. A person typically receives a pension from an employer after working for a certain number of years, reaching retirement age, or suffering an injury.

Employers who offer pensions usually withhold a small percentage of workers' salaries to deposit in the fund. Employers may also add their own contribution to the fund. Workers may put money into the fund for 30 or 40 years before they are ready to retire. Most of that money is invested in stocks and bonds. The pension fund makes its money from those investments. Government pension funds work in much the same way.

stop and think

What do finance companies and life insurance companies have in common? How is each different from a bank? Create a Venn diagram in your notebook to answer these questions.

Putting It All Together

How do families like yours benefit from the activities of banks and other financial intermediaries? How do business firms benefit?

Markets for Bonds and Stocks

Thinking on Your Own

Read the Focus Your Reading questions. Try to answer each question in at least one sentence in your notebook. As you read, check how close you came to the correct answer.

Every firm needs capital from time to time. Corporations have several ways of raising money. Most acquire the capital they need for expansion from corporate profits that have not been distributed to shareholders. Corporations can also raise money by issuing new shares of stock. In doing so, they are, in effect, expanding the number of people who own part of the company. Firms can also raise funds for development by issuing bonds.

Trading in Financial Assets

Certificates of deposit (CDs) and bonds are financial assets. They may be bought and sold in markets just as other goods and services are. There are two kinds of securities markets (or exchanges) — the primary market and the secondary market.

- **Primary market** Trade in newly issued financial assets takes place in **primary markets**. Most people know little about these markets, because the sale of new issues of bonds rarely involves the public. They are usually sold through an investment bank. An **investment bank** acts as a broker — an individual or firm that sells securities to the public.

focus your reading

What is the main difference between primary and secondary securities markets?

Explain how investors can assess the value of their assets.

What problem does a mutual fund try to solve?

vocabulary

primary market

investment bank

secondary market

capital market

money market

equities

securities exchange

over-the-counter market

Dow-Jones Industrial Average

Standard & Poor's 500

mutual fund

futures market

options

The investment bank is the intermediary between the corporation (the seller) and potential buyers.

Who buys from investment banks? Likely buyers include insurance companies and pension funds. When people buy an insurance policy or put money into a pension fund, that money is often invested in primary markets.

- **Secondary market** A **secondary market** is a market in which existing financial assets are resold. This market allows investors to sell an asset quickly and without penalty. The capital market is a secondary market, and so are money markets. A **capital market** is a market in which corporate and government bonds that must be kept for more than one year are bought and sold. A **money market** is a market in which bonds that will mature in one year or less are traded.

Stocks, Mutual Funds, and Futures

Financial assets are not the only purchase investors make in the securities market. They also buy equities. **Equities** are stocks that represent ownership in a corporation. Buyers and sellers trade stocks through organized **securities exchanges**—

The New York Stock Exchange

places where they trade securities. Members pay a fee to join, and trades can take place only on the floor of the exchange.

- **The securities market** The largest securities exchange is the New York Stock Exchange (NYSE) in New York City. NYSE has 1,366 seats, or memberships, that allow access to the trading floor. Large brokerage companies (firms that deal in stocks) may own as many as 20 seats at any time and pay as much as $2.5 million for a seat.

Online trading has opened investment opportunities for consumers and changed the role stock brokers play in personal investment.

Members have the right to elect their own directors and vote on the rules and regulations that govern the exchange. Those rules are designed to provide a relatively efficient way of conducting trades by as many people as possible. The NYSE lists 280 billion shares of stocks from more than 3,000 companies.

Another important exchange is the American Stock Exchange (AMEX), which is also located in New York City. It has approximately 1,000 listed stocks. Regional exchanges include the Chicago, Pacific, Boston, and Philadelphia exchanges. They meet the needs of smaller corporations in their regions. Stock exchanges can also be found in cities around the world, including London, Tokyo, Hong Kong, Singapore, Johannesburg, and Frankfurt.

Despite the importance of the organized exchanges, most stocks in the United States are traded on the over-the-counter market (OTC). The **over-the-counter market** is an electronic marketplace for securities that are not traded on an organized exchange. The National Association of Securities Dealers Automated Quotation (NASDAQ) is the listing that provides information on stocks traded over the counter.

Assessing Value

How do investors know how much to pay for a stock? Many consult two indicators. One is the **Dow-Jones Industrial Average** (DJIA), the most popular measure of stock market performance on the NYSE. It began in 1884, when the Dow-Jones Company published the average closing price of 11 industrial stocks. The price gave investors a way of gauging the overall strength or weakness of a particular stock, as well as of the market in general. In 1928, the number was increased to 30 stocks. Since then, new stocks have been added to the list and others removed, but the sample remains 30.

Another popular indicator is the **Standard & Poor's 500** (S&P 500). It uses the price changes of 500 representative stocks as an indicator of overall market performance. Unlike the Dow-Jones, the Standard & Poor's 500 includes stocks listed on the NYSE, AMEX, and OTC. Times when stock prices are high and the market is strong are known as bull markets (the market is as strong as a bull). Times when stock prices are low and the market is weak are referred to as bear markets (the market is as mean as a bear).

> **stop and think**
>
> If the laws of supply and demand are at work, when will stock prices be highest? When are they likely to be lowest? Answer these questions in full sentences in your notebook.

Minimizing Risk

Investing in the stock market is risky, particularly during a bear market. The stock market is risky because investors can lose a portion or all of their investments. To reduce their risk, some investors buy mutual funds. A **mutual fund** is a company that sells stock in itself to individual investors and then invests the money it receives in stocks and bonds issued by other corporations. Mutual fund stockholders receive dividends from these investments, just as other stockholders do. They can also sell their mutual fund shares the same way other stocks can be sold.

Mutual funds allow people to buy and sell stocks and bonds without putting all of their money into one or two companies. The large size of a mutual fund makes it possible to hire experts to analyze the market before buying and selling stock.

It also allows for a greater variety of stocks and bonds than most investors could otherwise afford. The market value of a mutual fund share is known as the net asset value (NAV). It is determined by dividing the net value of the mutual fund by the number of shares the fund has issued.

- **Trading in the future** Some investors participate in **futures markets**. These are markets in which contracts known as "futures" are bought and sold. A *futures contract* is an agreement to buy or sell a commodity or financial asset on a particular date at a predetermined price. The history of futures goes back to a time when farming was the main industry in the United States. Farmers and investors would agree on a specific price for corn that would be delivered at a future date. A futures contract would ensure that the farmer would get a good price for the crop at harvest time, even if the price of corn dropped in the meantime. The investor bought the contract in the hope that the price of corn would increase so he or she could resell it at a higher price.

The Chicago Mercantile Exchange was formed in 1898. Its four major product areas are interest rates, stock index futures, foreign exchange, and commodities.

Options are the right to buy or sell a commodity or financial asset at some point in the future at a predetermined price. Options are similar to futures in that they are based on a future event, but options give both the buyer and the seller an opportunity to back out. Options and futures are often sold in the same markets.

Putting It All Together

Rank the kinds of investments described in this lesson in two ways. First rank them by level of risk, and then by potential profits. What seems to be the relationship between risk and potential profit?

Chapter Summary

- In a **financial system**, savers, borrowers, and financial institutions transfer savings to borrowers.

- **Savings** and **investments** are critical to economic growth.

- **Savings accounts** and **certificates of deposit** are examples of **financial assets**.

- **Banks** safeguard money, transfer funds, and loan money, keeping a portion of it in **reserve**. Most **commercial banks** offer services to everyone.

- Banks, **thrift institutions**, and **credit unions** are **financial intermediaries**. Non-bank intermediaries include **finance companies**, **life insurance companies**, and **pension** funds.

- **Premiums** are payments on a life insurance policy.

- **Investment banks** serve as intermediaries in **primary markets**. **Capital markets** and **money markets** are examples of **secondary markets**.

- Buyers and sellers trade **equities** through organized **securities exchanges**.

- Most stocks are sold on the **over-the-counter market**.

- **Standard & Poor's 500** and the **Dow-Jones Industrial Average** gauge the performance of the stock market.

- **Mutual funds** help investors minimize risks; **futures markets** maximize risks.

- **Options** are the right to buy or sell a commodity or financial asset in the future at a predetermined price.

Chapter Review

1 Suppose you received a gift of $1,000. How much of it would you spend immediately? How much of it would you save? Write a paragraph explaining the choices you would make. Describe the short-term and long-term benefits of the gift.

2 Use what you have learned about the stock market to track one or two stocks each day. Track your chosen stock for at least one week. Report to the class how your company or companies perform.

Skill Builder

Read a Table

Tables and charts are often used to show comparisons between similar categories of information. Tables usually compare numbers. Follow these steps to learn how to understand and use tables.

- Read the title to learn what content is being presented.

- Read the headings in the top row. They describe the groups or categories of information to be compared. If the headings are abbreviated, look for a key that explains the abbreviations.

Newspapers, cable news stations, and Web sites report daily on the stock market. Figure 9.3 shows examples of stocks traded on the New York Stock Exchange.

Use the key and the table to answer the following questions.

The New York Stock Exchange   Figure 9.3

52-Week High and Low Highest and lowest prices reached by a stock over the past year, but not including yesterday

Dividends refers to the current annual rate of dividend payment, based on most recent declaration, unless indicated otherwise by footnote

Sales refers to the volume of shares, in hundreds

Last Last trade of the day in regular trading

Change Difference between last trade and previous day's price in regular trading

| 52 Week | | | | | SALES | | NET |
HI	LO	Stock(SYM)	Div		100s	LAST	CHG
29.99	20.88	Disney (DIS)	.24		39199	25.48	−0.14
25.91	12.75	Dominos (DPZ)	.40		11669	25.26	0.85
35.19	24.63	EKodak (EK)	.50		26894	25.74	−0.42
29.95	19.98	Footlocker (FL)	.30		37551	22.75	−0.13

1 What was the highest price paid for Disney over the past year? What was the lowest price?

2 What was EKodak's closing price? What was the percent of change over its closing on the previous day?

3 Why do you think it is important to know how much the price of a stock has changed in the course of a year?

10 LABOR MARKETS

Getting Focused

Skim this chapter to predict what you will be learning.

- Read the lesson titles and subheadings.
- Look at the illustrations and read the captions.
- Examine the charts and graphs.
- Review the vocabulary words and terms.

Have you ever participated in a labor market? You have if you have had a job or looked for a job. Use your own labor market experience to answer the following questions:

- What kinds of jobs were you qualified to hold?
- Were such jobs easily available or relatively scarce?
- Were many people competing for those jobs?
- Why do you think the job paid the wage that it did?

Write your answers in your notebook.

The labor market in the United States consists of everyone who is employed, regardless of skill or education.

Workers and Work

Thinking on Your Own

Create a three-column chart in your notebook. Label the columns "Jobs," "Sector," and "Skill Level." In the first column, list ten types of jobs. As you read, fill in the information for "Sector" and "Skill Level."

Anyone who has a job or is looking for one is a member of a labor force. A labor force describes all of the workers in a given area. The nation's labor force includes privates in the army, as well as generals. It also includes street sweepers, movie stars, major league baseball players, factory workers, and presidents of large corporations. If you have ever had a job, you've been part of the labor force.

Who Is in the Labor Force?

The **labor force** consists of the total number of people sixteen years old or older who are willing to work at all wage levels and are physically able to do so. As Figure 10.1 on page 155 shows, that number includes people in the armed forces and people who are unemployed but eager to find work, as well as those who have jobs.

The **civilian labor force** is shown in blue in Figure 10.1. It is made up of both employed and unemployed workers who are not in the military. It does not include those who are retired, or in school, or those who stay home to care for their children. Economists classify the civilian work force in the United States in a variety of ways, including by the **sector**, or section of the economy in which they are employed, and their level of training or education.

focus your reading

Who is included in the civilian labor force?

In what economic sector do most Americans work?

Explain how education affects the kinds of jobs available to Americans.

vocabulary

labor force

civilian labor force

sector

unskilled

semiskilled

skilled

professional

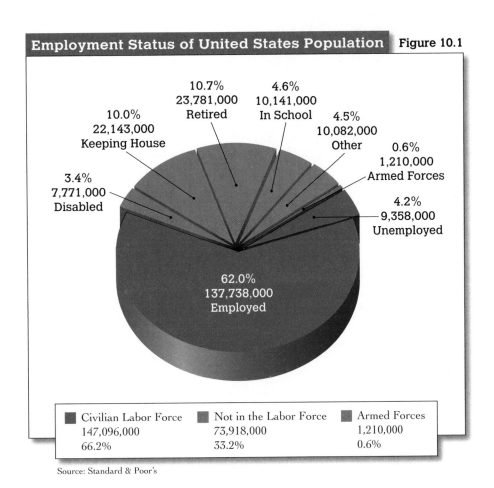

Employment Status of United States Population   Figure 10.1

10.0%
22,143,000
Keeping House

10.7%
23,781,000
Retired

4.6%
10,141,000
In School

4.5%
10,082,000
Other

0.6%
1,210,000
Armed Forces

3.4%
7,771,000
Disabled

4.2%
9,358,000
Unemployed

62.0%
137,738,000
Employed

Civilian Labor Force	Not in the Labor Force	Armed Forces
147,096,000	73,918,000	1,210,000
66.2%	33.2%	0.6%

Source: Standard & Poor's

Types of Work

Economists group workers into three main sectors: farming, manufacturing/construction, and service industries. The smallest sector in the United States today was once the largest. In the 1700s and 1800s, most Americans earned their living by farming. Over 90 percent of all Americans farmed in the early 1800s. Today, farmers make up less than three percent of all workers.

In the late 1800s and early 1900s, many farm workers began leaving the countryside to take jobs in construction and manufacturing. Some paved highways and laid track for railroads. Some built skyscrapers and factories. Others worked in mines and factories. They produced everything from nuts and bolts to automobiles and locomotives. By 1920, the manufacturing/construction sector of the economy was the largest of the three sectors.

Today, the third sector, once the smallest, is the largest. The service sector accounts for nearly two-thirds of the nation's economic activity. Hospitals and schools are a part of the

service sector. So is information technology —computer hardware and software as well as network, satellite, and telecommunications technologies. Workers in the service sector provide direct services to individuals and businesses. Computer technicians are service workers, and so are physicians, hairdressers, teachers, scientists, cooks, and bankers.

Which sector of the economy do each of these jobs represent?

Skill Levels

Another way workers are grouped is according to the skills their jobs require. A job that requires little or no special training is considered **unskilled**. A job clearing tables in a restaurant or working as a clerk in a store is defined as unskilled labor. Unskilled labor also includes digging ditches or answering the phone in a busy office. It is important to understand exactly what the term means. *Unskilled* does not mean that the worker has no skills. It also does not mean that the worker requires no training to do his or her job. It simply means that the skills required for the job are quickly learned. As a result, employers find it relatively easy to hire and replace unskilled laborers.

Work that is **semiskilled** requires more training. Semiskilled workers work on factory assembly lines, run machines, sort mail, and do construction work. Nurse's aides, telephone operators, and certain types of managers are also examples of semiskilled workers. The range of skills needed to do these jobs is narrow and can be learned in a relatively short amount of time.

Skilled jobs require extensive training and experience. Plumbers and electricians have specialized knowledge and skills. So do police officers, carpenters, cooks, and dental

assistants. Many of the skills required to do this type of work are learned on the job.

Some workers are considered **professionals**. They usually have a college degree, as well as one or more years of additional specialized training. Lawyers, physicians, engineers, teachers, and dentists are all professionals. Often, these jobs are known as white-collar professions.

stop and think

Why do farmers and manufacturing/construction workers make up a smaller percentage of the labor force than they used to? What changes in the economy can you think of that contributed to this? Compare your answer with a partner's and write it in your notebook.

Workers who hold jobs that require years of training or experience are difficult to replace. Doctors, lawyers, engineers and many other professionals also require ongoing education. This means that they must continue to take courses in order to learn new procedures or regulations. As a result, they generally earn more than workers whose jobs require fewer skills.

According to economists, the various types of labor—unskilled, skilled, and so on—do not directly compete with one another, because of differences in training, experience, or education. Each type of labor is essential to the economy. However, workers often want to move from one category to another. Someone who works in an unskilled job today may eventually become a professional—perhaps a lawyer or a teacher. A common way of progressing from one category to another is through education.

Putting It All Together

How would you categorize the following jobs? To which sector does each belong? What level of skill does each require? Add each job to the chart you began at the start of this lesson. Give reasons to support your choices.

- carpenter
- secretary
- accountant
- professional quarterback
- waiter
- toll collector
- scientist
- professor

Labor: Supply and Demand

Thinking on Your Own

As you read about the supply of and demand for labor, create a T-chart. In one column, list the things that affect the supply of labor. In the other column, list the things that affect the demand for labor.

Labor is a factor of production. Like other factors of production, labor can be bought and sold. In labor markets, individuals are the sellers and firms are the buyers. The laws of supply and demand affect the price paid for an hour's work, not only for unskilled workers but also for lawyers, business executives, and football players.

The Demand for Labor

The value of labor depends on the value attached to the product or service a worker helps produce. Therefore, the demand for computer programmers is derived, or arises from, the demand for software. If many people own computers, the **derived demand** for programmers will be high. The same is true in other industries. The demand for professional football players is derived from the popularity of the sport. If many people attend professional football games, the demand for players increases. According to the law of demand, as demand rises, price will also rise. **Wages** are the price paid for labor.

Another factor that affects the demand for labor is productivity. The more productive workers are, the more money firms are willing to pay for their labor. Productivity depends in part on such capital resources as tools and other machines. It also depends on the education, training, and skills of the workers. A worker with little or no training will not be able to use a sophisticated new machine as well as a co-worker who not only has been trained to run the machine, but also has the skills to maximize its potential.

The Supply of Labor

Just as the law of demand can be applied to the labor market, so can the law of supply. What affects the supply of labor? Population is one factor. The more people there are in a particular labor market, the lower the wages tend to be. Why? The supply is greater than the demand.

Use what you know about productivity and training to describe the job shown here. For example, what tools will this chef use to do her job?

recall

The **law of supply** states that if all other things are equal, the higher the price of a product or service, the more of it suppliers will offer for sale; as the price falls, so will the quantity supplied.

Elasticity refers to the responsiveness of supply or demand to changes in price.

Wages are also a factor. However, wages do not work in exactly the same way that prices do in other markets. Look carefully at the supply curve in Figure 10.2 on page 159. Notice that, at first, the quantity supplied rises as wages rise, but then, at point I, it begins to decrease.

Why can a rise in wages have a negative effect on supply? Assume you have a part-time job, and your boss raises your hourly rate. She also tells you that you are free to choose the number of hours you will work. You may decide to work more hours, so that you will earn even more money. The opportunity cost of your free time has become more expensive. You are experiencing what economists call the **substitution effect**. In this case, you are substituting extra time at work for your free time. Your decision is reflected in the rise in the supply curve in Figure 10.2.

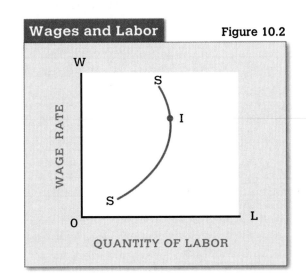

Wages and Labor   Figure 10.2

(Graph: vertical axis labeled W and WAGE RATE, horizontal axis labeled L and QUANTITY OF LABOR, origin O. Supply curve labeled S at bottom and S at top, with point I marked.)

Acting against the substitution effect is the **income effect**. As your income rises, you start to think about spending some of your raise on tickets to a concert or a weekend at the beach

with friends. Working fewer hours suddenly seems very attractive. In the case shown in Figure 10.2, on page 159, the income effect eventually outweighed the substitution effect and the labor supplied declined despite the rise in wages.

Yet another factor that affects the supply of labor—particularly, the supply of skilled labor—is its lack of elasticity in the short run. If teachers' pay tripled tomorrow, the number of applicants for teaching jobs would rise only slightly. Anyone who did not have the necessary education and experience would have to return to school to qualify for a teaching license. It might take several years for the supply of teachers to increase significantly. On the other hand, if the pay at a fast-food restaurant tripled, the number of applicants would rise almost immediately. You do not need years of training or a college education to work at the local fast-food restaurant.

Another factor that contributes to the inelasticity of labor is location. If a job—even one that includes a significant increase in salary—requires a move from one section of the country to another, many people may hesitate to take the job. People often have strong ties to their community. Some may also have a spouse who is unwilling or unable to give up his or her job for a move. Their children may also be reluctant to start over in a new community. The family as a whole may enjoy living near relatives and friends.

Putting It All Together

Draw a diagram that shows how the laws of supply and demand affect the labor market. What does your diagram suggest happens to wages when the demand is high and supply is low? What happens when demand is low and the supply is plentiful? Write a sentence or two describing how other factors may affect both supply and demand.

The Costco Way

To be competitive, firms try to keep costs as low as possible—particularly labor costs. Is doing so a good idea? *BusinessWeek* compared the way two large warehouse stores—Costco and Sam's Club—paid their workers and came up with a surprising finding. Stanley Holmes and Wendy Zellner write:

BusinessWeek ran through the numbers from each company to compare Costco and Sam's Club, the Wal-Mart warehouse unit that competes directly with Costco. We found that by compensating employees generously to motivate and retain good workers, one-fifth of whom are unionized, Costco gets lower turnover and higher productivity. . . .

Look at how Costco pulls it off. Although Sam's $11.52 hourly average wage for full-timers tops the $9.64 earned by a typical Wal-Mart worker, it's still nearly 40% less than Costco's $15.97. Costco also shells out thousands more a year for workers' health and retirement and includes more of them in its health care, [retirement], and profit-sharing plans. . . .

In return for all this generosity, Costco gets one of the most productive and loyal workforces in all of retailing. Only 6% of employees leave after the first year, compared with 21% at Sam's. That saves tons, since

WAREHOUSE STORES must compete for employees by offering excellent benefits.

Wal-Mart says it costs $2,500 per worker just to test, interview, and train a new hire. Costco's motivated employees also sell more: $795 of sales per square foot vs. only $516 at Sam's and $411 at BJ's Wholesale Club Inc., its other primary club rival. . . .

Wal-Mart defenders often focus on the undeniable benefits its low prices bring consumers, while ignoring the damage it does to U.S. wages. Costco shows that with enough smarts, companies can help consumers and workers alike. ∎

"Commentary: The Costco Way" by Stanley Holmes and Wendy Zellner. *BusinessWeek*, April 12, 2004.

reading for understanding

How does Costco benefit from paying its employees higher wages than Sam's Club does?

How do workers benefit?

How do the laws of supply and demand affect the decision Costco made?

Wages in Labor Markets

Thinking on Your Own

Look at the vocabulary words for this lesson. How many words do you already know? Write a sentence in your notebook that includes as many familiar words as possible. Compare your sentence with that of a partner. Which of you had more words?

When people apply for a job, they usually ask about the wage rate. A **wage rate** is the standard of pay for a particular job. Wage rates differ from one occupation to another and from one region of the country to another. Sometimes they differ even within the same occupation. For example, a new teacher usually makes less money than an experienced teacher. What causes those differences? This lesson looks at several explanations.

focus your reading

How do the laws of supply and demand affect wages?

What is a negotiated wage?

How does discrimination affect wages?

vocabulary

wage rate

equilibrium wage rate

labor union

negotiate

labor contract

collective bargaining

strike

lockout

discrimination

Supply, Demand, and Wages

Why do professional athletes make more money than teachers or doctors? Supply and demand provides one answer. Figure 10.3A, on page 163, shows what happens when a relatively large number of ditchdiggers compete in a market in which demand is low. Figure 10.3B, on page 163, shows what happens to wages when a relatively small number of professional athletes compete in a market in which demand is high. On both graphs, the point at which the line showing supply crosses the line showing demand is known as the **equilibrium wage rate**—the rate at which the market has neither a surplus nor a shortage of workers. This is why it is known as the rate that "clears the market."

For the most part, the more education and training a job requires, the smaller the supply of workers and the higher the average wage rate. There are exceptions, however. Some highly qualified workers have difficulty finding jobs. Some unqualified or unproductive workers are paid relatively high salaries. Other factors can also affect wages.

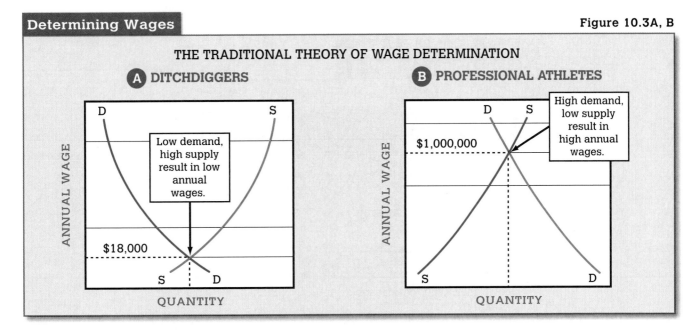

THE TRADITIONAL THEORY OF WAGE DETERMINATION

A DITCHDIGGERS — Low demand, high supply result in low annual wages. $18,000

B PROFESSIONAL ATHLETES — High demand, low supply result in high annual wages. $1,000,000

The Power of Negotiation

To improve wages and working conditions, many workers join **labor unions**. The labor movement in the United States began in the mid-1800s among skilled workers. To protect their wages, they tried to limit the number of new workers entering the skilled trades. In time, semiskilled factory workers also formed unions to demand higher wages and safer workplaces. Workers as individuals had little power compared to that of the factory owners who employed them.

Acting on behalf of its members, a labor union seeks to **negotiate** with an employer. Instead of one employee demanding a raise, the demand comes from a union that represents all or most of the workers in the company. When unions and businesses negotiate, they try to reach an agreement through give-and-take. Each side gives up something in order to work out differences.

The goal of a negotiation between employees and their employer is a **labor contract**—a document that spells out wages, the length of a workday, working conditions, and benefits for a given period of time. The process is known as **collective bargaining**. Figure 10.4, on page 164, shows the benefit to union members of a negotiated wage. Weekly salaries are considerably higher for union workers than for nonunion workers. The only occupations for which the difference in wages is relatively minor are highly skilled occupations.

Median Weekly Wages by Job and Union Affiliation		Figure 10.4
Occupation	Represented by Unions	Nonunion Workers
Managerial and Professional Specialty	$834	$836
Precision Production, Craft and Repair	778	570
Government Workers	726	609
Operators, Fabricators, and Laborers	602	411
Technical, Sales, and Administrative Support	590	497
Farming, Forestry, and Fishing	506	325

Source: Bureau of Labor Statistics, 2001

If efforts to work out differences fail, unions may call for a **strike** — the refusal to work until the firm meets workers' demands or the two sides return to the bargaining table. A failure to work out differences can also lead to a lockout of employees. A **lockout** is when an employer refuses to let its employees do their jobs until the union meets the company's demands or the two sides return to the bargaining table.

Preferences and Discrimination

Many employers are willing to pay more for workers who have a diploma, an advanced degree, or some other indicator of superior ability. Why would a business pay more for an employee who has a college degree than one with a high school diploma if both employees would do the same work? The answer lies in the way many businesspeople view a college degree. They see it as a sign of intelligence, hard work, and the willingness to complete a long-term goal. These are qualities they value in an employee.

stop and think

Study Figure 10.4. For which occupations is the difference in wages between unionized and nonunionized employees greatest? For which occupations is the difference relatively small? How do you account for the variations?

Employers may have other preferences as well. Some employers prefer to hire or promote individuals based on their race, religion, national origin, or gender. This kind of preference is known as **discrimination**. Choosing one employee over another based on skin color, gender, or religion, rather than on education or ability, does not maximize, or make the most of, an employer's investment in labor. Yet throughout the nation's history, many employers routinely discriminated against women, African Americans, Latinos, and other minority groups. Today, discrimination violates both federal and state laws. Employers are required to offer all of their employees the same employment opportunities.

How do the courts decide whether an action by an employer is discriminatory? Treating one employee differently from others violates Equal Employment Opportunity (EEO) laws *only* when the treatment is based on a characteristic protected under the law (for example, discrimination based on race, gender, or age), rather than on job performance or an employee's character.

The laws have opened new opportunities for groups that have traditionally been discriminated against. Yet, the 2000 census suggests that gaps in salary still exist. According to data gathered as part of the census, the average annual income in 1999 was $43,000. White Americans earned an average of $46,000, while African Americans earned $33,000. Asian Americans on average earned slightly more than whites—$47,000. The average wage for Latinos was $31,000 a year.

Economists have suggested that about one-half to three-quarters of the gap in wages between men and women can be explained by differences in experience and education. For example, many women drop out of the labor market to raise a family, while men rarely do. That leaves from one-quarter to one-half of the gap to be explained by discrimination or other reasons. The same is also true for the gap in wages between various minority groups and white Americans.

Over the last 40 years, governments have tried to end discriminatory practices. They have outlawed discrimination in hiring, firing, and employment. The 2000 census suggests that more work needs to be done.

Putting It All Together

How do the laws of supply and demand affect wages? What other factors affect how much money a worker earns? In your opinion, which factor is the most important? Discuss these questions with a partner. Then answer them using full sentences in your notebook.

Economics and You

Education and Earnings

How will your education affect your earnings? The U.S. Department of Labor found that college graduates over the age of twenty-five earn twice as much as workers who have only a high school diploma. High school graduates also have an unemployment rate that is about twice the rate of college graduates.

reading for understanding

What effect does dropping out of high school have on weekly earnings?

How does level of education affect the unemployment rate—the percentage of workers who do not have jobs?

Write a sentence explaining the main idea of each graph.

Earnings and Unemployment for Persons Twenty-five and Over   Figure 10.5

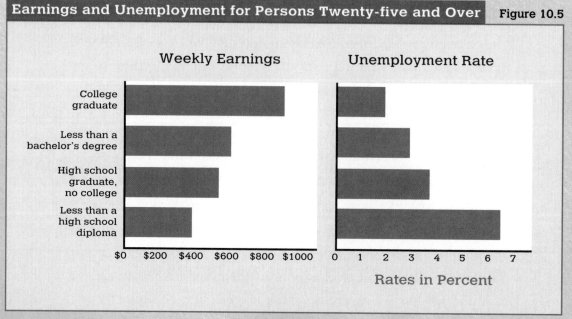

Source: Bureau of Labor Statistics, 2000 annual averages

Chapter Summary

- The **labor force** includes both employed and unemployed workers.

- The **civilian labor force** is divided into three **sectors**: farming, manufacturing/construction, and service industries.

- Workers include those who are **unskilled, semiskilled,** and **skilled,** as well as **professionals**.

- The **wages** offered for a job may be based on **derived demand**.

- The **substitution effect** and the **income effect** have opposite impacts on the quantity of labor supplied.

- The **wage rate** that clears the market is known as the **equilibrium wage rate**.

- **Labor unions** work with employers to **negotiate** a **labor contract**.

- **Strikes** and **lockouts** result from failures in **collective bargaining**.

- **Discrimination** accounts for part of the wage gap between white male workers and women and minority workers.

Chapter Review

1 Wages should be based solely on the laws of supply and demand. Do you agree or disagree? Take a side and prepare an argument you can use in a debate with someone who takes the opposite view. Be sure to provide facts and logical arguments in support of your position.

2 What role does education play in labor markets? What does it add to the wages employers are willing to pay a worker? What does it add to the productivity of a worker?

3 Look through the want-ads section of your local newspaper with a partner. Find four examples of service jobs, one for each type of work: unskilled, semiskilled, skilled, and professional. Which jobs pay the best? For what reasons?

Skill Builder

Determine Averages: Mean and Median

Economists often use averages to make comparisons. There are two ways to figure out the average: by using the mean or by using the median. The mean is the mathematical average of a series of items. For example, when the government wanted to find out the mean annual income in 1999, the Census Bureau added up the salaries of all workers and then divided by the total number of workers. They discovered that the mean salary was $43,000. If the Census Bureau had wanted to find the median salary, it would have listed all of the salaries from lowest to highest and then found the one in the middle.

Determining Mean and Median

Figure 10.6

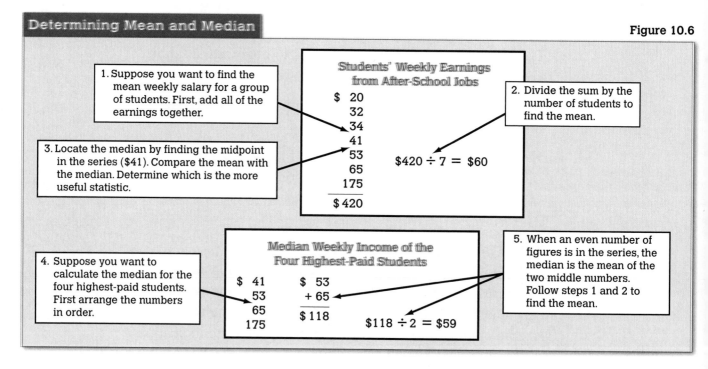

1. Suppose you want to find the mean weekly salary for a group of students. First, add all of the earnings together.

2. Divide the sum by the number of students to find the mean.

3. Locate the median by finding the midpoint in the series ($41). Compare the mean with the median. Determine which is the more useful statistic.

Students' Weekly Earnings from After-School Jobs

$ 20
32
34
41
53
65
175
——
$ 420

$420 ÷ 7 = $60

4. Suppose you want to calculate the median for the four highest-paid students. First arrange the numbers in order.

Median Weekly Income of the Four Highest-Paid Students

$ 41 $ 53
53   + 65
65   ——
175   $ 118

$118 ÷ 2 = $59

5. When an even number of figures is in the series, the median is the mean of the two middle numbers. Follow steps 1 and 2 to find the mean.

Use the information above to answer the following questions.

1 What is the mean salary for all seven students?

2 What is the median salary for all seven students?

3 How do you explain the difference between the two numbers?

4 In this case, which is the more useful number? For what reasons?

Chapter 11

GOVERNMENT

Getting Focused

Skim this chapter to predict what you will be learning.

- Read the lesson titles and subheadings.
- Look at the illustrations and read the captions.
- Examine the graph.
- Review the vocabulary words and terms.

What is the role of government in a market economy? Examine the headings and subheadings in this chapter. What do they suggest about the role of government? What do the illustrations suggest? Discuss your ideas with a partner.

The U.S. Capitol, in Washington, D.C., is the home to the Senate and the House of Representatives. These two legislative groups make up Congress.

Making Rules

Thinking on Your Own

To *govern* is to make rules. Using this definition, how is your school governed? In your notebook, list five major school rules. Then identify the person or people who made them.

You need rules to play basketball, baseball, football, or any other game. Without rules and a referee or umpire to settle disputes, there is no game. The same is true of a market economy. It also needs rules and a referee. Governments supply both. They set the rules by which markets operate and settle disagreements about the meaning of those rules.

focus your reading

What basic rights are necessary for the success of a market economy?

Name two effects of standards set by governments on buyers and sellers.

How do governments build confidence in markets?

vocabulary

private property rights

copyright

trademark

standard

Protecting Property

Among the most important rules or laws in a market economy are those that define and protect **private property rights**—the rights of individuals and businesses to own land and other resources. Within limits, the law allows you to do whatever you wish with your property. You can sell it, rent it, or use it as security for a loan. And you can make investments in your property, knowing that any profits from those investments will also belong to you.

recall

A **patent** is the grant of a property right to the inventor of a product or process for a period of 20 years.

The government protects ideas as well as resources. It issues patents to inventors and developers of new products and methods. It also allows writers and other artists to copyright their books, music, art, and other creative works. Like a patent, a **copyright** provides the owner with an exclusive right to reproduce, sell, or distribute a work. The government also safeguards **trademarks**—words, phrases, symbols, or designs, or a combination of words, phrases, symbols, or designs that identify and distinguish goods produced by one firm from those produced by others.

Maintaining Standards

The government protects buyers and sellers in other ways as well. One way is by setting standards. A **standard** provides a basis for comparisons. Government standards mean that a quart container of milk contains exactly the same amount of milk, no matter where in the country you buy it. Those standards also let you know that the pump at your local gas station will deliver exactly the amount of gasoline you pay for. Similar standards affect everything that you purchase by weight, length, area, volume, or some other measure. Those standards do not change when you move from one state to another.

You do not have to walk around with tape measures, balances, and measuring cups to be sure that you are not being cheated. City and state workers do that job for you. These officials inspect local businesses to be sure that scales and pumps are accurate. They rely on information provided by the National Institute of Standards and Technology (NIST) near Washington, D.C.

The government ensures that the amount of gas shown on the pump is accurate.

NIST sets the standards that businesses rely on. Its atomic clock is one of the most accurate in the world. It will neither gain nor lose a second in 30 million years. Long-distance telecommunications companies depend on that clock because their equipment demands accuracy within 100 billionths of a second. Banks and stock exchanges use the clock as well. They rely on it in order to correctly stamp the exact time of each of the millions of electronic financial transactions that occur each day.

The NIST staff also helps set standards so that firms can produce products that will work with items produced by other companies. For example, if you buy an AA battery, you can be sure that no matter what brand you purchase, it will work in your flashlight. The same is true of the sheets on your bed. All twin beds are exactly the same size. Therefore, any set of sheets that are for

Researchers at the National Institute of Standards and Technology

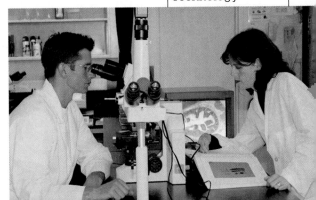

a twin bed will fit. Lightbulbs, shoes, nails, screwdrivers, and other items are all made to a standard.

NIST staff members also participate in more than 100 voluntary organizations that help industries develop their own standards and encourage international acceptance of those standards. As a result, American companies are better able to expand the market for their products by producing goods that meet not only American standards but also those set by other countries.

stop and think

Make a list of five to ten food items kept in your refrigerator or pantry at home. How many were packaged or priced by weight, length, area, or volume? How would your family react if these products did not contain the amount stated on the label?

Building Confidence

As a result of these and other government efforts, you are able to enter a bank and hand over your savings to someone you have never met before without fear of losing your money. You know that your savings are protected, not only by the bank but also by the government.

Consumer confidence is extremely important, especially in the banking industry.

You are also able to go online and purchase a CD, an airline ticket, or a pair of shoes from a business located in another state or even another country. If you send a check, the firm will cash the check and send you the product. If you use a credit card to make the purchase, you know that the company will get paid and you will receive the product you purchased in the mail. Your confidence in the system, as well as the confidence of the companies you do business with, comes from knowing that the government will see to it that the laws are obeyed and the rights of both buyers and sellers are protected.

Putting It All Together

You are a consumer of goods and services. Give four examples of how government regulations affect the products and services you purchase. Which of these roles is most important to you and your family?

Market Failures

Thinking on Your Own

Imagine seeing the following headline in your newspaper: MARKET FAILURE UNCOVERED! Write a sentence or two in your notebook explaining what you think this news story will be about.

A market economy is based on the idea that the market is the most efficient way of answering the basic economic questions—what to produce, how to produce, and for whom to produce. Like any other system, the market does not always work. **Market failures** occur as a result of imperfect competition and **externalities**—gaps between the private cost and the social cost of behaviors or actions.

Imperfect Competition

Unfair business practices are one cause of market failures or imperfect competition. In the past, some businesses have formed monopolies to limit competition. Others have engaged in **price discrimination**—the practice of charging one customer more than another for the same product. As you learned in Chapter 7, the U.S. government sets rules to prevent unfair business practices. In 1914, Congress passed the Clayton Antitrust Act, which outlawed price discrimination. That same year, Congress also created the Federal Trade Commission (FTC). It can issue **cease and desist orders**—rulings that force a company to stop an unfair practice.

focus your reading

Name two causes of market failure.

Name two effects of market failure.

How do negative externalities affect the need for public goods?

vocabulary

market failure

externality

price discrimination

cease and desist orders

minimum wage laws

negative externality

positive externality

tax

tax credit

recall

Imperfect competition is the name given to market structures that lack one or more of the conditions for perfect competition.

A **monopoly** is a market structure in which a single seller controls an entire industry.

In addition to antitrust laws, the federal government also regulates a number of industries. State and local governments also control various industries through rules that protect consumers, promote efficiency, or encourage competition.

One market that requires regulation is the labor market. Over the years, both federal and state governments have passed laws that set health and safety standards in various industries, outlawed child labor, banned discrimination in the workplace, and protected the right of workers to form unions and, in some states, their right not to join a union.

State and federal governments have also passed **minimum wage laws**. These laws set the lowest legal hourly wage that may be paid to most workers. The aim is to protect the lowest-paid workers. Many of them have no one to bargain for them and may be taken advantage of by employers. Most economists agree that a price floor—which is what a minimum wage is—is less efficient than a wage determined by supply and demand. They disagree over whether the law does more harm than good.

Some maintain that minimum wage laws increase unemployment because employers tend to hire fewer workers if they have to pay them more. Others point out that the demand for unskilled labor tends to be inelastic, and therefore demand is unlikely to be affected by a minimum wage law. They also insist that the law is not about efficiency, but about providing workers with wages they can live on.

Market Externalities

The government also tries to minimize the effects of negative externalities. What is a **negative externality**, and how can it result in market failure? Suppose your neighbor buys a set of drums from a nearby store. At the end of their transaction, your neighbor and the storekeeper are satisfied with the deal they struck. The problem is that not all of the people who are affected by the purchase were in the shop when the deal was made. The social cost of the transaction—the noise the drums make—is the price you and other neighbors may pay for a purchase that does not benefit you.

The drum set is a relatively small problem—unless you live next door to the owner. Other negative externalities can be more serious. Suppose a factory dumps waste products into the town water supply. Although the firm's action endangers the community's drinking water, there is no market solution to the negative externality caused by the dumping. The company can produce its products more cheaply by dumping waste than by disposing of it properly. Most of its customers live far away and don't know or care about the pollution. They do, however, appreciate the way the company keeps its prices low. So they reward the firm by buying more of its products. The most likely solution to the negative externality is action by the government. If dumping waste in a water supply is illegal, individuals or the community as a whole can take the factory to court.

Not all externalities are negative. If you enjoy listening to drums, your neighbor's drum set is a **positive externality**. You get a free concert every evening. The factory that pollutes the environment may employ hundreds of workers who spend their paychecks at local shops, restaurants, and banks. The factory is a positive externality for the owners of those businesses—that is, they receive economic benefits even though they paid nothing for those benefits.

Public parks are an example of a positive externality.

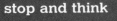
stop and think

Based on your own experiences, give an example of both a positive externality and a negative externality. Share your examples with a partner.

Government Responses

Governments respond to negative externalities in a variety of ways. They can outlaw the behavior that is causing the problem. For example, most communities have laws that ban loud music and other noises after 10 or 11 P.M.

Governments can also use the tax system to lessen the effects of a negative externality. A **tax** is a required payment for the support of a government. For example, if a government taxes factories that pollute the water supply, several things happen. First, the government has the money it needs to clean up the environment. Second, the factory's cost of production increases, because taxes are counted as expenses. The rise in production costs means that the price of the product is likely to increase. When prices are high, consumers buy less.

Figure 11.1, on page 176, shows how a tax of one dollar on every unit of output actually works. The original supply curve is marked "S," and the supply curve with the tax added is marked "S + tax." Notice that the price increases by 60 cents with the tax. That means that the company paid 40 cents of the tax and passed the rest on to the consumer. As the price rises, the quantity sold decreases from six to five. Economists call this use of the tax system "internalizing an externality," because it forces the firm and its customers to pay the cost of pollution.

The government can also use taxes to motivate firms to develop new products and services that have positive externalities. A **tax credit** is a reduction in taxes for taking a particular action. It is often used as an incentive for developing renewable energy sources—the use of the sun, wind, wood, and other forms of energy that cannot be used up the way gas, coal, and oil can.

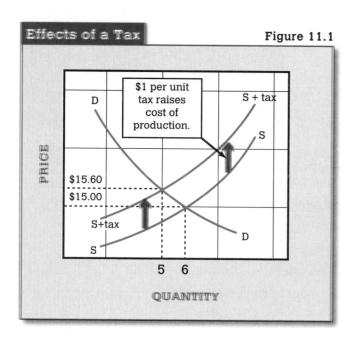

Effects of a Tax

Figure 11.1

$1 per unit tax raises cost of production.

S + tax

S

D

$15.60

$15.00

S+tax

S

D

5   6

QUANTITY

PRICE

Putting It All Together

Newspapers contain many examples of market failures at home and abroad. Find an example of a market failure in a newspaper or magazine. Identify the cause and the effects. What role did the government play in efforts to ease the effects? How successful were those efforts?

Tax Credits Put Wind in the Sails of Renewables

At a time when the price of gasoline and oil is rising, the federal government is offering tax credits to producers of "green energy"—energy resources that do not harm the environment. Wind is a green resource. John Carey of *BusinessWeek* writes:

Fickle breezes pose a challenge for Steven Zwolinski, president of GE Wind Energy. But in 2004, he was also hit by the [unpredictable] winds of politics. A tax credit for wind energy, expected to be renewed, expired in 2003 after being caught up in the congressional stalemate over a comprehensive energy bill. As a result, new wind farm development came almost to a halt. By summer, Zwolinski had no orders and nearly $300 million in inventory, forcing layoffs and factory closings. . . .

But what governments take away, they can also give. In September, Congress renewed the wind tax credit and extended credits to most other types of renewable energy. In addition, 19 states now require that electricity providers offer a certain percentage of green energy. . . .

The biggest winner: wind. . . . With the tax credit, wind power has plunged from 45 cents per kilowatt-hour in 1980 to less than 3 cents today, making it competitive with natural gas- or coal-fired plants. Power providers are rushing to take advantage of the credit before it is scheduled to disappear again in 2006. . . .

GOVERNMENT INCENTIVES are crucial to the development of wind farms and other sources of renewable energy.

Similar incentives are fueling solar power, which remains more costly than fossil fuels and is even more dependent on government incentives. . . . Forecasters see more than 30% growth per year for the next decade.

The renewable industry is largely the creation of government policies, and there's always a chance that the political winds could shift. But given environmental pressures and more competitive green energy prices, it's a good bet that the boom in renewables will continue. ∎

"Tax Credits Put Wind in the Sails of Renewables" by John Carey.
BusinessWeek, January 10, 2005.

reading for understanding

What was the effect on GE Wind Energy when Congress ended tax credits?

Explain how the company and the industry reacted when the tax credits were restored.

Why does the author describe the renewable industry as "largely the creation of government policies"?

Why do you think the government is providing incentives to companies that offer wind energy?

Providing Public Goods

Thinking on Your Own

There is an adage that states "There is no such thing as a 'free lunch.'" Make a list in your notebook of three products or services that you have used in the past year that did not cost you anything. Compare your list with that of a partner. Were they really free? Explain why you believe the items on your list were free.

Public goods are products and services whose benefits are spread among an entire community. They are relatively rare. The best examples of a pure public good are national defense and the nation's system of property rights. Both are important to society as a whole rather than to a few individuals or even a group within a community.

focus your reading

What are the two main characteristics of public goods?

Give three examples of a public good.

What is a public "bad"?

vocabulary

public goods

private goods

Characteristics of Public and Private Goods

Public goods are often compared with **private goods**—the products and services people use every day. Private goods have three important characteristics. The first is that a person's enjoyment of these goods reduces the amount available to others. The second is that a seller can attach a price to these goods and services and reject consumers who are unwilling to pay that price. In addition, potential buyers can reject the good or service if they are unwilling to pay the price or would prefer to buy something else.

Cookies are an example of a private good. They can be divided into bags or boxes of various sizes and sold. If you buy a bag,

Supermarkets offer many examples of private goods.

The Pentagon provides the public good of national defense.

there is one fewer bag for everyone else who wants one. If you don't like cookies, you do not have to buy or eat them.

A fireworks display is an example of a public good. Whether you see fireworks alone or with thousands of other people, your enjoyment does not take away from anyone else's pleasure. It would be nearly impossible to deny someone access to a fireworks display, whether they paid to see the lights or not.

A public good is, therefore, any product or service that is in demand, but its use does not limit the supply available to others. Sellers cannot keep consumers from using the product, even if consumers are unwilling to pay for it. Consumers are unable to reject the product, even if they have no interest in using it.

Consumers are said to get a "free ride" from public goods, because they enjoy the benefits without paying the costs. Therefore, businesses are unlikely to produce those goods because they cannot be sure of making a profit from them. Once they exist, they are there for all to use. If these goods are to be provided, the government will usually have to provide them.

Government in Charge

Governments use a variety of methods to provide public goods. Many local governments provide public transportation, run public parks, supply households with clean water, or collect the trash. As you learned in Chapter 7, governments can also provide a public good by awarding a monopoly franchise to a single company. With such a franchise, the business can provide a needed public good without worrying about competition. Electric and gas companies have government franchises in many communities.

Governments can also use subsidies to provide public goods. A subsidy is a government payment to an individual, business, or other group to encourage or protect a certain type of economic activity. Subsidies lower the cost of production, encouraging current producers to remain in the market and new producers to enter. For example, some state

Economics and You

Subsidizing a College Education

Both state and federal governments offer students help in paying for a college education. Both consider an education a public good. The U.S. Department of Education offers advice on paying college costs in a publication called *Funding Your Education*. It points out that about two-thirds of all student financial aid comes from Department of Education grants, work-study, and loan programs. The publication explains the differences among the three types of aid:

- You don't have to pay back grants (unless, for example, you withdraw from school and owe a refund).

- Work-study allows you to earn money for your education.

- Loans allow you to borrow money for school. You must repay any money you borrow.

More detailed information on federal student aid programs is available from various government Web sites. To learn about state aid programs, contact your state's higher education agency, or check with a high school counselor or the college or professional school you plan to attend. You might want to use a search engine on the Internet, using keywords such as "financial aid," "student aid," or "scholarships." Also, check the reference section of your local library, using the same words to search.

and local governments subsidize the building of new sports stadiums. The federal government subsidizes a wide variety of projects to encourage energy conservation, find cures for diseases, explore outer space, and aid thousands of other research efforts.

Air pollution is a public "bad."

Public "Bads"

The opposite of public goods are what some economists refer to as public "bads." These are goods and services with negative externalities. Similar to public goods, public "bads" affect everyone who is exposed to them. They include water and air pollution, the trade in dangerous drugs, and sales of liquor and tobacco.

The government outlaws the manufacture, sale, and use of a number of public "bads." Others are closely regulated, and some, as in the case of tobacco and liquor, are heavily taxed. The tax rate on these goods and services is often set particularly high in order to decrease demand for these goods.

Putting It All Together

Go back to the list that you made at the beginning of this lesson. Add more public goods to your list. Then write a paragraph explaining why you think the government should or should not be involved in providing these goods.

Chapter Summary

- Governments define and protect **private property rights**.

- The government protects ideas as well as resources by issuing patents, **copyrights**, and **trademarks**.

- The government sets **standards** to support industries and protect consumers.

- Government regulation can build the confidence of buyers and sellers in markets.

- **Market failures** occur as a result of imperfect competition and **externalities**.

- To deal with the effects of imperfect competition, Congress outlawed **price discrimination**, allowed the Federal Trade Commission to issue **cease and desist orders**, and established **minimum wage laws**.

- Governments try to minimize the effects of **negative externalities** and encourage **positive externalities**.

- **Taxes** are required payments to the government.

- **Tax credits** are given to some businesses as incentives to do what the government wants.

- In many respects, **public goods** are the opposite of **private goods**.

- Governments provide some **public goods**. They issue monopoly franchises and grant subsidies to provide other **public goods**.

Chapter Review

1 Draw a diagram that shows the various roles that government plays in a market economy. Write a caption that explains your diagram.

2 Look carefully at your diagram. Highlight what you consider to be the most important role of government in a market economy. Then write a paragraph defending your choice. Be sure to support your ideas with reasons and examples.

Skill Builder

Categorize Information

One way to keep track of what you read is by organizing information into groups of related facts and ideas. To categorize information:

- Look for information with similar characteristics.

- List those characteristics or categories as the headings on a chart.

- Fill in details from the reading under the proper category on the chart.

Read the following paragraph, which appears in this chapter. Identify the three categories discussed in the paragraph, and then answer the questions that follow.

> The government protects ideas as well as resources. It issues patents to inventors and developers of new products and methods. It also allows writers and other artists to copyright their books, music, art, and other creative works. Like a patent, a copyright provides the owner with an exclusive right to reproduce, sell, or distribute a work. The government also safeguards trademarks—words, phrases, symbols, or designs, or a combination of words, phrases, symbols, or designs that identify and distinguish goods produced by one firm from those produced by others.

1 Create a chart that identifies the three categories, and provide information about each.

2 How do the three differ from one another?

3 In what way are the three categories similar to one another?

UNIT 4

THE NATIONAL ECONOMY

Unit 3 focused on four key institutions within a market economy: businesses, financial institutions, labor markets, and government. Unit 4 looks at the ways these institutions affect the nation's economy as a whole. You will explore how they work together to promote national economic growth. You will also examine the challenges in the nation's economy.

Chapter 12

MEASURING ECONOMIC PERFORMANCE

Getting Focused

Skim this chapter to predict what you will be learning.

- Read the lesson titles and subheadings.
- Look at the illustrations and read the captions.
- Examine the graphs and charts.
- Review the vocabulary words and terms.

Economists measure how well the nation's economy is performing. Three important indicators are economic output or productivity, the rate of inflation, and business fluctuations. As you skim this chapter, look for ways economists measure each of these. Briefly describe each one in your notebook.

The nation's economy is always in the news. Politicians and citizens alike are concerned with inflation, interest rates, and the future of the economy. The U.S. government uses GDP to measure the nation's economy.

Measuring Output and Income

Thinking on Your Own

Have you had a good year or a bad year financially? What measures would you use to answer this question? Would they allow you to compare this year with last year? If so, which year was better?

When people think about how well they are doing financially, they often focus on their salaries. Did they make more money this year than the past year? Or they may think about how much they had to produce or how hard they had to work. Economists measure a nation's economic performance in similar ways.

Measuring Output

The United States government uses **gross domestic product** (GDP) to measure total output or production in the nation in a single year. GDP is determined by multiplying the quantity of all goods and services by their prices for three broad categories—consumer spending, government spending, and investments. The results are added together to form GDP, the most important gauge of the strength of the economy. It includes everything from the production of guided missiles to rock concerts, tractors to prom dresses, medical care to movies.

Defining GDP

To combine such very different goods and services into a single number, economists focus on the value of the various products

---

focus your reading

What is included in GDP?

How does GDP differ from GNP (gross national product)?

Name four other measures of economic performance.

vocabulary

gross domestic product

final product

intermediate goods

secondhand sales

nonmarket transaction

underground economy

gross national product

net national product

national income

personal income

transfer payments

disposable personal income

and services rather than the quantity produced. GDP is the dollar value of all of the final goods and services produced in a nation in a single year.

A **final product** is a good or service that requires no additions or changes before being used. For example, when you buy a new car, you get factory-installed seat belts, a steering wheel, a battery, tires, side-view mirrors, and windshield wipers. The values of these individual items are included in the price of the car. Items like seat belts and tires that carmakers buy for resale or use in producing other goods are known as **intermediate goods**. They are not included in GDP.

Some goods are both intermediate goods and final products, depending on who buys them and for what purpose. For example, if your car needs a new tire or windshield wiper, your purchase will be counted as part of GDP. Why? The replacements are considered a final product, because you did not buy them to resell or to produce another product.

GDP includes only products and services produced within a nation. If an American company has a factory in Mexico, the goods produced there are not included in the U.S. GDP, but are included in Mexico's GDP. Similarly, if a Mexican company opens a factory in Texas, the goods produced in that factory are counted as part of the U.S. GDP.

GDP includes only goods and services produced in a single year. **Secondhand sales**—the sales of used goods—are excluded. These products were counted in the year they were originally sold and will never be counted again. Only first sales count.

For the most part, GDP does not include nonmarket transactions. A **nonmarket transaction** is one that takes place outside organized markets. For example, jobs done at home—mowing the lawn, preparing meals, or doing laundry—are nonmarket transactions. They are counted only when someone outside the family does these chores for pay. If you order a pizza for dinner, that pizza is counted in the nation's GDP. However, if you make a pizza and serve it to your family for dinner, it is not counted. GDP also does not include unpaid

labor. Volunteering at the senior center will be appreciated, but not counted in GDP. Bartering is also excluded. If you mow your neighbor's lawn for a month in exchange for a used bicycle, that transaction is not included in GDP.

Some nonmarket transactions are excluded because they are illegal and therefore not reported. These activities include smuggling and drug dealing. They also include gambling in places where it is illegal. Illegal activities are considered part of the **underground economy**. This term is used to describe market exchanges that are unreported because they are illegal or because those involved want to avoid paying taxes on their exchanges. Economists estimate that the underground economy may amount to 10 percent or more of the U.S. GDP. It may be an even larger percentage in other countries.

Limits on GDP

Although GDP is the most comprehensive measure of output in the U.S. economy, it does not tell economists everything about the economy. Because it includes only transactions in organized markets, work done outside those markets is uncounted. As a result, comparing the GDPs of various nations can be difficult. Countries differ in the amount of

activity that takes place in organized markets. In the United States, the amount is very large; in less developed countries, the amount is often quite small. People are more likely to barter for the things they need than to purchase them with money.

Another limitation on GDP is that it counts public "bads" as public goods. For example, hurricanes and tornadoes can cause billions of dollars worth of damage. Yet these disasters are likely to raise GDP, because consumers, businesses, and governments spend huge sums of money to rebuild, repair, and replace damaged highways, power lines, homes, stores, offices, and factories. Wars are yet another disaster that can raise GDP. Nations are not usually better off as a result of a hurricane or a war. Yet an increase in GDP would indicate that they are better off economically.

GDP tells economists very little about how the nation's production of goods and services affects the quality of life. Machines that reduce pollution are counted along with those that pollute the environment. Still, economists regard GDP as a measure of the overall strength of the economy because it is a count of voluntary transactions, which take place only when both the buyer and seller feel they will be better off as a result of their deal. Therefore, if GDP increases from one year to the next, it suggests that more people feel they are better off today than they were the previous year.

Other Measures

GDP is not the only measure of economic performance. **Gross national product** (GNP) measures the value of final goods and services produced by a nation in a given year. The

National Income and Product Accounts — Figure 12.1

Gross Domestic Product (GDP)	$	10,226.8
Plus: Payments to American citizens who employ resources outside the U.S.	+	360.2
Less: Payments to foreign-owned resources employed inside the U.S.	–	367.2
Gross National Product (GNP)	$	10,219.8
Less: Capital consumption allowances and adjustments (depreciation)	–	1,318.6
Net National Product (NNP)	$	8,901.2
Less: Indirect business taxes and subsidies	–	736.2
National Income (NI)	$	8,165.0
Plus: Transfer payments to persons, personal interest income, and Social Security receipts	+	2,572.8
Less: Undistributed corporate profits, corporate income taxes, and Social Security contributions	–	2,183.6
Personal Income (PI)	$	8,554.2
Less: Personal taxes and nontax payments	–	1,372.2
Disposable Personal Income (DPI)	$	7,182.0

(in billions of current dollars)

Source: *Bureau of Economic Analysis,* June 2001 (data for first quarter)

difference between GNP and GDP lies in a single word. GDP measures the output *in* a country—no matter who owns the business. GNP measures the output *by* residents of a country—no matter where they live.

Figure 12.1 shows the relationship between GDP and GNP. In Figure 12.1, GNP is a smaller number than GDP. Why? Because Americans paid more to acquire factors of production outside the U.S. than Americans received from foreign-owned resources in the U.S. If the U.S. were a closed economy—one that did not do business outside its borders—GDP and GNP would be identical.

GNP is one of five income measures included in National Income and Product Accounts (NIPA). The second measure is **net national product** (NNP). It is GNP with depreciation subtracted. Depreciation is the decrease in the value of tools and other equipment from wear and tear and the passage of time.

The third measure is **national income** (NI). It is the income that remains after all taxes, except those on corporate profits, have been subtracted from NNP.

The fourth measure is **personal income** (PI). It is the total income earned by consumers before paying individual income taxes.

Personal income is measured by making four adjustments to national income. The first three are subtractions from income. They include income taxes, individual contributions to Social Security, and undistributed corporate profits (profits firms use for reinvestment in new plants and equipment). The final adjustment is the addition of all of the individual's transfer payments. **Transfer payments** are payments that do not require any goods or services in return. Social Security benefits, unemployment compensation payments, insurance, and welfare checks are all examples of transfer payments.

Personal income is one measure of GDP.

The fifth and smallest measure of income is **disposable personal income** (DPI). It is the total income the consumer has after paying personal income tax. DPI is an important measure, because it is the actual amount of money individual consumers have to spend.

Putting It All Together

Briefly explain in your own words each of the measures of economic performance introduced in this lesson. Which do you think reveals the most about the strength of the economy? Why do you think so? Give reasons for your answer.

Inflation and GDP

Thinking on Your Own

Have you ever heard someone say, "A dollar is not worth what it used to be"? How will a lesson on inflation help explain why this is usually true?

When is a dollar not a dollar? During periods of inflation, the purchasing power of a dollar declines. **Inflation** is a rise, over time, in the general level of prices. As a result, a dollar buys less. **Deflation**—a drop, over time, in the general level of prices—may also affect GDP. However, deflation is very rare.

Inflation and Buying Power

Figure 12.2, on page 193, shows how inflation distorts economic statistics. Notice that the quantity sold in Year 1 is identical to the quantity sold in Year 2. The difference is that in Year 2, the inflation rate (the percent of price change usually calculated on a monthly or yearly basis) is at 10 percent. As a result, the GDP rises 10 percent, even though the quantity sold does not change.

focus your reading

Explain why economists try to correct for inflation.

How does a price index work?

Describe the difference between real GDP and current GDP.

vocabulary

inflation

deflation

consumer price index

base year

market basket

producer price index

implicit GDP price deflator

nominal GDP

real GDP

Measures of Inflation

The government measures inflation in a number of ways. The three methods most commonly used are the consumer price index, the producer price index, and the implicit GDP price deflator.

Consumer price index The **consumer price index** (CPI) is a measure of the monthly changes in price of a specific group of goods and services that consumers use regularly. It includes the prices of food, clothing, shelter, fuel, transportation fares, doctors' and dentists' services, medicines, and other goods and services that people buy for day-to-day living.

To create a price index, the U.S. Bureau of Labor Statistics (BLS), which compiles the CPI each month, identifies a **base year**—a year that will be used as a point of comparison. Then a **market basket** is chosen. This refers to goods that reflect the day-to-day purchases of consumers. Figure 12.3 shows that the items in the market basket are grouped into eight major categories: food and beverages (milk, eggs, cereal, etc.); housing (includes rent or mortgage payments and items purchased for the home or apartment); clothing; transportation (automobiles and insurance, plane tickets, and gasoline); medical care; recreation (includes pets, sports equipment, and televisions); education and communication; and other goods and services (includes tobacco and smoking items, and services such as haircuts).

The number of goods and services in the market basket has to remain fixed after the selection is made in order to identify overall trends in prices. The price of items in the basket is recorded and then totaled. The sum of the contents of the market basket in the base year is valued at 100 percent. The CPI in each of the years that follow indicates the percentage of change from the base year. For example, the CPI was 190.3 in December 2004. That number would mean that the cost of

Estimating Gross Domestic Product

Figure 12.2

	Product	Quantity (millions)	Year 1		Year 2	
			Price (per 1 unit)	Dollar Values (millions)	Price (per 1 unit)	Dollar Values (millions)
Goods	Automobiles	6	$ 20,000	$120,000	$22,000	$132,000
	Replacement Tires	10	$60	$600	$70	$700
	Shoes	55	$50	$2,750	$55	$3,025
	...*	...*	...*	...*	...*	...*
Services	Haircuts	150	$8	$1,200	$10	$1,500
	Income Tax Filing	30	$150	$4,500	$160	$4,800
	Legal Advice	45	200	$9,000	$220	$9,900
	...*	...*	...*	...*	...*	...*
Structures	Single Family	3	$75,000	$225,000	$80,000	$240,000
	Multifamily	5	$300,000	$1,000,000	$330,000	$1,650,000
	Commercial	1	$1,000,000	$1,000,000	$1,100,000	$1,100,000
	...*	...*	...*	...*	...*	...*

NOTE: ...* other goods, services, and structures

Total Gross Domestic Product = $9 trillion

Total Gross Domestic Product = $9.9 trillion

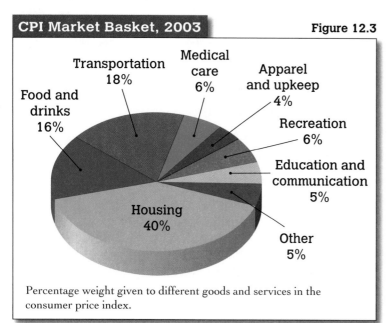

CPI Market Basket, 2003   **Figure 12.3**

Transportation 18%

Medical care 6%

Apparel and upkeep 4%

Recreation 6%

Food and drinks 16%

Education and communication 5%

Housing 40%

Other 5%

Percentage weight given to different goods and services in the consumer price index.

Source: U.S. Bureau of Labor Statistics

goods and services increased 90.3 percent (190.3 − 100 = 90.3) since the base year, in this case 1982.

The CPI reports on price changes for about 90,000 items. It is compiled every month by the U.S. Bureau of Labor Statistics and published for the economy as a whole. There is also a regional index for each part of the country.

Producer price index The **producer price index** (PPI) measures the monthly change in prices paid by producers in the United States for their outputs. The PPI is based on a sample of about 100,000 commodities, and uses 1982 as the base year. The index is broken into various categories, including farm products, fuels, chemicals, rubber, paper products, and processed foods. A rise in the PPI often precedes an increase in consumer prices. Manufacturers who have to pay more for their raw materials are likely to pass on their increased costs to the consumer in the form of higher prices. A rising PPI can be an indicator that inflation is on its way.

Implicit GDP price deflator The **implicit GDP price deflator** measures price changes in GDP. It is calculated every three months and has a base year of 2000.

Real GDP

Many economists believe that GDP is a good indicator of price changes that consumers face because it includes thousands of items. To compare GDP over time, economists have to distinguish between changes in GDP caused by the effects of

inflation and changes caused by different rates of production and income. When **nominal GDP**, or current GDP, is adjusted to remove the effects of inflation, it is called **real GDP**, or GDP in constant dollars. It shows what GDP would have been if prices had not changed from what they were in the base year. To calculate real GDP, GDP is divided by the implicit GDP price deflator and then multiplied by 100. For 2004, GDP was $11,735 billion. Real GDP, measured in 2000 prices, was $10,842 billion.

Real GDP is useful for making comparisons. It is also a way to make sure that an increase in GDP was not simply the result of inflation.

Putting It All Together

In your notebook, write a two- or three-sentence answer for each of the following questions: Why does a dollar buy less as a result of inflation and more because of deflation? Why is a rise in the PPI often bad news for consumers? Why is real GDP a better measure of economic performance than current, or nominal, GDP?

Statistician

Do you like to solve puzzles? Would you enjoy searching for clues to solve a scientific or economic mystery? If so, you may want to think about becoming a statistician.

The Work

Statisticians work in a variety of fields, including medicine, government, education, agriculture, business, and law. In business and industry, statisticians play an important role in quality control and product development and improvement. Some statisticians are involved in deciding what products to manufacture, how much to charge for them, and to whom those products should be marketed. Statisticians are also employed by nearly every government agency. They may develop surveys that measure population growth, consumer prices, or unemployment.

Qualifications

Although some jobs are open to individuals with a college degree in statistics, a master's degree is usually the minimum educational requirement for most statistician jobs. Beginning positions in industrial research often require a master's degree combined with several years of experience.

Career Connections

Business Cycles

Thinking on Your Own

Select three of the terms from the vocabulary list. Write them in your notebook. Under each, write what you think the term means. As you encounter each word while you read, correct or add to your definition.

GDP does not move in a steady unbroken pattern from one year to the next. It may rise steadily for several years and then drop sharply. A few years later, real GDP may begin to increase again, only to slow or stop a short time later. These **fluctuations** (ups and downs) of real GDP are known as the **business cycle**.

The Ups and Downs of the Business Cycle

Figure 12.4, on page 197, is a model of a business cycle. The model divides the business cycle into phases, or parts. The cycle moves from a **trough**—a low point from which real GDP starts to rise—and eventually reaches a **boom**—a period of prosperity marked by the opening of many new businesses, and older ones producing at full capacity.

In time, real GDP begins to decline and the economy enters a period of **contraction**—a time when business activity slows. If the contraction lasts at least six months, it is considered a **recession**. In a recession, real GDP does not grow, and business activity falls at a rapid rate throughout the economy. If the slowdown is severe enough, the recession may deepen into a **depression**—a major slowdown in economic activity. It is a time when the economy operates far below its capacity.

focus your reading

Identify the phases of the business cycle.

Name five causes of ups and downs in the business cycle.

What are the major economic indicators?

vocabulary

fluctuations

business cycle

trough

boom

contraction

recession

depression

expansion

inventories

economic indicators

leading indicators

coincident indicators

lagging indicators

At some point, the downward direction of the economy levels off and activity slowly begins to increase. That increase in economic activity is called an **expansion**, or recovery. Consumer spending picks up and factories increase production to meet the demand. The recovery continues until the economy reaches another peak and a new cycle begins.

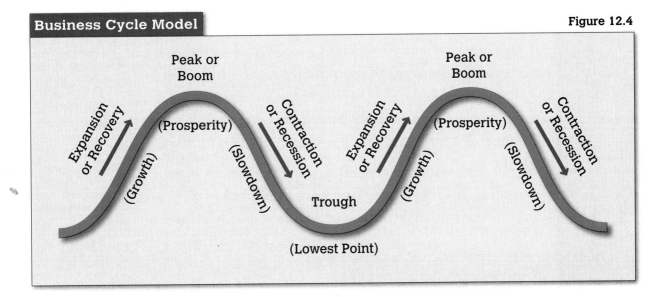

Business Cycle Model   Figure 12.4

Figure 12.4 is a model. In the real world, business cycles are not as regular and as predictable as the model shows. As Figure 12.5 shows, however, the peaks and troughs are clear.

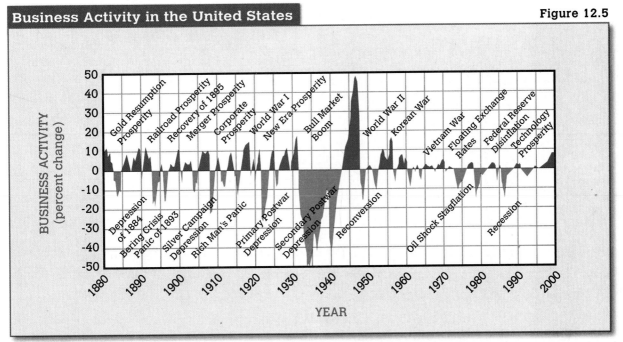

Business Activity in the United States   Figure 12.5

Sources: *American Business Activity from 1790 to Today*, 67th ed., AmeriTrust Co., January 1996; plus author's projections

Causes of Business Fluctuations

What causes the economy to move up and down? Economists tend to believe that changes in economic activity can be linked to five main forces: business decisions, external events, innovation and imitation, government policies, and psychological factors.

Business decisions When the economy is expanding, many businesses expect future sales to soar, so they invest in capital goods. They buy new tools, build new plants, and purchase other capital resources. When their expansion is complete, they begin to pull back on capital investments. As a result, layoffs may occur in capital goods industries, signaling the beginning of a recession.

At the first sign of a recession, some businesses cut back on inventories. **Inventories** are goods held in reserve, including finished goods waiting to be sold and raw materials purchased for use in production. Those same businesses restock at the first sign of a recovery. Either action can result in changes in real GDP—and cause either a boom or a contraction in the economy.

After Hurricane Katrina in 2005, the price of gasoline rose sharply due to damaged oil rigs in the Gulf of Mexico.

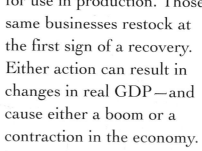

stop and think

Make a list of the reasons the economy moves up and down. Add to this list as you read the rest of this lesson.

External events A war, the discovery of new oil reserves, or a natural disaster can cause a shock to markets. Some of these events promote economic growth, while others may have a negative effect on business activity.

Innovation and imitation Innovations are yet another reason for changes in business activity. An innovation may be a new product or a new way of producing a product or service. When a business comes up with a new idea, it gains an advantage over its competitors and sales rise. Innovations also tend to improve productivity and promote growth. Other businesses in the same industry respond by copying or imitating the innovation or coming up with an even better idea. The result is often greater investment in capital goods. Once the innovation is in place, further investments are not needed and economic activity may begin to slow.

Government policies

Decisions made by the government can affect economic activity. High taxes or government regulations may slow an expansion; low taxes or a reduction in regulations may speed up a recovery. The government can also make it easier or harder for businesses to borrow money. Both have an effect on business activity. The government is also a purchaser of goods and services. Spending on highways, offices, arms, and other goods can stimulate the economy. A reduction in government spending may slow economic activity.

Psychological factors The

prospect of war may cause both consumers and producers to

Major Economic Indicators	Figure 12.6

Leading Indicators

1. Average weekly hours for production workers in manufacturing
2. Weekly initial claims for unemployment insurance
3. New orders for consumer goods
4. Speed with which companies make deliveries (the busier a company, the longer it will take to fill orders)
5. Number of contracts and orders for plants and equipment
6. Number of building permits issued for private housing units
7. Stock prices
8. Changes in money supply in circulation
9. Changes in interest rates
10. Changes in consumer expectations

Coincident Indicators

1. Number of nonagricultural workers who are employed
2. Personal income minus transfer payments
3. Rate of industrial production
4. Sales of manufacturers, wholesalers, and retailers

Lagging Indicators

1. Average length of unemployment
2. Size of manufacturing and trade inventories
3. Labor cost per unit of output in manufacturing
4. Average interest rate charged by banks to their best business customers
5. Number of commercial and industrial loans to be repaid
6. Ratio of consumer installment debt to personal income
7. Change in consumer price index for services

fear for the future. A scientific breakthrough may lead to feelings of confidence and optimism. Both sets of feelings can influence the business cycle. During the Great Depression that began in 1929, President Franklin D. Roosevelt told Americans, ". . . the only thing we have to fear is fear itself." He was trying to help people understand that the basic economic institutions of the nation were sound.

Economic Indicators

Is a rise in prices a signal that a recession is coming? Or is the rise due to bad weather or a temporary shortage of a key resource? Business leaders and government officials study a variety of economic indicators to help them figure out the answers to these and dozens of similar questions.

Economic indicators are statistics that measure variations, or changes, in the economy. Every month, the U.S. Department of Commerce compiles statistics for 78 economic indicators that examine all aspects of the U.S. economy.

Leading indicators Statistics that point to what will happen in the economy are called **leading indicators**. They seem to lead to a change or trend. The ten indicators of most concern to economists are listed in Figure 12.6, on page 199.

Coincident indicators Economists also study **coincident indicators**—statistics that occur at the same time as changes in overall business activity. These indicators are signs that a contraction or expansion has begun.

Lagging indicators A third set of indicators seems to lag behind changes in business activity. The amount of changes in these **lagging indicators** offers clues as to how long a phase in the business cycle will last.

Putting It All Together

News stories boast of recoveries and warn of contractions in the economy. How do these economic phases affect you, your family, and your neighbors, in terms of job opportunities, the prices you pay for goods and services, and your ability to borrow money? Write a paragraph explaining how the business cycle affects your life.

Our Murky Crystal Ball

Economists use economic indicators to figure out how the economy is doing and what may lie ahead. In December 2004, *BusinessWeek Online* offered its predictions for 2005. In June 2005, Mira Serrill-Robins checked to see how accurate those predictions turned out to be.

It seems like only yesterday that the winter winds blew, the holiday season was ending, and *BusinessWeek Online* boldly offered its predictions for 2005. . . .

With 2005 close to its midpoint, we thought it would be illuminating and fun to look at those predictions, which serve as a vivid reminder of how world and national events can change in six months' time—and how sometimes the more things change, the more they remain the same. . . .

Prediction . . . GDP growth for 2005 will clock in at around 4%.

In the first quarter of 2005 the economy grew by an annual rate of 3.5%, according to the government. On June 8 the White House announced that it expects growth of 3.4% in the second half. Later that same day, the Federal Reserve Bank of Philadelphia's semiannual Livingston survey of economists forecast U.S. economic growth at an annual adjusted rate of 3.3% in the first half of 2005 and 3.6% in the second. We're in the ballpark. . . .

Prediction . . . The price of oil will drop below $40 a barrel sometime during the year and stay in the $40 range through year end.

Ugh! Oil prices hit a new record high today of $58.47 a barrel. . . .

Prediction . . . At least one airline company will disappear, as air travel demand continues to sag and oil prices remain high.

Glad we were wrong—so far. . . . Oil prices are near record-highs, and airlines are still in trouble, but they're holding on and trying to work fast to boost revenues during the summer travel season. ∎

"Our Murky Crystal Ball" by Mira Serrill-Robins. *BusinessWeek Online*, June 17, 2005.

reading for understanding

Which predictions turned out to be correct?

Which predictions turned out to be incorrect?

What does the author mean when she writes that the predictions are "a vivid reminder of how world and national events can change in six months' time—and how sometimes the more things change, the more they remain the same"?

Chapter Summary

- **Gross domestic product** (GDP) is the dollar value of all of the final goods and services produced in a nation in a single year. GDP does not include **intermediate goods, secondhand sales, nonmarket transactions,** or the **underground economy.**

- Other measures of the economy include **gross national product** (GNP), **net national product** (NNP), **national income** (NI), **personal income** (PI), and **disposable personal income** (DPI).

- **Transfer payments** include Social Security benefits, unemployment payments, insurance, and welfare checks.

- During periods of **inflation**, the purchasing power of a dollar declines, and during periods of **deflation**, purchasing power rises.

- In compiling the **consumer price index** (CPI), a **base year** is identified and a **market basket** selected.

- The **producer price index** (PPI) and the **implicit GDP price deflator** also help economists measure inflation.

- When **nominal GDP** is adjusted to remove the effects of inflation, it is called **real GDP**.

- **Fluctuations** of real GDP are known as the **business cycle**. It includes **troughs** and **booms**, as well as **contractions** and recoveries.

- **Economic indicators** include **leading indicators, coincident indicators,** and **lagging indicators.**

Chapter Review

1 How do you and your family contribute to GDP? How accurate is GDP as a measure of your total contribution to the economy? You may want to start by making a list of items that you and your family buy on a weekly or monthly basis.

2 Some economists have compared the business cycle to a roller coaster. In what respects is the cycle similar to a roller coaster? What are the most significant differences? Be sure to support your ideas with reasons and examples.

Skill Builder

Nominal and Real Values

To make comparisons between the prices of things in the past and those of today, you have to distinguish between nominal, or current, values and real values—values adjusted for inflation. To calculate the real value of any item, follow these steps.

- Identify the nominal price of the item today and its nominal price in the year of comparison. Subtract the comparison price from the current price.

- Divide the increase by the original price and then multiply by 100 to express the nominal percentage increase.

- Find the rate of inflation or percent of change in CPI.

- Subtract the percentage increase in CPI from the percentage increase in the nominal price to determine real value.

Determine the Real Value of a Bicycle

Figure 12.7

Purchase price of bicycle in 2000: $100 CPI in 2000: 100	
Purchase price of bicycle in 2006: $200 CPI in 2006: 200	
Step 1—subtract 2000 comparison price from 2006 comparison price	$200 − $100 = $100
Step 2—divide increase and then multiply to find percent change	100/100 = 1 1 × 100 = 100%
Step 3—find inflation rate or percent change in CPI	200 − 100 = 100 100/100 = 1 1 × 100 = 100%
Step 4—subtract percentage increase in CPI from percentage increase in the nominal price	100% − 100% = 0%

Answer the following questions.

1 Suppose that last year you earned $10 per hour. This year you receive a 5 percent raise. The CPI is 3.2 percent higher this year than it was last year. What is the real value of your raise?

2 To receive a real 5 percent raise in a year with 3.2 percent inflation, what would your nominal raise need to be?

Chapter 13

GOVERNMENT AND THE ECONOMY

Getting Focused

Skim this chapter to predict what you will be learning.

- Read the lesson titles and subheadings.
- Look at the illustrations and read the captions.
- Examine the graphs and charts.
- Review the vocabulary words and terms.

As you preview the chapter, look for clues about the role of the government in the nation's economy. Create a list of questions that you expect the chapter will answer.

The mission of the United States Department of the Treasury is to "promote the conditions for prosperity and stability in the United States and encourage prosperity and stability in the rest of the world."

Government Spending

Thinking on Your Own

Governments enforce laws and provide basic services. They also purchase goods and services. In your notebook, list three items or services regularly purchased by the government of your city.

The United States has three levels of government: local, state, and federal. Each plays an important role in the U.S. economy. In Chapter 11, you learned that governments make rules for markets and make sure that those rules are enforced. In addition, they encourage competition and try to minimize the effects of negative externalities. In this lesson, you will learn that the government is also a major consumer of goods and services. Government spending can be divided into three main categories: purchases of goods and services, transfer payments, and interest payments.

focus your reading

What kinds of goods and services does the federal government purchase?

Give an example of a transfer payment.

What is an interest payment?

vocabulary

goods and services

Social Security

Medicare

grant

interest payment

recall

Negative externalities are harmful side effects of an activity that impact people who are not involved in the activity.

Public goods are products and services whose benefits are spread among an entire community.

Gross domestic product (GDP) is the total output or production in a nation in a single year.

Purchases of Goods and Services

In the first years of the twenty-first century, government spending accounted for about one-third of the gross domestic product (GDP). Figure 13.1, for example, shows that in 2004, the federal government purchased $2.3 trillion worth of goods and services—about 20 percent of the GDP. State and local governments purchased another $1.5 trillion worth of products and services.

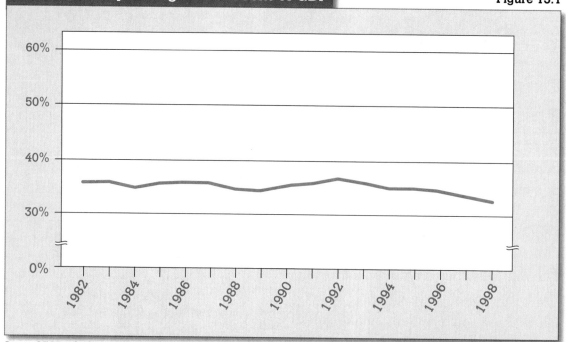

Source: OECD, calendar-year data

How do governments spend their money? **Goods and services** are items that the government purchases to use, or consume, directly. As Figure 13.2 on page 207 suggests, the federal government is a consumer of a wide range of goods and services. It buys computers for government agencies, scientific equipment for research, and everything from missiles to uniforms for the armed forces. The government also builds and maintains national parks, highways, bridges, tunnels, buildings, and other infrastructures.

In addition, governments purchase labor. Over 2.7 million people worked for the federal government in 2004. That number does not include members of the armed forces or employees of local and state governments. Their salaries are included in nondefense government purchases. Money earned by members of the armed forces is included under national defense spending.

stop and think

Look carefully at the categories of spending in Figure 13.2. What categories did you expect to find? What categories surprised you? Share your thoughts with a partner.

Transfer Payments

The largest category of spending in Figure 13.2 is for transfer payments. A transfer payment is a cash payment from a government to an individual, group, or another level of government for which nothing is required in return. **Social Security** benefits, **Medicare** payments, and unemployment compensation payments are all examples of transfer payments.

How the Government Spent Its Money, 2004

Figure 13.2

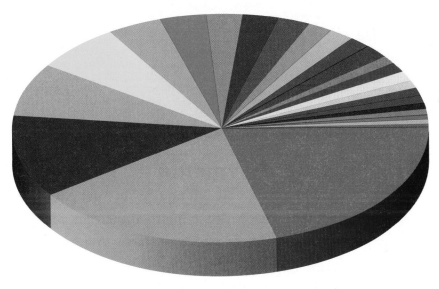

FEDERAL BUDGET: EXPENDITURES
Outlays by function in billions of dollars, fiscal year 2004

- Social Security $495.5 (21.6%)
- National defense $455.9 (19.9%)
- Medicare $269.3 (11.8%)
- Medicaid $176.2 (7.7%)
- Interest on debt $160.2 (7.0%)
- Other retirement and disability $94.8 (4.1%)
- Education, employment, and social services $87.9 (3.8%)
- Transportation $64.6 (2.8%)
- Health $63.9 (2.8%)
- Veterans' benefits $59.7 (2.6%)
- Justice system $45.5 (2.0%)
- Housing assistance $45.5 (2.0%)
- Unemployment $42.4 (1.8%)
- Food and nutrition assistance $40.7 (1.8%)
- Earned Income Tax Credit $33.1 (1.4%)
- Supplemental Security Income $31.2 (1.4%)
- Natural resources and the environment $30.7 (1.3%)
- International affairs (includes foreign aid) $26.8 (1.2%)
- Family support (includes TANF) $24.2 (1.1%)
- Science, space, and technology $23.0 (1.0%)
- General government $21.8 (0.9%)
- Other income security $20.9 (0.9%)
- Agriculture $15.4 (0.7%)
- Community development $15.7 (0.7%)
- Commerce and housing credit $5.2 (0.2%)

Note: Federal outlays totaled $2.29 trillion in fiscal year 2004, which includes the subtraction of $58.5 billion (or -2.5 percent) in "undistributed offsetting receipts," which are collections deducted from outlays rather than added to receipts.

Source: Budget of the United States Government, Fiscal Year 2006

So are federal grants to state and local governments as shown in Figure 13.2, on page 207. A **grant** is financial assistance that does not have to be repaid.

Social Security is the nation's largest federal program. It provides retirement benefits and medical insurance (Medicare) benefits to eligible workers. More than 50 million retired or disabled workers,

Senior citizens can take advantage of the health benefits offered by the Medicare program.

their families, and surviving family members of deceased workers receive Social Security benefits each month. Those benefits cost the government a total of about $430 billion each year.

Interest Payments

The government also spends money on interest payments. **Interest payments** are cash payments to holders of government bonds. Bonds are loans that individuals and firms make to the government. Interest is the amount the borrower (in this case, the government) pays for the privilege of using the lender's money. Interest is usually calculated as a percentage of the loan. The percentage rate may be fixed for the life of the loan, or it may vary, depending on the terms of the loan.

In 1970 and 1980, interest payments made up between 1 and 2 percent of government spending. In 1990, that percentage nearly doubled. As Figure 13.2 shows, by 2004, interest payments made up 7 percent of government spending.

Putting It All Together

In your notebook, write a paragraph that compares the three categories of government spending. How are they alike? Which category differs most from the other two? Give reasons for your answer.

Taxes

Thinking on Your Own

To purchase goods and services, governments must have income. List three ways that your city government receives income.

Taxes provide the money for the tanks the Defense Department needs, the computers government workers rely on, the devices the Department of Homeland Security uses to screen passengers at airports, and the office buildings that house government agencies. State and local governments also depend on taxes to purchase the goods and services they provide.

Who Pays?

As Figure 13.3 on page 210 shows, individual and corporate income taxes accounted for over half of all government revenue in 2004. Social Security taxes accounted for almost all of the rest. Almost everyone who is employed in the United States must pay Social Security taxes. Those taxes are used to provide retirement benefits and medical insurance (Medicare) benefits. Employers deduct these taxes from each employee's wages and add their own contributions.

Other than income taxes and Social Security taxes, the only other major source of government revenue is the excise tax. An **excise tax** is a tax on the purchase of a specific good or service—for example, taxes on tobacco products, gasoline, or telephone services. Such taxes accounted for less than 4 percent of all revenues in 2004. An array of other taxes provided the rest of the

> **focus your reading**
>
> What are the two principles of taxation?
>
> What is the main difference between a progressive tax and a regressive tax?
>
> Give an example of a proportional tax.

> **vocabulary**
>
> excise tax
>
> income tax
>
> sales tax
>
> property tax
>
> principle of benefits received
>
> principle of ability to pay
>
> deduction
>
> progressive tax
>
> regressive tax
>
> proportional tax

> **recall**
>
> A **tax** is a required payment of a percentage of income, property value, or the value of a purchase for the support of a government.

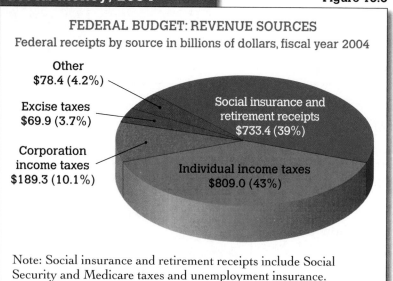

Where the U.S. Government Got Its Money, 2004

Figure 13.3

FEDERAL BUDGET: REVENUE SOURCES
Federal receipts by source in billions of dollars, fiscal year 2004

Other $78.4 (4.2%)

Excise taxes $69.9 (3.7%)

Corporation income taxes $189.3 (10.1%)

Social insurance and retirement receipts $733.4 (39%)

Individual income taxes $809.0 (43%)

Note: Social insurance and retirement receipts include Social Security and Medicare taxes and unemployment insurance. Other includes estate and gift taxes and customs and duties fees.

Source: Budget of the United States Government, Fiscal Year 2006

government's income. These included taxes on goods brought into the United States from other countries and taxes on the property of people who recently died.

Many states have **income taxes**. States also rely on two taxes that the federal government does not use: the sales tax and the property tax. A **sales tax** is a tax on purchases. Most states and many local governments tax purchases. The rates vary, as do the items subject to the tax. For example, some states tax all purchases; others tax everything but food and medicine. A **property tax** is a tax on the value of property—both real property, like houses and land, and personal property, like stocks and bonds.

stop and think

Make a list of all the kinds of taxes you pay in the course of a year. If you work, you probably pay federal income tax and Social Security tax. What other taxes do you pay? Share your list with a partner.

Justifying Taxes

How do lawmakers decide who will pay which tax and how much he or she will pay? How do they try to ensure that the system of paying taxes is fair? Lawmakers use two general principles to justify tax payments: the principle of benefits received and the principle of ability to pay.

The **principle of benefits received** links a tax directly to the benefit taxpayers receive from it. A gas tax is a good example. The government taxes gasoline to pay for building and maintaining the roads used by drivers of cars, buses, and trucks. The more you drive, the more gas you consume, and the more

tax you pay. That seems fair. Yet no one would expect people on welfare to pay a tax that will be used to pay for welfare payments. And how does any nation determine how much benefit an individual receives from national defense, public schools, or fire protection? Clearly, it is not always possible to divide up the benefits of a government service.

As a result of such dilemmas, many taxes are based on the **principle of ability to pay**. The idea is that almost everyone benefits from the work of government. Therefore, nearly everyone should pay for the services it provides, but those who have larger incomes or more assets should pay more.

Economists generally believe that no matter what principle is used to create a tax, the tax itself should be

The money to maintain roads often comes from a gasoline tax paid by drivers.

Personal Income Tax

At some time or another, everyone pays income taxes. How much will you pay in taxes? Figure 13.4 can help you figure it out.

1 How much tax will you owe if you earn $17,000 a year?

2 How much tax does someone who earns $40,000 pay?

3 Your boss offers to raise your salary from $17,500 to $18,000. How will the raise affect the amount of tax you pay?

Figure 13.4

SINGLE INDIVIDUALS 2005				
IF TAXABLE INCOME ...		THEN THE TAX IS ...		
IS OVER	BUT NOT OVER	THIS AMOUNT	PLUS THIS %	OF THE EXCESS OVER
	7,300		10%	
7,300	29,700	730.00	15%	7,300
29,700	71,950	4,090.00	25%	29,700
71,950	150,150	14,652.50	28%	71,950
150,150	326,450	326,548.50	33%	150,150
326,450		94,727.50	35%	326,450

Economics and You

broad, simple, and fair. A tax that is broad is one that places a relatively small tax on a very large group of people. A tax that is broad in scope is hard to escape, and since the tax is relatively low, there is less incentive to avoid it. A simple tax is one that is easy to understand and to pay.

A tax is considered fair if two similar individuals pay similar taxes. The key word is *similar*. Income tax is a good example. Imagine two people who work at the same job and earn exactly the same salary. They might pay the same amount of tax, but they might not. For example, suppose that one of the two has no children and the other is the parent of four children. Should they pay the same amount? The U.S. government has decided that they should not be taxed the same amount. The parent receives a **deduction**—a reduction in taxes—for each of his or her four children.

Types of Taxes

Taxes are classified in the United States based on their effect on the income of the taxpayer. There are three main types.

A **progressive tax** takes a larger percentage of income from high-income groups than from low-income groups. The federal income tax is a good example of a progressive tax. The more you earn, the higher your tax rate.

A **regressive tax** requires that everyone pay the same rate. Therefore, it takes a larger percentage of income from low-income groups than from high-income groups. A sales tax is an example of a regressive tax. Suppose you bought a car that cost $10,000 and the sales tax was 5 percent ($500). If you earn $100,000 a year, $500 is one-half of one percent of your total income. If you earn $20,000 a year, $500 is 2.5 percent of your total income.

A **proportional tax** takes the same percentage of income from everyone regardless of how much (or little) a person earns. As Figure 13.5 on page 213 shows, Social Security taxes are proportional. In 2005, the Social Security tax for employees was 6.2 percent of income up to $90,000 in earnings. Above $90,000, the tax is regressive. Only those with earnings less than $90,000 pay a tax on their entire earnings.

Tax	Description	Type
Personal income	Tax is a percentage of income and a major source of federal revenue; some states also levy	Progressive at the federal level, but is sometimes proportional at the state level
Social insurance	Taxes covered by the Federal Insurance Contributions Act (FICA); second-largest source of federal revenue	Proportional up to $90,000 in 2005, regressive above that (as estimated by the Social Security Administration)
Corporate income	Federal tax as a percentage of corporate profits; some states also levy	Progressive up to $10 million at the federal level, proportional above that
Excise	Tax paid by the consumer on the manufacture, use, and consumption of certain goods; major federal taxes include alcohol, tobacco, and gasoline; some states also levy	Regressive if people with higher incomes spend a lower proportion of income on taxed items
Estate	Federal tax on the property of someone who has died; some states also levy	Progressive; rate increases with the value of the estate
Inheritance	State tax paid by those who inherit property	Varies by state
Gift	Federal tax paid by the person who gives a large gift	Progressive; rate increases with the value of the gift
Sales	Tax paid on purchases; most states and local governments also levy; items taxed vary	Regressive if people with higher incomes spend a lower proportion of income on taxed items
Property	State and local tax on the value of property; both real (buildings, land) and personal (stocks and bonds) may be taxed	Proportional; rate is set by state and local governments
Customs duties	Tax on imports; paid by the importer	Proportional

Putting It All Together

Create a three-column chart that describes the kinds of taxes you or your family has paid. Describe the tax in the first column, indicate the principle involved in the second column, and state the type of tax in the third column. Compare your chart with that of a partner.

BusinessWeek

A Housing Boom Built on Folly

Christopher Farrell, an editor at *BusinessWeek*, described the role of the capital-gains tax in a boom in the housing market. A capital-gains tax is a tax on profits from the sale of capital assets, like a house or stocks and bonds. The capital gain is the difference between the selling price and the original purchase price of the asset.

What accounts for the housing boom? Economists have cited a number of fundamental factors, including low interest rates, favorable demographics, and restrictions on development. But the unappreciated force that may have infected a strong housing market with home-buying mania is bad tax policy. Specifically, I mean the Taxpayer Relief Act of 1997.

Under a set of easily met limitations— mainly that a home has been a primary residence for two out of the past five years— a family can exempt the first $500,000 in profit on the sale of the home from capital-gains taxes. The comparable figure for a single filer is $250,000.

In sharp contrast, capital gains on stocks and bonds carry a 13% [tax]. . . . The powerful lure of tax-free profit is one reason that home prices have risen at a nearly 7% annual rate, vs. about 4% for the stock market since 1997. . . .

As much as possible, the tax code shouldn't bias investment decisions. As it is, the tax code is too heavily weighted in favor of housing. The Urban Institute calculates that the government provides about $147 billion in subsidies to homeowners, including the mortgage-interest deduction and capital gains exemption. . . .

Congress could level the investment playing field by treating capital gains on real estate, stocks, bonds, and other assets the same. I say levy the same 13% rate on all capital gains— regardless of how they're realized.

Doing so would also reduce the incentive for speculative investment in real estate and remove some disincentive to investing in the stock market. My guess is that investors would shift more of their money into Corporate America, especially innovative companies that create the wealth of the future. ■

"A Housing Boom Built on Folly" by Christopher Farrell. *BusinessWeek*, July 26, 2005.

reading for understanding

For what reasons does the writer consider the Taxpayer Relief Act of 1997 unfair?

Explain what the writer sees as a consequence of that law.

What does the argument the writer makes suggest about the role tax laws play in the economy?

Budgets, Surpluses, and Deficits

Thinking on Your Own

Select three of the terms from the vocabulary list. Write them in your notebook. Under each, write what you think the term means. As you encounter the word when you read, correct or add to your definition.

In 2004, the U.S. government spent $2.3 trillion! How does the government spend that much money in one year's time? How does it plan and track its spending? The government does what millions of American families and businesses do: it prepares a budget. A **budget** is an estimate of income and expenses for a specific period of time—usually one year.

focus your reading

Describe the first step in the budget process.

What are the consequences of a budget surplus?

What are the consequences of a budget deficit?

vocabulary

budget

mandatory spending

discretionary spending

fiscal year

deficit

surplus

national debt

Creating a Budget

If your family is like most, it has two kinds of expenses—fixed expenses and discretionary spending. A fixed expense is one that reoccurs on a regular basis. Mortgage payments and rent are fixed expenses. So are loan payments on a car or insurance payments on your house or car. Governments also have fixed expenses. Those expenses are known as mandatory spending. **Mandatory spending** refers to payments required by law. They continue without the need for annual approvals. Social Security is an example of mandatory spending. So are interest payments on debts. About two-thirds of the federal budget is mandatory spending.

The remaining third is discretionary spending. **Discretionary spending** requires approval by

Employees at the U.S. Government Printing Office unpack copies of the fiscal year 2006 budget.

Congress. Discretionary spending is often divided into three categories: defense (which funds the military activities of the Department of Defense), international (which includes spending for economic and military aid to other countries), and domestic (which includes, among other things, the government's science, transportation, law enforcement, and education programs). The money needed to pay Congress, the president, the courts, and other federal workers also falls under the heading of discretionary spending.

Preparations for a new budget begin 18 months before the start of a new fiscal year. A **fiscal year** is an accounting period. The fiscal year for the federal government begins on October 1 and ends on September 30. It is designated by the calendar year in which it ends. That means the 2008 fiscal year begins on October 1, 2007, and ends on September 30, 2008.

Figure 13.6 summarizes the process of preparing the federal budget. That process begins in the Office of Management and Budget (OMB). For nearly a year, OMB employees work on a first draft of the budget. They meet with the president to be sure that the budget reflects his or her ideas. Then they estimate how much money each department will need and how much revenue the government will collect. That plan is then sent to federal agencies and departments for review. Each has an opportunity to respond to the preliminary budget with particular requests.

The Federal Budget Process

Figure 13.6

Steps in the Budget Process

February–September 2006
Agencies in the executive branch develop requests for funds and submit them to the Office of Management and Budget (OMB).

September–December 2006
The OMB and the president review the requests and make decisions on what is included in the budget. The budget is printed and formally submitted to Congress.

January–September 2007
The House of Representatives and the Senate Budget Committees review the proposed budget. By April 15, these committees prepare an initial resolution for the budget that goes to Congress for debate. By September 25, the congressional budget should be finalized and passed by the House, which approves spending and revenue bills.

October 1, 2006
The fiscal year begins.

October 1, 2006–September 30, 2007
Agency program managers implement the budget and disperse funds.

October–November 2007
Data on actual spending and receipts for the completed fiscal year become available. The General Accounting Office audits the fiscal-year outlays.

stop and think

Write a paragraph in your notebook to explain why you think the budget process involves both the president and Congress.

Deficits and Surpluses

Part of the difficulty lawmakers and other government leaders have in agreeing on a budget is related to the central economic problem: scarcity. Like individuals and businesses, governments do not have enough resources at any given time to satisfy the nation's long list of needs and wants. Like individuals and businesses, governments must make choices. Decisions about the federal budget have consequences. They affect the quality of highways in your community, what you will pay for prescription drugs, and whether you can get a loan for college. They also impact how much money you will take home each week after taxes have been deducted.

Neither the president nor Congress controls every budget decision. Some choices depend on events beyond anyone's control. Nearly everyone agrees that the government had to respond to the terrorist attacks on September 11, 2001. That response was reflected in the 2003 federal budget, which gave the Department of Defense $50 billion more than in 2002. The war in Iraq had a similar effect on the 2004 budget and on those that followed. Since 2002, funding for defense has increased each year. The money has been used for expenses such as weapons, military housing, and military pay.

When creating a budget, the goal is to have expenses equal revenue. In 1998, the United States had its first balanced budget after years of **deficits**—years when government expenses were greater than income. Many people predicted a ten-year **surplus**—years when the government would take in more money than it spent. As Figure 13.7 on page 218 shows, the predictions were wrong. A weak economy and an increasingly expensive war resulted in deficits. When deficits occur, the government raises extra money the same way many families do—by borrowing.

The National Debt Clock in New York City keeps track of the money owed by the federal government.

The government borrows money by selling bonds and other securities to individuals and businesses. When you buy a savings bond, you are loaning the government money. Each year, the government creates new debt by issuing new securities. At the same time, it pays off bonds, notes, and other bills that have come due. The total amount the government owes is called the **national debt**.

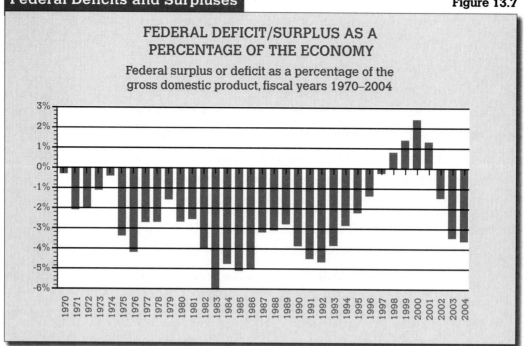

FEDERAL DEFICIT/SURPLUS AS A
PERCENTAGE OF THE ECONOMY

Federal surplus or deficit as a percentage of the
gross domestic product, fiscal years 1970–2004

Source: Budget of the United States Government, Fiscal Year 2006

The Effects of Deficits

Do deficits matter? Some economists think that if well
managed, a deficit can help the economy recover from a
recession. After all, additional spending increases demand and
creates jobs.

Other experts disagree. They argue that it is a bad idea for
anyone, including the government, to borrow money to pay
bills that come due on a regular basis. They point out that
government borrowing raises interest rates, increasing the cost
of car loans and home mortgages. That borrowing also limits
the government's ability to create new programs and improve
ongoing ones. Still other economists maintain that surpluses
and deficits have little meaning in an economy as large as the
U.S. economy. They think it is more dangerous for Congress
to focus on program cuts or higher taxes in an effort to balance
the budget.

Putting It All Together

How is the national budget similar to and different from an
individual's budget? List the similarities and differences in a
Venn diagram in your notebook.

Chapter Summary

- Government spending includes purchases of **goods and services**, transfer payments, and **interest payments**.

- **Social Security** benefits, **Medicare** payments, and federal **grants** are all examples of transfer payments.

- Taxes provide governments with income. Those taxes include **excise taxes**, **income taxes**, **sales taxes**, and **property taxes**.

- Lawmakers use two general principles to justify tax payments: the **principle of benefits received** and the **principle of ability to pay**.

- Many taxpayers are allowed **deductions**.

- The United States has three main types of taxes: **progressive**, **regressive**, and **proportional taxes**.

- The federal **budget** includes both **mandatory spending** and **discretionary spending**.

- The **fiscal year** for the federal government begins on October 1 and ends on September 30.

- In the United States, budget **deficits** are more common than **surpluses**.

- A deficit can lead to an increase in the **national debt**.

Chapter Review

1 Governments are major consumers of goods and services. Create a poster showing how spending by the Department of Defense or the Department of Education can shape the supply and the demand for resources and products.

2 Look carefully at Figure 13.2, on page 207. Identify some of the factors that may have shaped government spending. What are the opportunity costs of those decisions? For example, how might a reduction in interest on debt affect social programs?

3 Politicians often disagree about the nation borrowing money and creating a deficit. In your notebook, create a T-chart that compares the advantages and disadvantages of having a national deficit. Then write a persuasive paragraph to argue your opinion about the national deficit.

Skill Builder

Understand Percentages

Has this happened to you? You decide to buy a book that is marked $9.99. When you hand the clerk a $10 bill, he or she asks you for an additional 49 cents. Why? To pay a 5 percent sales tax. The word *percent* refers to a ratio that compares a number to 100 and uses the % sign. So, 5% means the same thing as $\frac{5}{100}$ or .05. The following examples show how to calculate and use percentages.

Step 1

- To find how much a 4% sales tax is on a $30 pair of shoes, multiply the price of the shoes by the percent of the sales tax. Be sure to change the percent to a decimal before you multiply.

  Price of a pair of shoes $30.00
  4% sales tax $\times$ .04
                                  $1.20

Step 2

- Find the real price of the shoes by adding the amount of the tax to the marked price of the shoes.

  Price of a pair of shoes $30.00
  Sales tax   + 1.20
                             $31.20

In 2004, the U.S. government collected $809 billion in individual income taxes. In 2005, the government estimated it would collect $893.7 billion. To figure out the percent of increase:

Step 1

- Subtract the amount the government collected in 2004 from the amount it estimated would be collected in 2005.

  2005 income taxes $893.7
  2004 income taxes   − 809.0
                        84.7

Step 2

- Determine the percent of change by dividing the arithmetical difference by the original amount. Multiply by 100 to change the decimal to a percent.

  Percentage change $\frac{84.7}{809}$ = .105 $\times$ 100 = 10.5%

  Note: .105 is a rounded number.

Answer the following questions.

1 You decide to buy a computer that is advertised for $500. Sales tax in your community is 7 percent. How much will the computer cost?

2 The government collected $70 billion in excise taxes in 2004. It expects to collect $74 billion in 2005. What is the percent of change?

14 MONEY AND BANKING

Getting Focused

Skim this chapter to predict what you will be learning.

- Read the lesson titles and subheadings.
- Look at the illustrations and read the captions.
- Examine the charts.
- Review the vocabulary words and terms.

In your notebook, make one list of what you know about money and another about banks. After skimming the chapter, list what you think you will learn in the following pages about each. Share your list with a partner. What else would you like to know?

The U.S. Mint at Philadelphia was established in 1792. Coins in the United States are minted—or created—at one of the several facilities of the U.S. Mint in Philadelphia, Denver, or San Francisco. Paper money is printed at the U.S. Bureau of Engraving and Printing, which has facilities in Ft. Worth and Washington, D.C.

Money

Thinking on Your Own

As you read this lesson, identify three roles that money plays in a market economy and explain the importance of each role.

Long ago, most people bartered for goods and services. Bartering is not an easy way to get the things you want or need. To **barter**, you have to find someone who not only has the goods or services you want, but is also willing to exchange them for whatever it is that you have to offer.

Suppose you want to buy a hamburger and all you have to offer in exchange is a plate of brownies. You would have to find someone with a hamburger who would like brownies. The other problem is that the objects have to be of comparable value. How many brownies are equal to one hamburger? How would you make change if the exchange wasn't equal?

The Changing Forms of Money

When bartering proved inconvenient, people turned to money. **Money** is any item that can be used to purchase goods or services or to settle other financial obligations, including the payment of taxes.

Over the years, money has taken many different forms. In ancient times, the Maya used cloth and cocoa beans as money. Wheat was used as money in ancient Egypt, and silk was once used as money in China. The Romans used salt and cattle as money. In fact, the word *salary* comes from the way Roman soldiers were paid. Their wages consisted of bags of salt. In early colonial Virginia, people used tobacco as money.

focus your reading

Name at least two advantages of using money instead of bartering.

How does money serve as a store of value?

What makes money valuable?

vocabulary

barter
money
commodity money
representative money
fiat money
legal tender
medium of exchange
store of value
purchasing power
unit of account

These various items had two things in common. First, each was relatively scarce. Scarcity tends to increase the value of money. Second, these items had an alternative use as an economic good or commodity. For example, silk could be woven into cloth, and wheat could be ground to make flour for bread. Today, this kind of money is known as **commodity money**—money that has an alternative use. A commodity is an item that can be bought and sold.

Representative money is money backed by a valuable item such as gold or silver. The amount of representative money in use is limited because it is linked to gold or some other scarce resource. In the 1800s and early 1900s, the United States issued representative money in the form of silver or gold certificates. At that time, people could cash in those certificates at a local bank for a specific amount of silver or gold.

In 1934, the U.S. government stopped issuing gold certificates and purchased the gold reserves held by banks. Today, the United States issues **fiat money**. A fiat is an order or decree. Those small pieces of paper in your wallet with green printing on them are considered money only because the U.S. government says they are. If you look at the face of a dollar bill, you will see the following statement: "This note is legal tender for all debts, public and private." **Legal tender** consists of the paper money and coins that are used within a nation. The law requires that people accept legal tender in payment of all debts. As long as the government is in power and people have confidence in that government, the money will be accepted.

Commodity money can consist of salt, cattle, or wheat. It was commonly used many years ago, before modern systems of currency were developed.

The Roles Money Plays

No matter what form money takes, it serves three important functions, or roles, in an economy. It is used as a medium of exchange, a store of value, and a unit of account.

Medium of exchange As long as you have money, you do not need to find something to barter in exchange for a haircut,

Around the world, money serves the same purpose. It is a medium of exchange, a store of value, and a unit of account.

a hamburger, or a ticket to a ball game. Instead, you can use bills and coins to purchase these and other goods and services. In doing so, you are using money as a **medium of exchange**, or a way of purchasing goods and services.

Store of value The idea that money functions as a **store of value** means that it holds its value over time. Suppose you receive $100 as a special birthday gift and decide to save the money. You will deposit your $100 in a savings account only if you are confident that the money will not lose its purchasing power. **Purchasing power** is measured by what a dollar can buy at a given time. If, for example, prices rise dramatically in a month or two, the $100 you saved will lose some of its value.

Money as a store of value also allows for purchases on credit. For example, if you use a credit card to buy a sweater today and pay off the debt over the next six months, you and the storekeeper are using money as a store of value. You are both assuming that a dollar will be worth about as much in six months as it is today.

Unit of account Money also serves as a **unit of account**—a reliable way of understanding prices. In the late 1700s, the United States adopted the Spanish unit of currency, which was known in English as the dollar. The dollar has provided Americans with a consistent way of understanding prices and measuring the relative value of goods and services.

You use money as a unit of account every time you compare prices. If you have ever gone shopping and compared the prices of items, you used money to gauge the value of a product. If you have ever walked away from an item because it wasn't worth the price, you have used money in a similar way.

stop and think

Think of various times that you used money as a medium of exchange, as a store of value, and as a unit of account. Record an example of each use in your notebook.

What Makes Money Valuable

Money can be any item that people are willing to accept in exchange for goods and services. At various times in history, people have used gems, tobacco, cotton, shells, and other items as mediums of exchange. Each item has characteristics that make it more or less useful as money. For example, lugging around bales of cotton or dozens of seashells is awkward at best. On the other hand, it is relatively easy to carry gems, but not so easy to divide them into smaller units. To carry out each of its functions, money should have the following characteristics:

Money comes in various colors, shapes, and sizes, but most money is backed by the country that issued the currency.

- **Widely accepted** The most important characteristic of money is its acceptance as a medium of exchange by almost everyone. You can use dollars to pay bills throughout the United States. If you travel to another country, your dollars can be exchanged easily for Mexican pesos, Canadian dollars, or another currency.

- **Holds value** The value attached to the money should not change rapidly. Money, like everything else, loses value if there is a surplus.

- **Durable** Money should be reasonably durable. That is, it should withstand the wear and tear of being passed from person to person. Paper money lasts only about 18 months and can be easily replaced.

- **Portable** Money must be easy to carry. It should also be easily transferred from one person to another.

- **Divisible** Money should be easily divided into smaller units, so that people can use only as much as they need. For example, gems used as money were readily accepted, held their value, and were extremely durable. However, they could not be divided easily into smaller units. With coins and bills, people today can make purchases of any amount.

Putting It All Together

Which of the following is money, as defined in this lesson: one ounce of gold, a one-dollar bill, a one-carat diamond? Explain in your notebook why each does or does not qualify as money.

Money in the United States Today

Thinking on Your Own

Money is used as a medium of exchange. Yet people who have no cash can still buy things. What do they use in place of money?

What is money? In Lesson 1, you learned that money has three main characteristics: it is usable as a means of payment, it is a store of wealth, and it can be used to compare prices. Those characteristics fit a wide range of assets in the U.S. economy. However, not all of those assets are money. The **money supply** is the amount of money available for purchasing goods and services at any one time. The supply is usually considered in terms of three overlapping categories: M1, M2, and M3.

focus your reading

Explain the main differences between M1, M2, and M3.

How do economists measure liquidity?

Describe what economists include when they measure the size of a nation's money supply. What do they exclude?

vocabulary

money supply

M1

currency

traveler's checks

checkable deposit

liquid assets

M2

M3

Defining M1

M1 is sometimes called transactions money. It consists of assets that are easily used as payment for goods and services. **Currency**—bills and coins—is part of M1. But only currency that is in circulation is included. *In circulation* means that the money is being used; it is found in cash registers, ATMs, and wallets. If you collect pennies in a jar, they will not be counted as part of M1 because they are not in circulation. The same is true of the cash you deposit in a savings account.

M1 also includes traveler's checks. **Traveler's checks**—often used by people when traveling, instead of carrying large amounts of cash—are like currency,

Traveler's checks are safer to carry while traveling because they are insured by the issuer.

except that they have a form of insurance linked to them. The issuer of a traveler's check will reimburse you if the check is lost or stolen.

The third item in M1 consists of checkable deposits. A **checkable deposit** is a deposit on which a check can be written. These are bank accounts that allow consumers to withdraw their funds at any time without advance notice or penalty.

Figure 14.1 shows the M1 money supply for the U.S. economy. Notice that a little over one-half of M1 is currency in circulation. The rest consists mostly of checkable deposits. Traveler's checks make up only a tiny portion of M1. M1 had a value of $1,353 billion in January 2005.

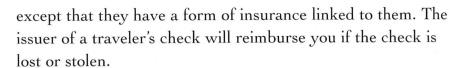

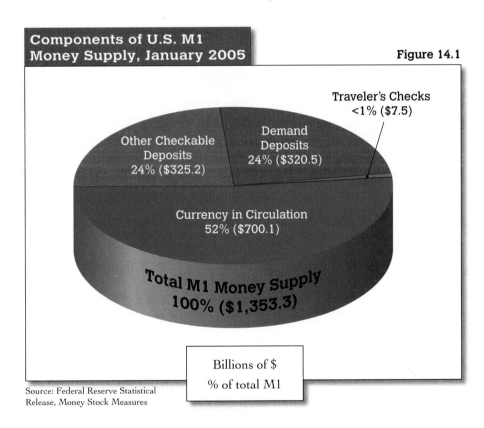

Source: Federal Reserve Statistical Release, Money Stock Measures

If checkable deposits are money, are checks a form of money? The answer is no. To figure out why, think about what happens when someone writes a check.

Suppose a friend goes to the mall and buys a pair of shoes. The shoes cost $50 and he writes a check for that amount. That check is a written instruction to the bank to transfer your

Cash has been replaced by credit cards as a means of purchasing goods and services.

friend's money to the storekeeper. The storekeeper takes the check to the bank and deposits it in the store's account. That account has grown by $50 and your friend's account is smaller by $50. In writing the check, your friend has simply transferred his money to another person. The check itself was never money.

Is a credit card money? A credit card is an identification card—an ID card—that allows you to borrow money at the time you make a purchase. When you buy an item using a credit card, you sign a credit card sales slip that creates a debt

Comparing Credit Cards

Think about how you would use a credit card. Would you expect to

- **pay your monthly bill in full?**   • **carry over a balance?**   • **get cash advances?**

Once you have decided how you would use a credit card, you can use this checklist to compare cards. Information about most of the features is given in the disclosure box that is included in all printed credit card applications.

What are the annual percentage rates (APRs)

- for purchases?
- for cash advances?
- for balance transfers?
- if you pay late?

What type of interest does the card have? How long is the grace period (the number of days you have to pay your bill in full without triggering a finance charge)

- if you carry over a balance?
- if you pay the balance each month?
- for cash advances?

How is the finance charge calculated? For example, does it include new purchases? Is there a minimum finance charge?

What are the fees?

- annual
- late payment
- set-up
- over the credit limit

What are the cash advance features?

How much is the credit limit?

Does the card offer other features?

- rebates
- insurance
- frequent-flyer miles
- other

stop and think

Why is a traveler's check considered money even though neither a check nor a credit card is considered money?

in your name. In signing the sales slip, you are agreeing to pay for the purchase when the credit card company sends you a bill. Once you receive a statement from the company, you have to make at least the minimum payment that is due. To make that payment, you write a check or send cash to the company. Neither a credit card nor a check is money. Both act as substitutes for money.

M2 and M3

M1 is money used for everyday transactions—for paying bills, buying groceries, and shopping at the mall. M1 consists of **liquid assets**—assets that are easily spent. You probably know how easy it is to spend the cash you carry in your pocket.

M2 and **M3** are broader measures of money. They include all of M1 and a number of other assets that are less liquid. These assets tend to reflect the idea of money as a store of value. For example, M2 includes savings accounts and certificates of deposit (CDs). However, M2 does not include retirement accounts, because the money in these accounts will be spent much later. M3 includes not only all of M2, but also assets that are even less liquid than those in M2. For example, M3 includes retirement accounts and other assets that are difficult to convert to cash.

Why does the U.S. government use several different measures to determine money supply? One reason is to find out how much purchasing power consumers have. How much spending a person can do depends not only on how much cash he or she has on hand, but also on how willing he or she is to write a check, make a trip to the bank, or change various assets into cash.

Putting It All Together

Create a three-column chart in your notebook. In column one, list each type of money supply in the U.S. today. In column two, define each type. In column three, give an example of each type.

How Banks Work

Thinking on Your Own

Suppose that you have $500 in savings. Does it matter, so far as the economy is concerned, whether you deposit it in a bank or lock it up in a burglar-proof safe at home? Discuss this with a partner. Then explain in your notebook why you think it does or does not matter.

In Chapter 9, you learned that when you deposit your money in a bank, the bank makes a promise to return that money to you. You also learned that the bank uses your deposit and those of its other customers to make loans. Those loans play an important role in the economy because they increase the money supply. How do banks increase the amount of money in an economy? The process begins with deposits made by bank customers.

focus your reading

Name two ways the money supply can grow or shrink.

What are excess reserves?

How does the simple money multiplier work?

vocabulary

reserves

reserve ratio

excess reserve

simple money multiplier

aggregate demand

How Banks Create Money

Suppose you deposit $100 in a savings account. That money becomes part of the bank's reserves. **Reserves** are a bank's holdings, which consist of deposits and currency. The deposits are usually kept in an account at a national bank like the Federal Reserve. By law, the bank cannot lend the entire amount in its reserves. It has to put aside a percentage of the money. The percentage a bank is required to keep on hand is called the **reserve ratio**.

A bank can loan its **excess reserve**—the amount of money above the reserve ratio. If the reserve ratio is 20 percent and you deposited $100, the excess reserve is $80. That money is the starting point for expanding the money supply. Follow Figure 14.2, on page 231, step by step to see how the process works.

Notice that Figure 14.2 begins with your deposit of $100 in Bank A. In making that deposit, you reduce your supply of cash by $100 and increase your bank account by $100. The bank now has $100 in reserves. It keeps $20 in reserve as the law requires and lends the excess reserve of $80 to Abe, another customer. At this point, the bank has not created any new money, but pay careful attention to what happens next.

Creating Money by Making Loans

Figure 14.2

Bank	Depositor	Borrower	Change in Transaction Accounts	Change in Total Reserves	Change in Required Reserves	Change in Excess Reserves	Change in Lending Capacity
A	You	Abe	$100.00	$100.00	$20.00	$80.00	$80.00
B	Bob	Brad	80.00	80.00	16.00	64.00	64.00
C	Carla	Carol	64.00	64.00	12.80	51.20	51.20
D	Diane	David	51.20	51.20	10.24	40.96	40.96
E	Earl	Ellen	40.96	40.96	8.19	32.77	32.77
F	Frank	Fran	32.77	32.77	6.55	26.22	26.22
G	Greg	Gene	26.22	26.22	5.24	20.28	20.28
If loans made and deposited continued to Bank Z:							
Z			0.40	0.40	0.08	0.32	0.32
Cumulative, through Bank Z			500.00	100.00	100.00	0.00	400.00

Abe uses his loan to buy a TV from Bob. Abe writes a check for $80 on his account at Bank A, and Bob deposits it in Bank B. Bank B now has a new deposit of $80. Bank B does not have to keep the entire $80 as reserves; it only needs to hold $16. So it lends $64 to Brad, who uses the money to buy in-line skates from Carla. She deposits his check in Bank C. Bank C now has a new deposit of $64, of which it can lend $51.20. The $80 that Bank A lent to Abe has now grown to $195.20 (80 + 64 + 51.20) and it will continue to grow.

The process continues, but with amounts that get smaller and smaller. In the end, the money supply will have increased by $400. Keep in mind that even though your $100 set the ball rolling, it alone did not increase the amount of money. The increase in the entire money supply was solely the result of new deposits created by bank loans.

stop and think

Why are the accounts created by bank loans considered money? How do they fit the criteria you used in Lesson 2?

The Simple Money Multiplier

Banks are able to create money, but they cannot create as much as they would like. The amount that they can create depends on the required reserve ratio. In Figure 14.2, a $100 cash deposit creates $400 of new spending capacity based on a 20 percent reserve ratio.

The **simple money multiplier** measures how much the money supply will increase as a result of bank loans. The size of the multiplier depends on the reserve ratio—the percentage of reserves that banks are required to keep on hand. In other words, it is calculated by dividing total bank deposits by the reserve requirement. In Figure 14.2, the money multiplier is 5: 100 (the total bank deposits) divided by the reserve requirement (20%) equals 5. To figure out how much money will be created with a $100 deposit if the reserve ratio is 20 percent, you multiply excess reserves ($80) by the money multiplier (5). The total is $400.

The loans given by banks and other lending institutions serve to increase the money supply and generate revenue for the lending institution.

Loans in the real world are more complicated than the model shown in Figure 14.2 for two reasons. First, the required reserve ratio is usually much smaller—about 10 percent. Second, not all of the loans that banks make return to a bank in the form of reserves. Some remain outside the banking system in the form of currency in circulation. The fact that the real reserve ratio is smaller means that the real-world multiplier is larger than the example suggests. The fact that some of the money remains in circulation makes the real-world multiplier much smaller.

Banks have a powerful effect on the economy because their actions alter the size of the money supply. The money supply affects aggregate demand. **Aggregate demand** is the total demand for goods and services within an economy. It is the quantity of all goods and services demanded at different price levels. An increase in the quantity of money tends to increase aggregate demand. In the short run, an increase in aggregate demand tends to increase both the level of prices and real GDP.

Putting It All Together

Use the explanation that you wrote at the beginning of this lesson to write a paragraph explaining how bank loans create money.

Cell Phones vs. Credit Cards: The Battle Begins

Olga Kharif, a writer for *BusinessWeek*, reports on new technology that may affect banks and credit card companies. She writes:

For the past several years, European wireless service providers have allowed subscribers to charge vending machine purchases onto the users' mobile phone bills. Now, U.S. service providers are starting to follow suit. . . .

Lots of analysts believe that cell phones will soon turn into our virtual wallets. We'll be able to use them to pay for purchases everywhere: at stores, restaurants, amusement parks. Perhaps we'll even consolidate our gas and water charges onto our wireless bill.

If that happens, banks and credit card companies will lose out on the fees they currently charge for facilitating financial transactions. Today, every time you pay a merchant with your credit card, that seller has to, in turn, pay Visa or MasterCard 1% to 2% of the purchase price.

Perhaps in the future, they will pay that fee to wireless service providers, instead. Such a set-up might especially appeal to young people, who seem to never part with their mobile phones. Also, some estimated 10 million to 20 million U.S. households without bank accounts—but with cell phones—might jump at the chance to use the wireless . . . service.

CELL PHONE technology is rapidly changing the way of life in many countries around the world.

In fact, I think it's quite possible that cell phone companies could, eventually, become banks, keeping customer money, helping users pay bills and to pay for purchases. . . . And that could shake the credit card and banking industries to the core. ∎

"Cell Phones vs. Credit Cards: The Battle Begins" by Olga Kharif. *BusinessWeek*, June 28, 2005.

reading for understanding

According to the writer, what technological change will "shake the credit card and banking industries to the core"?

If the writer's prediction comes true, will cell phone companies be able to create money? Give reasons for your answer.

What functions of a bank are most unlikely to change? For what reasons?

Chapter Summary

- When **bartering** proved inconvenient, people turned to **money** to pay for goods and services.

- Over the years, people have used **commodity money**, **representative money**, and **fiat money** to settle accounts.

- Money is used as a **medium of exchange**, a **store of value**, and a **unit of account**.

- Individuals, firms, and governments are concerned about the **purchasing power** of their **legal tender**.

- **Money** should hold its value and be widely accepted, durable, portable, and easily divisible.

- The **money supply** is usually categorized by the liquidity of various assets.

- **M1** includes all **liquid assets** such as **currency**, **traveler's checks**, and **checkable deposits**.

- **M2** and **M3** are broad measures of money that are less liquid than M1.

- A **reserve ratio** limits how much of its **reserves** a bank can lend.

- Loans made from **excess reserves** increase the money supply.

- A **simple money multiplier** measures the amount of money banks can create.

- A change in the money supply affects **aggregate demand**.

Chapter Review

1 Imagine that you received a $100 bill as a birthday present and you decided to place the bill in a box under your bed. Suppose millions of other Americans did the same thing. What effect would these decisions have on the money supply? On the economy as a whole?

2 Review the laws of supply and demand. How do you think they affect the purchasing power of money? For example, why might prices tend to rise faster when more money is available? What is likely to happen if less money is available?

Skill Builder

Make Inferences

To infer is to draw a conclusion based on what you already know and on that alone. Rather than a direct statement, an inference is a judgment or conclusion based on reasoning. In making inferences, it is important to apply related information you already know to the stated facts.

You make inferences every day. You wake up in the morning and notice the ground is wet. What inference are you likely to make? Later in the day, you notice that a number of people are carrying umbrellas. You know that many people use umbrellas as protection from the rain. What conclusion do you draw?

Read the passage below and then answer the questions.

About two-thirds of American households have debit cards. Debit cards are also known as check cards. Debit cards are different from credit cards. While a credit card is a way to "pay later," a debit card is a way to "pay now." When you use a debit card, your money is quickly deducted from your checking or savings account.

Debit cards are accepted at many locations, including grocery stores, retail stores, gasoline stations, and restaurants. You can use your card anywhere merchants display your card's brand name or logo. Debit cards offer an alternative to carrying a checkbook or cash.

1 What characteristics of money do debit cards have? How are they different from money?

2 Is a debit card a type of money? Explain your reasoning in a well-developed paragraph.

3 What effect do you think debit cards have on the money supply?

Chapter
15 THE FEDERAL RESERVE

Getting Focused

Skim this chapter to predict what you will be learning.

- Read the lesson titles and subheadings.
- Look at the illustrations and read the captions.
- Examine the maps, graphs, and charts.
- Review the vocabulary words and terms.

In this chapter, you will learn about the Federal Reserve System. It is the national bank of the United States and it plays a major role in not only regulating the nation's banking system, but also in shaping its monetary policy. Look over the major headings, charts, and photos in this chapter for clues about the Federal Reserve and how it works. List as many facts as you can in your notebook.

The Federal Reserve Bank in Washington, D.C.

How the Federal Reserve Works

Thinking on Your Own

Why do we need a central banking system? In your notebook, answer this question as best you can. Check your answer as you read.

The Federal Reserve System is the central bank of the United States. A **central bank** serves as a bank for other banks and for the federal government.

The Need for a Central Bank

At the beginning of the twentieth century, the United States lacked a central bank. The Bank of the United States had once served that purpose. President Andrew Jackson closed the bank in 1836 when he vetoed a bill to renew its charter and later withdrew its government deposits. In 1863, Congress created a new national banking system. It provided the nation with a uniform currency but gave the government little control over the supply of money. In good times, it could not increase the supply of currency to meet the expanding needs of business. When a banking panic occurred, it could not shift money from healthy banks to banks that were in trouble.

In 1907, a banking panic caused several New York City banks to close their doors. The **panic** was the result of the banks investing too much money in stocks. After a downturn in the stock market, depositors rushed to withdraw their savings. They had lost confidence in the banks and feared that they would go out of business. As the banks only had to keep 10 percent of their deposits as a cash reserve, the withdrawals

A **recession** is a period of time when a contraction lasts at least six months.

Inflation is the term used to describe a rise, over time, in the general level of prices.

quickly used up the banks' available cash. That forced them to close. The panic caused a brief, but sharp, downturn in the economy.

In 1912, Congress turned its attention to the nation's flawed banking system. Reformers wanted to place banks under federal control, with the currency system owned and operated by the U.S. Treasury. Conservatives in and outside of Congress called for a privately owned central bank not regulated by the government. After a heated debate, Congress passed the Federal Reserve Act.

A crowd gathers outside the Nineteenth Ward Bank in New York City during the 1907 bank panic.

The Federal Reserve Act of 1913 was a **compromise**—both sides gave up something to achieve a goal. It left the nation's banking system in private hands. However, it created a Federal Reserve Board appointed by the president to set policies governing the system. Over the years, Congress has expanded its power and added new responsibilities, but the goals of the Federal Reserve System, known as the Fed, have remained the same. The Fed is responsible for

- carrying out the nation's **monetary policies**—strategies for controlling the size of the money supply and the price of credit.

- supervising and regulating banks and protecting consumers' credit rights.

- keeping the nation's financial system sound.
- providing financial services to the U.S. government, the public, financial institutions, and foreign financial institutions.

Organization

Although Congress gives the Federal Reserve System its authority, it is not a government agency. Lawmakers set up the Fed as "an independent entity within the government." Neither the president nor Congress has any say over its decisions. It does not receive funding from Congress, although lawmakers do oversee its activities and can change its responsibilities if they choose to do so.

The Reserve Banks The Fed is national in its scope, but it is organized regionally. As Figure 15.1 shows, the Fed is divided into 12 districts and has branches in 25 additional cities.

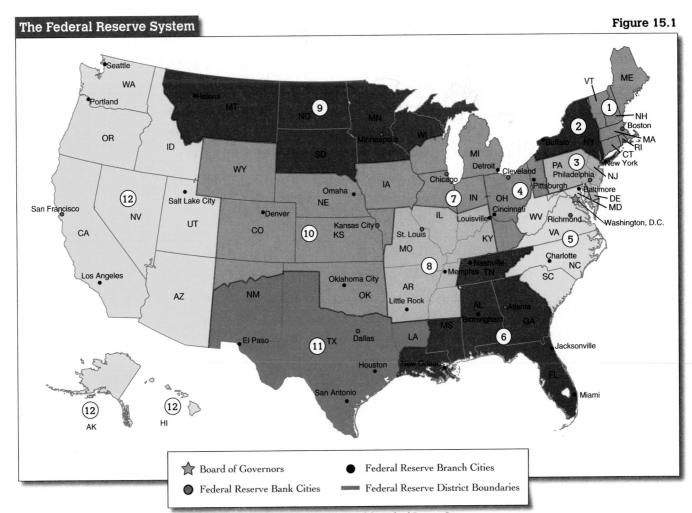

The Federal Reserve System Figure 15.1

Legend:
- ⭐ Board of Governors
- ● Federal Reserve Bank Cities
- ● Federal Reserve Branch Cities
- ▬ Federal Reserve District Boundaries

Source: *Federal Reserve Bulletin*, Board of Governors of the Federal Reserve System

Each Federal Reserve bank has its own president and board of directors. Each keeps a close watch on the economy and financial institutions in its district and provides a variety of services to the U.S. government and to its member banks. **Member banks** are commercial banks that hold stock in the Fed. Banks chartered, or established, by the federal government are required to belong to the Fed. Banks chartered by the states can join if they wish to do so.

stop and think

Look carefully at Figure 15.1, on page 239. In which federal district do you live? In what city is the Federal Reserve bank for your district? If there are branch banks in your district, where are they located? Record your answers in your notebook.

Each Federal Reserve bank issues shares of stock in much the same way corporations do. However, owning Reserve bank stock is very different from owning stock in a private company. The Reserve banks do not try to earn a profit. No one buys shares in hopes of making money. Ownership of a certain amount of stock is, by law, a requirement for membership. That stock cannot be sold, traded, or used as security for a loan. Instead, shareholders receive a 6 percent dividend each year.

The Board of Governors As Figure 15.2 on page 241 shows, the Board of Governors heads the Fed and sets policy for all 12 Federal Reserve banks. In addition, it keeps Congress informed on how the economy is doing on a regular basis. The chairman also meets regularly with the president and the secretary of the treasury. Board members testify before congressional committees and meet with members of the **President's Council of Economic Advisers** and other key officials.

Alan Greenspan, chairman of the Federal Reserve from 1987–2006

The president appoints all seven members of the Board of Governors, but the Senate has to confirm those appointments. The seven members serve for 14 years; their terms are staggered so that there are always experienced people on the board. One term expires on January 31 of each even-numbered year. The president, with Senate approval, also decides which members will serve as chairman and vice chairman. This term of office is a period of four years.

The Federal Open Market Committee The Federal Open Market Committee plays a key role in controlling the size of the nation's money supply and the price of credit. The committee

has 12 members—the seven members of the Board of Governors and five Reserve bank presidents, one of whom is the president of the Federal Reserve Bank of New York. The other presidents serve one-year terms on a rotating basis, and all presidents participate in each meeting.

Structure of the Federal Reserve System

Figure 15.2

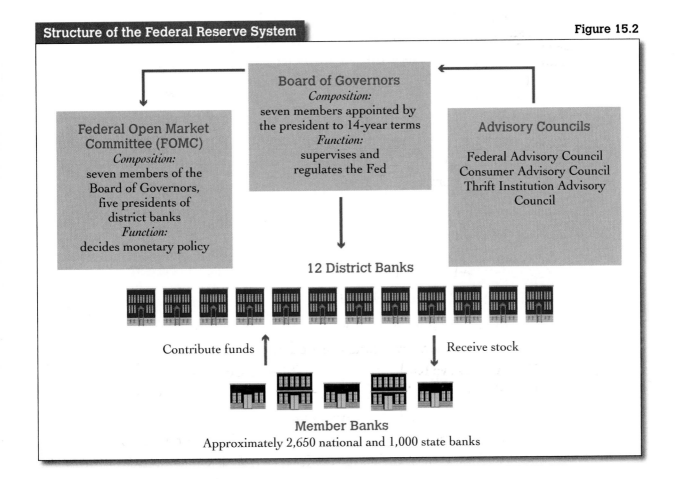

The Federal Advisory Council The Board of Governors also consults with the Federal Advisory Council. Every year, each of the 12 Reserve banks chooses one person to represent its district on the council. Members usually serve three one-year terms and elect their own officers. The council meets at least four times a year as required by the Federal Reserve Act.

Putting It All Together

Having read about the purpose of the Federal Reserve System, expand the answer that you wrote at the beginning of this lesson for the Thinking on Your Own question into a full paragraph.

The Nation's Money Manager

Thinking on Your Own

The Federal Reserve is a banking system. It manages the nation's money. What does the term "managing money" mean in this instance? Write a one-sentence answer to this question in your notebook.

The most important responsibility of the Federal Reserve is managing the nation's money. In this role, the Fed tries to balance the size of the money supply and the price of credit—interest rates—with the needs of the economy. In doing so, the Fed helps set the nation's monetary policy.

A Balancing Act

In earlier chapters, you learned that too much money in the economy can lead to inflation, while too little can prevent economic growth. As the nation's money manager, the Fed tries to achieve a balance by controlling the money supply and the availability of credit. Credit, like other goods and services, has a cost. The cost of credit is the interest that must be paid to the lender. The laws of supply and demand affect interest rates in much the same way they affect the costs of other goods and services. As the cost of credit rises, the quantity demanded decreases. As the cost decreases, the quantity demanded rises.

As Figure 15.3 on page 243 shows, the Fed uses the laws of supply and demand to control the money supply and the price of credit. If the economy is slowing down, the Fed may carry out a **loose money policy**—a strategy designed to encourage borrowing and business expansion. In fact, a loose money

focus your reading

Explain fractional reserve banking.

How does the Fed expand the money supply?

What is the effect of tight money policies?

vocabulary

loose money policy

expansionary policy

tight money policy

contractionary policy

fractional reserve banking

discount rate

government securities

open market operations

policy is sometimes called an **expansionary policy**. When the economy is expanding too quickly, the Fed tries to slow the economy with a **tight money policy**—one that makes credit harder to obtain. This policy is sometimes called a **contractionary policy** because it is designed to reduce, or contract, the availability of credit. The Fed relies on three important tools in its efforts to expand or contract the nation's money supply—reserve requirements, the discount rate, and open market operations.

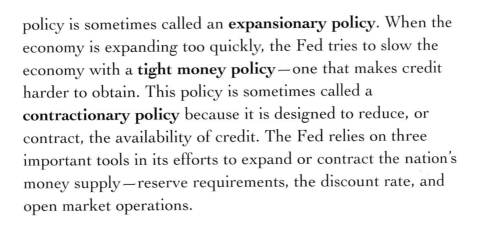

Balancing Monetary Policy   Figure 15.3

Inflation

1. Borrowing is easy.
2. Consumers buy more.
3. Businesses expand.
4. More people are employed.
5. People spend more.

Loose Money Policy

1. Borrowing is difficult.
2. Consumers buy less.
3. Businesses postpone expansion.
4. Unemployment increases.
5. Production is reduced.

Recession

Tight Money Policy

Reserve Requirements

In Chapter 14, you learned that banks expand the money supply by lending money. The Fed controls the amount banks can loan by raising or lowering the reserve ratio—the amount of money a bank has to keep in reserve. A system that requires banks and other financial institutions to keep a percentage of their deposits in reserve is known as **fractional reserve banking**.

Changing the reserve ratio can affect the flow of money and credit in a very powerful way. Recall from Chapter 14 how loans made on a $100 deposit could eventually increase the money supply by $400 based on a reserve ratio of 20 percent. A lower reserve ratio means that banks can lend, and therefore create,

> **recall**
>
> A **reserve ratio** is the percentage of a deposit a bank is required to keep on hand.

even more money. Higher reserve ratios require financial institutions to keep a greater percentage of each deposit, which means that money does not enter the economy.

The Fed rarely uses the reserve requirement as a tool of its monetary policy. One reason is that its other tools work better. Another is that its effect on the economy can be very dramatic—perhaps too dramatic for a system that tries to maintain a delicate balance. Figure 15.4 shows just how quickly a $1,000 deposit can increase the money supply to $10,000 if the reserve ratio is 10 percent. It also shows much slower growth when the ratio is set at 40 percent.

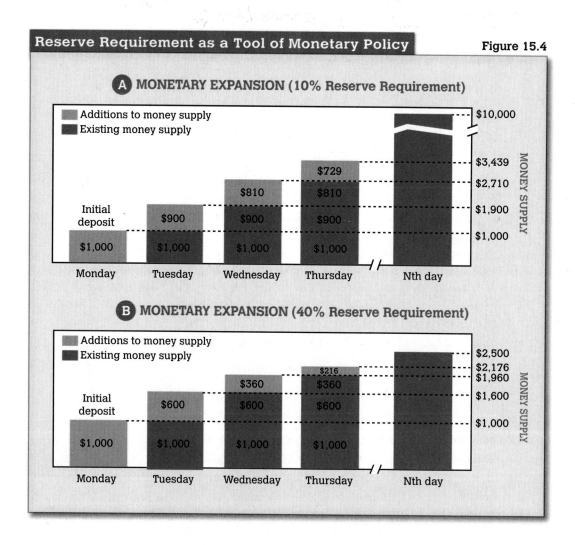

Reserve Requirement as a Tool of Monetary Policy Figure 15.4

Discount Rate

The Fed can also control the supply of money and the price of credit by changing the **discount rate**—the rate of interest it charges on loans to member banks. If the Fed raises the

discount rate, the higher cost of borrowing reserves will probably result in fewer bank loans. Therefore, the money supply will grow more slowly.

If the Fed lowers the discount rate, banks may be willing to make additional loans because of the lower cost of borrowing. However, if banks have access to funds from other sources, a change in the discount rate won't directly affect the flow of money and credit. Even so, a change in the discount rate can be an important signal of a change in the direction of the Fed's monetary policy.

Open Market Operations

The Fed also buys and sells **government securities**—short- and long-term bonds that the government sells to pay for its programs. These acts of buying and selling are known as **open market operations**. When the Fed decides to increase the supply of money and credit, it buys government bonds. When it wants to decrease supply, it sells them. The flexibility of open market operations makes it the most important of the Fed's monetary policy tools.

At its regular meetings, the Federal Open Market Committee (FOMC) sets goals that determine whether the Fed will buy or sell securities. Once those goals are set, Fed officials at the trading desk at the Federal Reserve Bank of New York go to work. They buy and sell bonds daily to meet the FOMC's goals. The desk is there because New York is the center of the nation's financial markets.

Open market operations affect the supply of money by affecting the amount of excess reserves in the system. If, for example, the Federal Reserve wanted to increase the supply of money, it might purchase $1 billion in government securities from a securities dealer. The Fed would then pay for the securities by adding $1 billion to the account the security dealer's bank keeps at the Fed. In turn, the bank would credit the dealer's account for that amount. Although the bank must keep a percentage of the money in reserve, it can lend and invest the rest. As these funds are spent and re-spent, the stock of money eventually increases by far more than $1 billion.

The process is reversed if the Fed wishes to decrease the money supply. If the Fed sells $1 billion in government securities to a dealer, that amount would be deducted from the reserve account of the dealer's bank. In turn, the bank would deduct $1 billion from the account of the dealer. The end result would be less money in the economy.

stop and think

What effect do you think a major purchase of government securities by the Fed would have on interest rates? What effect would a major sale of government securities have? Give reasons for your answers.

The Importance of the Money Supply

How does the supply of money affect the economy? A healthy economy requires that consumers have enough money to buy, at current prices, all of the goods and services the economy can produce using all of its available resources. If there is too little money available, the result is likely to be a recession. Too much money in the economy generally means that demand will exceed current output, resulting in inflation—a rise in the general level of prices.

Immediate Effects A change in the money supply will have an immediate effect on interest rates—the price of a loan. When the Fed expands the money supply, the cost of credit goes down. This relationship is shown in Figure 15.5. Like other demand curves, the demand curve for money shows that

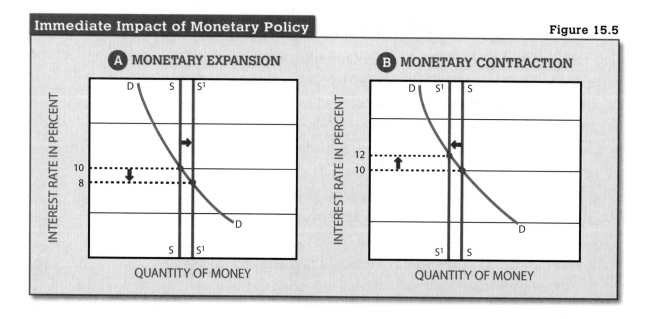

Immediate Impact of Monetary Policy   **Figure 15.5**

the quantity demanded rises as the price of credit falls. The supply curve, however, does not look like other supply curves you have examined. It is not a curve at all but a straight vertical line, which means that the supply of money is fixed at a given time.

The line labeled *S* in Graph A shows the demand at 10 percent. The line labeled *S'* shows an increase in the supply. Notice that when the supply is increased, the interest rate falls to 8 percent. Graph B shows a contraction in the economy. In this case, the interest rate is raised from 10 to 12 percent. This time, the supply is decreased and the price of credit goes up.

Those shifts have real meaning for consumers who need a loan to pay for college or to buy a house or car. They also have meaning for business owners who would like to update or replace tools and other capital resources.

Long-term Effects Over time, changes in interest rates affect the general level of prices. They can also affect the way scarce resources are distributed. For example, high interest rates may encourage people to delay major purchases. Rather than secure a high-interest loan today to make a major purchase, they may decide to save enough to buy the item without securing a loan. The overall effect is that the use of some tools and other resources is decreased or put off until the future.

Putting It All Together

What is the purpose of the Fed's monetary policy? How do each of the major tools of the Fed's monetary policy help it achieve its goal?

Other Responsibilities of the Federal Reserve

Thinking on Your Own

Select three of the terms from the vocabulary list. Write them in your notebook. Under each term, write what you think the term means. As you encounter the word, correct or add to your definition.

Managing the nation's money supply is just one of the responsibilities of the Federal Reserve. It also has other responsibilities. The Fed provides a variety of services to the nation's bankers. It also serves as the banker for the U.S. government—the nation's largest banking customer. In addition, the Fed supervises and regulates the nation's financial institutions.

focus your reading

Describe three responsibilities of the Federal Reserve.

Explain how the Fed serves member banks.

Describe the three types of electronic fund transfers.

How does the Fed regulate and supervise the nation's banks?

vocabulary

check clearing

electronic fund transfer

direct deposit

A Banker's Bank

Each of the 12 Federal Reserve banks provides services to banks and other financial institutions in its district. These services are similar to the ones that member banks provide to businesses and individuals. Member banks deposit some of their reserves at the Fed. They can also turn to the Fed for a loan. A bank that is experiencing an unexpected drain on its deposits can borrow from its Reserve bank. The loan not only enables the bank to make it through a tough time, but also prevents a problem at one bank from spreading to other banks.

The Fed also helps ensure that checks and other transfers of funds are handled efficiently and safely. The Fed processes the checks of its member banks. As a result, it clears more than one-third of all of the checks written in the United States— a total that exceeds $14 trillion each year. **Check clearing** is the

movement of a check from the bank at which it was deposited back to the bank on which the check was written. Figure 15.6 shows the key role the Fed plays in the process.

Clearing a Check   Figure 15.6

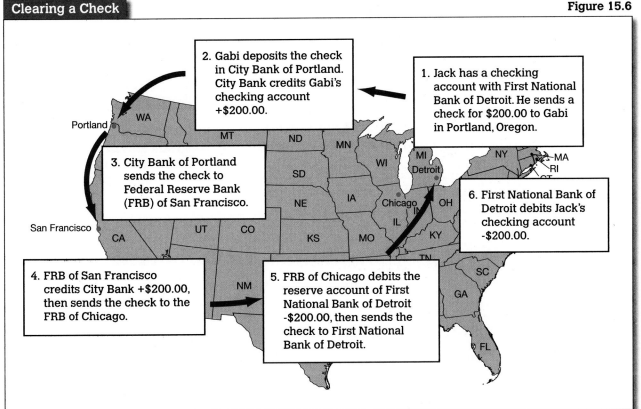

2. Gabi deposits the check in City Bank of Portland. City Bank credits Gabi's checking account +$200.00.

1. Jack has a checking account with First National Bank of Detroit. He sends a check for $200.00 to Gabi in Portland, Oregon.

3. City Bank of Portland sends the check to Federal Reserve Bank (FRB) of San Francisco.

6. First National Bank of Detroit debits Jack's checking account −$200.00.

4. FRB of San Francisco credits City Bank +$200.00, then sends the check to the FRB of Chicago.

5. FRB of Chicago debits the reserve account of First National Bank of Detroit −$200.00, then sends the check to First National Bank of Detroit.

Even more money is transferred electronically, through debit cards, electronic check deposits and withdrawals, and electronic banking. The Fed estimates that the volume is more than $343 trillion a year. Electronic banking works in a similar fashion, but the process is much faster.

Electronic banking is known as an **electronic fund transfer** (EFT). An EFT is initiated through special cards or codes that allow you to access your account or authorize someone else to do so. If you have ever used a debit card to get cash from an ATM (automated teller machine), you have made an EFT. Other examples of electronic fund transfers include:

- **direct deposit**—an electronic fund transfer into a checking or savings account. Many companies use direct deposit for ongoing, regularly scheduled payments, such as salary, retirement benefits, dividends, and annuity payments. To enable a company or a government agency to pay you by direct deposit, you must sign a form authorizing the company to credit your account.

- **personal computer banking**—the use of a computer for banking transactions. For instance, you can view your account balance, request transfers between accounts, and pay bills electronically.

- **point-of-sale transfers**—the use of a debit card to pay for purchases. A debit card looks like a credit card. However, when you use a debit card, you are not borrowing money. You are paying for a good or service by transferring money from a checking or savings account.

stop and think

In your opinion, what are the advantages of electronic banking? What are the disadvantages?

A Bank for the U.S. Government

The Federal Reserve provides services for the nation's largest banking customer—the United States government. In much the same way that your family keeps an account at a local

Checklist

Protecting Privacy on the Internet

The Internet is a public network. So if you bank online, you will want to protect your privacy. Simple safety measures are essential:

- Tell no one your password or other confidential information unless you are sure of his or her identity. Hackers sometimes impersonate technical support workers or others over the phone and in e-mail to obtain private information.

- Keep your password out of sight.

- Select a password that is hard to guess; avoid Social Security numbers, birth dates, or other obvious choices. Good passwords are unique. Try using capitalization, non-letter characters, and other symbols with significance only to you.

- Be sure to change your password periodically.

Keep in mind that once someone has access to your account number, he or she has access to your money and personal financial information.

bank, the U.S. Treasury keeps a checking account with the Federal Reserve. Federal Reserve banks handle incoming federal tax deposits and outgoing government payments. The Fed also sells and redeems U.S. government securities, such as savings bonds and Treasury bills.

The U.S. Treasury, through its Bureau of the Mint and Bureau of Engraving and Printing, actually produces U.S. coins and paper money. However, it is the Federal Reserve that distributes that money to financial institutions. The currency periodically comes back to the Fed banks, where it is counted and checked for wear and tear. If it is in good condition, it is eventually sent back into circulation. Worn-out bills, however, are shredded. On average, a dollar bill circulates for about 18 months before it is destroyed.

The new $100 bill

Supervisor and Regulator

The Fed oversees the activities of banks and other financial institutions. As a regulator, it sets the rules for financial institutions. As a supervisor, the Federal Reserve sees to it that those rules and federal laws that deal with the banking industry are enforced. Each Federal Reserve bank is responsible for monitoring companies that own one or more banks and state member banks that belong to the Fed and are based in its district. For example, it checks to make sure those banks are maintaining the required level of reserves.

In addition, the Fed monitors the activities of the more than 60 foreign banks that do business in the United States. If a bank does not act in accordance with American law, the Fed can order it to close its operations in the United States. The Fed tries to ensure that all banks in the United States act in the public's interest by ruling on applications from banks wanting to merge with other banks, buy other banks, or engage in non-banking activities. In making these rulings, the Fed takes into account the way a transaction may affect competition and the local community.

Deutsche Bank, one of the largest foreign banks operating in the United States, is based in New York City.

The Federal Reserve also enforces consumer laws that relate to banking. Some laws prohibit discrimination in making loans, while others provide consumers with information about the real cost of loans. For example, the Truth in Lending Act requires that retail stores, automobile dealers, and corporations, as well as banks, let customers who buy on credit know exactly how much their loan will cost. They have to explain the down payment required, the number of monthly payments, and the total amount of interest consumers must pay over the life of the loan.

Putting It All Together

Which of the Fed's areas of responsibility have the greatest impact on you and your family? Write a paragraph explaining your answer. Exchange paragraphs with a partner. How were your answers similar? How do you account for differences?

Hot Summer, Cool Prices, Rising Rates

Economists pay careful attention to the efforts of the Fed to manage the money supply and control the cost of credit. In the summer of 2005, economist David Wyss wrote:

The U.S. economy is heating up even more than expected this summer. Led by the consumer, . . . growth appears to be strengthening despite the drag of rising gasoline prices and the 10th consecutive Fed interest rate hike. . . . The economy is so far doing better than anticipated and seems likely to remain on a steady growth course. . . .

Even with the continued climb of oil prices to new records, the core consumer price index (excluding food and energy) is up only 2% from a year earlier, a deceleration from the rate in spring. High productivity growth and the recent strength in the dollar have kept inflation low, despite continued increases in health-benefit costs.

Having done so again on Aug. 9, the Federal Reserve will continue to raise interest rates. . . . We expect the Fed to continue to tighten, pushing the funds rate up to 4.25% by year-end. Energy is taking a bigger share of consumers' budgets, but Americans are offsetting that by saving less and borrowing more. Household debt hit a record 123% of after-tax income at the end of the first quarter. Most of the rise is in mortgage debt, but non-mortgage borrowing was up $14.5 billion in June (8.2% at an annual rate).

The ability to refinance at lower mortgage rates has contributed to the spending spree. Households took out $139 billion in cash-out refinancing last year and increased their home-equity loans by $158 billion. The added $315 billion was 3.7% of last year's household disposable income. Without that extra "income," spending might have been much weaker.

Consumers can't continue to live this far beyond their means. As interest rates rise, the cost of servicing the debt will increase (although only slowly, since most consumer debt is fixed-rate). The easy borrowing that's boosting spending today will come back to cut spending tomorrow. If interest rates rise slowly, as we . . . expect, the problem will be modest. But if they soar, consumer spending could drop sharply. ■

"Hot Summer, Cool Prices, Rising Rates" by David Wyss.
BusinessWeek Online, August 10, 2005.

reading for understanding

What link does the writer see between consumer spending and interest rates?

Discuss the fear of what will happen if interest rates rise sharply.

What problem does the writer infer that the Fed faces as it decides whether or not to raise interest rates?

Chapter Summary

- Congress created the Federal Reserve as a **central bank** to avoid **panics** like the one in 1907.

- Congress needed to **compromise** in order to set up the Federal Reserve.

- The Fed is responsible for carrying out the nation's **monetary policies**.

- The Fed is organized into 12 districts, each with its own **member banks**.

- The **President's Council of Economic Advisers** provides advice and analysis to the president on domestic and international economic issues.

- The Fed tries to balance the economy by alternating between a **loose money policy** and a **tight money policy**.

- An **expansionary (loose) policy** is designed to encourage spending and expand the economy. A **contractionary (tight) policy** is designed to limit the amount of credit available and slow economic expansion.

- **Fractional reserve banking** allows the Fed to control the amount banks can lend by changing the **discount rate**.

- The most flexible monetary policy tool is **open market operations**, which allow the Fed to buy and sell **government securities**.

- **Check clearing** is one of the Fed's responsibilities. It also oversees **electronic fund transfers**, including **direct deposits**.

Chapter Review

1 When Congress created the Federal Reserve, it wanted a central bank that would be independent of the government. Why was Congress concerned about the independence of its new central bank? How did it try to ensure that the Fed would be independent?

2 Create a diagram showing the cause-and-effect relationship between the Fed's tools for managing the money supply. Use your diagram to write a paragraph explaining that relationship and why it does not work perfectly.

Skill Builder

Evaluate Information

Two numbers can help you compare various lenders' prices. One is the finance charge—the amount you pay to use credit.

> **Example:** You borrow $100 for one year, and the interest is $10. If there is a service charge of $1, the finance charge will be $11.

The other number is the annual percentage rate (APR), the cost of credit on a yearly basis. It stays constant regardless of the amount you borrow or the time you have to repay your loan.

> **Example:** You borrow $100 for one year and pay a finance charge of $10. If you keep the $100 for a year and repay the $110 at year's end, you are paying an APR of 10 percent. If you repay the loan in 12 equal monthly installments, the $10 finance charge amounts to an APR of 18 percent.

Under the Truth in Lending Act, the creditor must tell you what each of these terms will be so that you can compare credit costs.

Suppose you buy a $7,500 car. You make a down payment of $1,500 and borrow $6,000. Compare the three credit arrangements in the chart.

Credit Options

Figure 15.7

	APR	Length of Loan	Monthly Payment	Total Finance Charge	Total of Payments
Bank A	14%	3 years	$205.07	$1,382.52	$7,382.52
Bank B	14%	4 years	$163.96	$1,870.08	$7,870.08
Bank C	15%	4 years	$166.98	$2,015.04	$8,015.04

1 Which bank is offering the lowest-cost loan?

2 If you can't afford to pay more than $175 a month, which loan offers the best deal? How much more will that loan cost you?

3 What other factors may affect the loan you choose? What would happen if you increased your down payment?

Chapter

16 ECONOMIC GROWTH

Getting Focused

Skim this chapter to predict what you will be learning.

- Read the lesson titles and subheadings.
- Look at the illustrations and read the captions.
- Examine the graphs.
- Review the vocabulary words and terms.

Chapter 16 explores the causes and the effects of economic growth. Think about what you have already learned about economic growth. What questions do you have about growth and its effects on you and your family? Record two questions in your notebook. Share those questions with a partner.

Although economists use various methods of determining economic growth, building and construction is one visible sign of economic growth.

Aggregate Supply and Demand

Thinking on Your Own

What comes to mind when you think about economic growth? Is it having more jobs to choose from or being able to buy more things? What else could economic growth mean for you?

Economists define economic growth as an increase in real gross domestic product (real GDP). They note that growth is not automatic even though everyone wishes it were. Economic growth expands a nation's production possibilities, but it does not solve the problem of scarcity. Remember that the list of things we want is limitless, while our ability to satisfy those wants is limited. To promote growth, economists study markets to find out how they work and what can be done to make them work even better. They begin with the interaction between supply and demand.

focus your reading

How does aggregate supply differ from supply in general?

How does aggregate demand differ from demand in general?

Explain macroeconomic equilibrium.

vocabulary

aggregate supply

aggregate supply curve

aggregate demand

aggregate demand curve

macroeconomic equilibrium

recall

Supply is the quantity of a good or service supplied at various prices.

Demand is the quantity of a good or service demanded at various prices.

Real gross domestic product (real GDP) is the total output or production of a nation in a single year, adjusted for inflation.

Aggregate Supply

The word *aggregate* means "total" or "combined." **Aggregate supply** is the total quantity of goods and services producers are willing and able to supply at various price levels in a specific time period. It is the sum of all of the goods and services produced in an economy in that time period.

Figure 16.1, on page 258, shows an **aggregate supply curve**. Like the supply curves you studied in Chapter 5, it is determined, at least in part, by the desire of firms to earn a profit. That is why the graph shows output increasing as the price level rises.

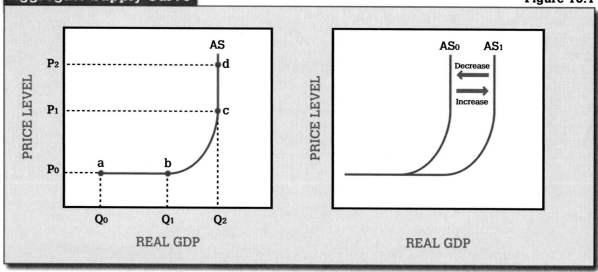

Aggregate Supply Curve

Figure 16.1

Notice that the aggregate supply curve is almost horizontal at first and then becomes increasingly steep. Why don't prices increase immediately? Because the model assumes producers have unused resources and can therefore increase production without raising prices. At some point—in this case, point *b*—prices begin to increase because costs have begun to rise. Producers may have to pay their workers overtime to meet demand. Or they may have to purchase additional resources to expand their production. The curve becomes almost vertical between points *c* and *d* as a result of the effects of rising costs.

What causes increases in the cost of production? The answer is many of the same factors that cause increases for an individual firm—higher labor costs or higher costs for key resources like energy. Each tends to result in price increases.

stop and think

What effect might higher taxes have on aggregate supply? Explain your reasoning to a partner. Then write your answer in one sentence in your notebook. As you read, also consider the effect of higher taxes on aggregate demand.

Aggregate Demand

Aggregate demand is a term that describes the behavior of all buyers in an economy. Specifically, it refers to the various quantities of goods and services that all people, taken together, are willing and able to buy at various price levels in

recall

Aggregate demand is the total demand for goods and services within an economy.

a specific period of time. It represents all of the demand within the economy. Like aggregate supply, aggregate demand can increase or decrease over time. Keep in mind that when economists speak of aggregate demand, they are referring to an average price level, not to the price of any single product.

To get a better understanding of aggregate demand, imagine that everyone is paid on the same day. With money in hand, they enter the market. How much they buy depends on prices. If prices are low on one payday, people are likely to buy more. If prices are higher on the next payday, people will be less able and less willing to buy as much. The amount of money people brought to the market did not change. What changed was how much they could buy with their paychecks.

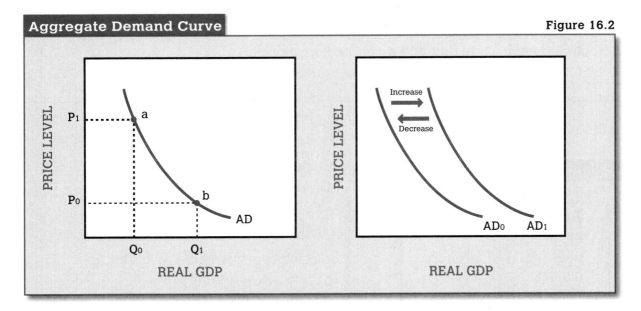

Aggregate Demand Curve   Figure 16.2

Figure 16.2 shows an **aggregate demand curve**. It slopes downward and to the right, much like the demand curve for individual industries. Notice that the drop in the general level of prices between points *a* and *b* results in an increase in demand. If the price level drops further, even more goods and services can be purchased, which is why the curve tends to shift to the right.

Among the factors that affect aggregate demand is a change in savings. If consumers save less and spend more, the increase in consumer spending increases aggregate demand. In much the same way, an increase in savings can result in a decrease in aggregate demand—leaving consumers with less money to spend. With less consumer spending, aggregate demand is likely to decrease and the aggregate demand curve shifts to the left.

Macroeconomic Equilibrium

The aggregate supply and aggregate demand curves look much like the other supply and demand curves you studied in earlier chapters. These particular curves, however, have special meaning. They are not a description of buyers and sellers in a single market. They are a summary of market activity for the whole economy. The word *macro* means "overall" or "total." The two curves show the total amount of goods and services that will be supplied or demanded at various price levels.

Aggregate supply and aggregate demand are at equilibrium when the quantity demanded is equal to the quantity supplied at a given price level. The word *equilibrium* means "in balance." Imagine a seesaw. If you and a friend decide to ride on one, and you weigh the same amount, the seesaw will balance. **Macroeconomic equilibrium** is the point at which aggregate supply balances aggregate demand. In Figure 16.3, equilibrium is reached at point *Q*—the point at which real GDP (aggregate supply) intersects with aggregate demand. It is the only place where the two curves meet. At any other level of output or price, adjustments have to be made. Therefore, all other price and output combinations tend to be unstable. They are not likely to last, and eventually the economy will return to point *Q*.

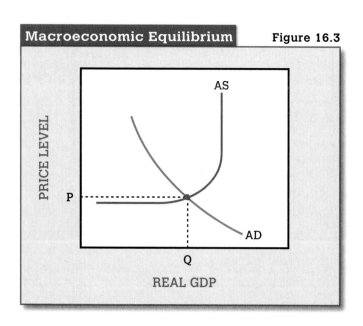

Macroeconomic Equilibrium   **Figure 16.3**

Putting It All Together

Review what you read about supply and demand curves in Chapter 5. Then write a paragraph comparing aggregate supply and aggregate demand with the supply and demand of a firm. Be sure to include at least one similarity and one difference.

Examining Economic Growth

Thinking on Your Own

Imagine a situation in which a nation's production of goods and services increases each year, but most people are economically worse off than they were the year before. How might you explain this result? Answer this question in your notebook.

Economic growth occurs whenever the production of goods and services increases at a rate faster than the rate of population growth. A **population** is a group of people living in a particular geographic area.

GDP and Population Growth

Have you ever ordered a pizza only to have a couple of hungry friends show up unexpectedly? If so, you know what happens when a population expands and the amount of food available stays the same. The more people who share a given amount of food, the smaller each share becomes.

focus your reading

How do economists measure economic growth?

Explain the relationship between population growth and economic growth.

Discuss the relationship between economic growth and a nation's standard of living.

vocabulary

population

economic regression

economic stagnation

real GDP per capita

standard of living

Population affects GDP in a similar way. If real GDP stays the same and the population increases, income and output per person decrease. The result is known as **economic regression**. To regress is to move backward.

If real GDP and the population increase at the same rate, the relationship between the two does not change. Economists refer to this condition as **economic stagnation**. When something is stagnant, it stands still and does not move or grow. Economic growth occurs only when the production of goods and services increases faster than the population.

To include population in real GDP, economists divide GDP by the total number of people in a country. The result is **real GDP per capita**. The term *per capita* means "per person." It indicates how much output the average person would receive if GDP were divided equally among the entire population.

Since GDP is not divided equally, you may wonder what difference real GDP per capita makes. To answer that question, study Figure 16.4. It compares real GDP with real GDP per capita. Notice that real GDP per capita increases more slowly than nominal, or current, GDP—particularly in periods when the population is growing. A growing population also means that periods of little or no growth in real GDP are more severe than they appear to be when the only measure is real GDP. Real GDP per capita gives economists a better idea of the effects of growth than real GDP does.

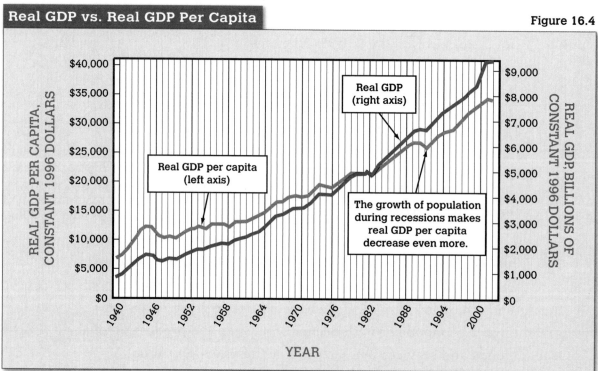

Real GDP vs. Real GDP Per Capita

Figure 16.4

Source: *Economic Report of the President*, various years

The standard of living in Brussels, Belgium (left), is very different from the standard of living in Cairo, Egypt (right).

GDP and Standard of Living

A country benefits from economic growth in many ways. One of the most important is that it raises the **standard of living**. The term *standard of living* refers to the overall quality of life. It is usually measured by real GDP per capita.

As a result of economic growth, the standard of living for Americans today is much higher than that of earlier generations. In the late 1900s, on average, Americans increased their production of goods and services by about 3 percent per year and their population by about 1 percent. Therefore, the rate of growth was about 2 percent per year. At that rate, the nation's per capita income doubles every 35 years. In 1950, real GDP per capita was $6,330. By 2004, it was $37,800—almost six times as much. The U.S. real GDP per capita in 2004 was more than five times higher than the world average.

A suburban community in the United States

Your home and others like it throughout the nation reflect the effects of a high real GDP per capita, even if your parents earn less than $37,800 per year. The nation's wealth is reflected in the amount and quality of clothes in your closet and the supply of food in your kitchen. It is also evident in the items found

A suburban community in Niger

throughout your house— radios, televisions, DVD players, computers, phones, indoor plumbing, and electric lights. The nation's standard of living is also evident in the number of cars on the road and in the quantity and quality of goods in department stores and supermarkets.

Unfortunately, the effects of a low standard of living are also easy to spot. Niger, a nation in central Africa, has one of the world's lowest standards of living. Real GDP per capita is about $900 per year. As a result, the average person in Niger can expect to live just 42 years, compared to 77 years in the United States. In Niger, the number of deaths per 1,000 live births (the infant mortality rate) is 122. That is, 122 infants out of every 1,000 live births die each year. In the U.S., seven infants die out of every 1,000 live births each year.

In 2005, newspaper headlines revealed a little more of what it means to have a very low standard of living. That year, almost one-third of Niger's population of 12.1 million—about 4 million men, women, and children—did not have enough food to eat as a result of a drought. In a country where most people have barely enough to eat in a year with plenty of rain, the consequences of a drought can be devastating. Young children were the most vulnerable. Some 800,000 children under the age of five were at risk of malnutrition and even starvation.

Putting It All Together

Experts often rely on real GDP per capita to measure the standard of living. How full a picture does it provide? Write a paragraph explaining what lies behind the numbers. What measures would you add to give a fuller picture of a nation's economic status?

Sources of Economic Growth

Thinking on Your Own

Assume that the nation's economy is growing at a healthy rate. If someone asked you why this growth is taking place, what answers could you give? List three possible reasons in your notebook.

Each of the four factors of production—natural resources, labor (human resources), capital resources, and entrepreneurship—contributes to economic growth. Sources of productivity gains include

- increases in the skills of workers.

- increases in the ratio of capital to labor.

- improved use of all factors of production.

- the development and use of better equipment and products.

focus your reading

Name four sources of economic growth.

Explain how improvement in the capital-to-labor ratio contributes to economic growth.

How does research and development contribute to economic growth?

vocabulary

on-the-job training

capital-to-labor ratio

research and development

More Productive Workers

Until the 1900s, most jobs required physical labor. Today, most of the work people do requires a variety of specialized skills and education. That shift has resulted in large increases in education.

As Figure 16.5 on page 266 shows, less than 8 percent of all U.S. workers in 1950 had a college education. By 2003, over 85 percent of all adults twenty-five and older had completed at least high school, and over 27 percent had graduated from college. Many workers who did not attend college learned a trade through **on-the-job training** or by participating in specialized training programs. That investment in education has allowed American firms not only to take advantage of improvements in technology but also to play a leadership role in the development of new technologies.

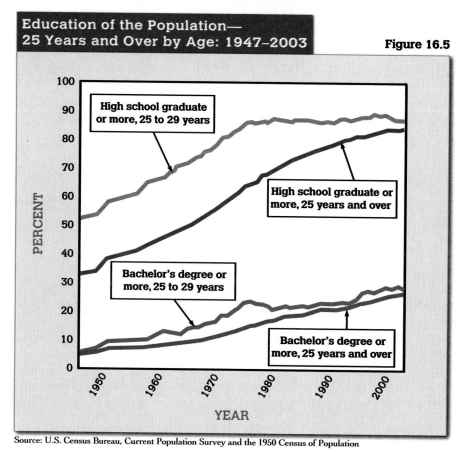

Education of the Population— 25 Years and Over by Age: 1947–2003

Figure 16.5

Source: U.S. Census Bureau, Current Population Survey and the 1950 Census of Population

Capital Investment

In the days when most jobs required physical labor, a worker's productivity depended mainly on his or her own strength and endurance. Today, however, a worker's productivity depends to a large extent on the quantity and quality of his or her tools and other equipment. A worker with no tools will not be very productive, no matter how well he or she is trained. Similarly, a worker with outdated equipment will not produce as much as an equally capable worker who is equipped with the latest machines and the newest technology.

Therefore, the key to improvements in labor productivity is the rate of capital investment. Economists are particularly concerned with the **capital-to-labor ratio**—the total capital stock divided by the number of workers. A high capital-to-labor ratio encourages economic growth because it enables individual workers to produce more than they could otherwise.

You may think of saving and investment as putting aside money to buy stocks, bonds, or mutual funds. You hope that their value will grow faster than inflation. To economists, however, saving and investment means setting aside a part of current income, or output, so that people can consume and produce more in the future. Therefore, the purchase of capital goods, like machinery, is an investment. A useful way to understand the relationship between future income and investment is by thinking about a farmer who sets aside a part of this year's crop (saving) to use as seed (investment) for next year's crop (future income).

The capital investment rate dropped in the 1970s from about 4 percent a year to about 2.5 percent a year and declined even further in the 1980s. As a result of that drop, productivity fell sharply even though the number of workers increased.

If an economy does not invest in capital equipment, productivity is likely to decrease and economic growth will slow. Indeed, if people consume their entire output, their productive capacity shrinks. They will not even be able to replace worn-out plants and equipment. An economy needs savings to finance investment.

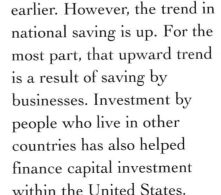

Capital investment is an important factor in economic growth.

A nation's savings rate has three key components: savings by households, businesses, and governments (both state and federal). The personal savings rate was down to less than 1 percent in 2004, and the overall rate of saving was less than it was 30 or 40 years earlier. However, the trend in national saving is up. For the most part, that upward trend is a result of saving by businesses. Investment by people who live in other countries has also helped finance capital investment within the United States.

stop and think

Make a list of the sources of economic growth described on page 265. In your own words, describe each in a sentence or two. Add sources and descriptions as you read.

Management

The actions of entrepreneurs also affect economic growth. They organize resources—natural, human, and capital—into a production process and then manage that process.

If a manager focuses only on short-term outcomes and ignores long-term effects, the firm will eventually fail. Effective managers take into account the long-term effects of their decisions, as well as the short-term consequences. They emphasize the quality of the goods and services they produce, as well as the quantity. Many managers involve workers in key decisions to take advantage of their insights and build goodwill.

"Marvels of a Marvelous Age"

In 1889, author Samuel Clemens, better known as Mark Twain, expressed his views on economic growth in a letter congratulating poet Walt Whitman on his 70th birthday:

"You have lived just the seventy years, which are greatest in the world's history and richest in benefit and advancement to its peoples. These seventy years have done more to widen the interval between man and the other animals than was accomplished by any of the five centuries which preceded them.

"What great births have you witnessed! The steam press, the steamship, the steel ship, the railroad, the perfect cotton gin, the telegraph, the phonograph, the photogravure, the electrotype, the gaslight, the electric light, the sewing machine and the amazing infinitely varied and innumerable products of coal tar; those latest and strangest marvels of a marvelous age. And you have seen even greater births than these; for you have seen the application of anesthesia to surgery-practice, whereby the ancient dominion of pain, which began with the first created life, came to an end on this earth forever. . . .

"Yes, you have indeed seen much—but tarry for a while, for the greatest is yet to come."

Reprinted in *Letters of a Nation*, edited by Andrew Carroll (Kodansha America, Inc., 1997).

reading for understanding

What are the "marvels of a marvelous age" that Mark Twain describes?

What effect does Twain suggest that those marvels had on the standard of living in the United States in the late 1800s?

What marvels would you list if you were to write a letter about the impact of recent innovations on the standard of living today?

Research and Development

A fourth source of economic growth is **research and development** (R&D). It includes scientific research, product development, innovations in production, and improvements in management. Some R&D takes place in research laboratories, while other R&D may be the result of discoveries made on the job. A worker may find a shortcut that saves time and money. In either case, R&D generally leads to new products and less expensive ways of producing them.

Economists estimate that R&D may have contributed 25 percent or more to the total growth in the U.S. economy between 1929 and 1982. Some economists believe that research may account for an even larger share of economic growth. That growth is hard to measure in the short run. Neither economists nor researchers can predict the long-term effects of current research projects, or even of those that took place in the 1990s.

Pharmaceutical companies routinely invest millions of dollars in research and development.

R&D and capital investment are closely linked. Part of a firm's investment in tools and other equipment is due to depreciation of or wear and tear on existing tools. However, the new machines that firms purchase are rarely identical to the ones they replace. More often than not, the new tools are based on the latest technology. Because of improvements in technology, firms are often motivated to buy new equipment before the old machines wear out. Those purchases contribute to economic growth.

Putting It All Together

Which source of economic growth do you consider most important? Write a paragraph that not only states your opinion, but also defends it with reasons and supports it with evidence.

The Power of Us

How do innovations aid or contribute to economic growth? A feature article in *BusinessWeek* offered some clues.

[Last year] the 35 employees at Meiosys Inc., a software firm in Palo Alto, Calif., . . . began using Skype, a program that lets them make free calls over the Internet, with better sound quality than regular phones, using headsets connected to their PCs. Callers simply click on a name in their Skype contact lists, and if the person is there, they connect and talk just like on a regular phone call. . . .

When users fire up Skype, they automatically allow their spare computing power and Net connections to be borrowed by the Skype network, which uses that collective resource to route others' calls. The result: a self-sustaining phone system that requires no central capital investment—just the willingness of its users to share. . . .

The nearly 1 billion people online worldwide—along with their shared knowledge, social contacts, online reputations, computing power, and more—are rapidly becoming a collective force of unprecedented power. . . .

Although tech companies may be leading the way, their efforts are shaking up other industries, including entertainment, publishing, and advertising. Hollywood is under full-scale assault by 100 million people sharing songs and movies online via programs such as Kazaa and BitTorrent. The situation is the same with ad-supported media: Google Inc.'s ace search engine essentially polls the collective judgments of millions of Web page creators to determine the most relevant search results. In the process, it has created a multibillion-dollar market for super-targeted ads that's drawing money from magazine display ads and newspaper classifieds.

Most telling, traditional companies, from Procter & Gamble Co. to Dow Chemical Co., are beginning to flock to the virtual commons, too. The potential benefits are enormous. If companies can open themselves up to contributions from enthusiastic customers and partners, that should help them create products and services faster, with fewer duds—and at far lower cost, with far less risk. ∎

"The Power of Us," *BusinessWeek*, June 20, 2005.

reading for understanding

The article focuses on an innovation. What is that innovation, and why is it new?

Describe how the innovation has improved productivity.

What does the article suggest about the reasons economists are not always able to measure the impact of an innovation accurately?

Chapter Summary

- **Aggregate supply** of a nation in one year is identical to real gross domestic product. It is the total quantity of goods and services producers are willing and able to supply at various price levels in a specific time period.

- **Aggregate demand** is the total quantity of goods and services in the economy demanded at various price levels.

- The intersection of the **aggregate supply curve** and the **aggregate demand curve** is known as **macroeconomic equilibrium**.

- An economy grows when the production of goods and services increases faster than the **population** grows.

- Economic growth is the opposite of **economic regression**.

- **Economic stagnation** occurs whenever the production of goods and services increases at the same rate as population growth.

- **Real GDP per capita** measures **standard of living**.

- **On-the-job training** helps people to obtain higher-paying employment.

- Labor productivity and **capital-to-labor ratio** are central to economic growth. So are management style and **research and development**.

Chapter Review

1 How are aggregate supply and aggregate demand similar to the supply and demand of individual firms and industries? What are the key differences?

2 Describe the effects of economic growth on you and your family. How does growth enrich your lives? How does it affect the opportunities you are likely to have in the future?

3 The standard of living varies in each country around the world. Use library resources or the Internet to locate information about the standard of living in six different countries. Then create a chart to present this information.

Skill Builder

Spot Trends

A trend is a change over time. Graphs are often used to show such changes. The following steps will help you identify and analyze trends.

Read the title and the labels on the graph. They tell you the topic, the items being compared, and how they are counted or measured.

Examine various points on the graph. Notice the date below each point on the horizontal axis and the quantity measured on the vertical axis.

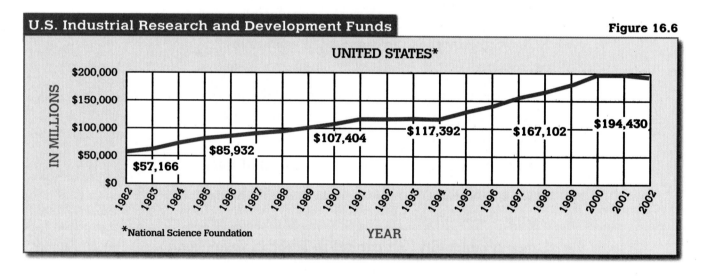

U.S. Industrial Research and Development Funds

Figure 16.6

UNITED STATES*

IN MILLIONS

$200,000
$150,000
$100,000
$50,000
$0

$57,166
$85,932
$107,404
$117,392
$167,102
$194,430

1982 1983 1984 1985 1986 1987 1988 1989 1990 1991 1992 1993 1994 1995 1996 1997 1998 1999 2000 2001 2002

*National Science Foundation

YEAR

Analyze the change over time to determine the main idea of the graph.

1 How much was spent on industrial R&D in 1982?

2 In what year did industrial R&D peak, or reach its highest point?

3 What trend does the graph illustrate?

4 What might the trend mean? Using what you learned in the last chapter, write a few sentences describing the effects of this trend on the U.S. economy.

17 ECONOMIC CHALLENGES

Getting Focused

Skim this chapter to predict what you will be learning.

- **Read the lesson titles and subheadings.**
- **Look at the illustrations and read the captions.**
- **Examine the graphs, charts, and maps.**
- **Review the vocabulary words and terms.**

Chapter 17 considers a few of the economic challenges that nations, communities, and individuals face today—the threat of inflation, unemployment, and poverty. What economic challenges do you face? How do you deal with these challenges? Record your strategies in your notebook. Share your thinking with a partner.

Unemployment is one issue that faces societies all around the world. In the United States, politicians and economists alike pay close attention to the unemployment figures that are released regularly.

Inflation

Thinking on Your Own

How do rising prices affect you? Imagine that prices will rise 10 percent during the next year while your income remains the same. How will this affect your monthly purchases?

The price of a movie goes up. You pay more for a gallon of gas than you did a few weeks ago. Is it inflation? The economy does not experience inflation every time the price of a movie ticket goes up. Inflation is an increase in the average level of price, not a change in a specific price.

Inflation distorts the way a market economy works. In a market economy, prices send signals to both buyers and sellers. Businesses rely on those signals to direct their resources to their most profitable products or services. That job is challenging even without inflation. With a high inflation rate, it is almost impossible to tell whether a change in price is part of the general increase in prices or specific to a particular product or service. As a result, the market does not work as well as it should. Some resources are wasted and some business opportunities are missed.

focus your reading

Describe how inflation differs from other price increases.

What are the causes of inflation?

What methods do governments use to reduce inflation?

vocabulary

demand-pull inflation

hyperinflation

cost-push inflation

Federal Reserve System

recall

Inflation is a rise, over time, in the general level of prices.

According to the **law of demand**, if all other things are equal, the higher the price of a product or service, the less people are willing to buy.

According to the **law of supply**, if all other things are equal, the higher the price of a product or service, the more suppliers will offer for sale.

Fluctuations are ups and downs in an economy.

Aggregate supply is the total value of all of the goods and services produced in the entire economy in a specific period of time at various price levels.

Causes of Inflation

The laws of supply and demand are helpful in understanding the causes of inflation. From time to time, aggregate demand increases. Consumers, businesses, and/or governments demand many more goods and services than the economy as a whole can produce. As a result, shortages occur and prices rise. Economists call this kind of inflation **demand-pull inflation**. An extreme increase in total or aggregate demand pulls up the level of prices.

As price levels increase, so does the demand for money. The government is under pressure to increase the supply. But if it gives in to those pressures and the increase is too great, the government may set off **hyperinflation**—an extreme form of inflation with increases of more than 500 percent a year. Germany experienced hyperinflation in the early 1920s. In 1921, a German newspaper sold for about one-third of a mark. Two years later, a newspaper cost 70 million marks! What happened? The government was printing money with reckless abandon. As a result, the mark lost so much value that it was cheaper for people to heat their homes by burning their money than to buy firewood.

Inflation can also be caused by an increase in costs. Such inflation is known as **cost-push inflation**. (Another term for this is *supply-shock inflation*.) In the 1970s, for example, the price of oil went from $5 a barrel to $35 a barrel. Because oil was used in almost every business, its rising price pushed up the cost of other goods and services.

Germany experienced hyperinflation during the 1920s.

An increase in labor costs can have a similar effect. If the job market is tight and few workers are unemployed, a general increase in wages tends to increase the demand for goods and services. Figure 17.1, on page 276, shows the rate of inflation from 1965 to the present. Notice that prices tend to rise faster during expansions and then slow down during recessions.

A number of economists believe that most forms of inflation—but particularly hyperinflation—will not last without a growing money supply to fuel the rise in prices. As people spend that money, they set off a demand-pull effect that drives up prices. On the other hand, if the price of gas or electricity goes up and the amount of money in the economy does not change, people will buy less of something else. So, while the price of gas or electricity remains high, the prices of other goods and services are unchanged.

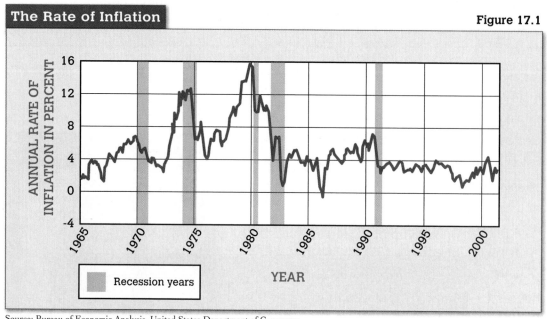

The Rate of Inflation

Figure 17.1

ANNUAL RATE OF INFLATION IN PERCENT

Recession years

YEAR

Source: Bureau of Economic Analysis, United States Department of Commerce

Many economists believe that no single sector of the economy—businesses, government, or consumers—is to blame for inflation. They argue that once wages and prices begin to rise, the process is difficult to stop. Higher prices force workers to ask for higher wages. If they receive higher wages, their employers try to recover the cost with even higher prices. As each group tries to improve its position with a larger price increase than the one before, the rate of inflation increases dramatically.

The Costs of Inflation

Inflation is costly for several reasons. First, the amount of goods or services people can buy for their money falls as prices rise. As a result, those who do not get automatic raises find that their money buys a little less each month. People who are retired and others who live on fixed incomes are especially affected.

Inflation has another important effect. Money helps people judge the value of goods and services in much the same way a tape measure helps them judge size. Imagine if the length of a foot was reduced each year by 10 percent. Judging length would become more complicated each year and people would gradually lose confidence in the system. The same is true for money. Inflation makes it harder to judge the value of goods and services from one year to the next.

During periods of inflation, firms find it more difficult to plan for the future. Many delay capital purchases and focus on projects that offer relatively quick profits.

Families also have trouble making plans. Many find that they have to change their spending habits. During the 1980s, for example, as interest rates—the price of borrowed money—rose along with other prices, many people were reluctant or unable to make major purchases. Sales of houses and automobiles fell. Other consumers rushed to spend their money before it became worthless. Instead of investing their money in stocks or bonds or saving it, they purchased luxury items like gemstones in the hope that they would keep their value.

The sale of homes dropped during the 1980s.

Inflation changes the way income is distributed. For example, suppose you received $1,000 as a birthday gift and you decided to keep the money hidden in a drawer. If inflation is at 10 percent a year, Figure 17.2, on page 278, shows that your money will be worth $909 a year later. If you kept it in the drawer for ten years, its value would drop to $386.

If the inflation rate is higher, your losses will be even greater. Inflation does not benefit savers or lenders. It does benefit borrowers. Anyone in Germany who got a fixed-rate mortgage in 1913 could have paid it off in 1923 for less than the price of a newspaper. As a result, bankers try to take inflation into account when they make loans. In the 1980s, they offered a new kind of loan—one with adjustable interest rates. Adjustable-rate mortgages (ARMs) stipulate an interest rate that changes during the life of the loan to keep pace with inflation.

Annual Inflation Rate   Figure 17.2

Year	2 percent	4 percent	6 percent	8 percent	10 percent
2005	$1,000	$1,000	$1,000	$1,000	$1,000
2006	980	962	943	926	909
2007	961	925	890	857	826
2008	942	889	840	794	751
2009	924	855	792	735	683
2010	906	822	747	681	621
2011	888	790	705	630	564
2012	871	760	665	584	513
2013	853	731	627	540	467
2014	837	703	592	500	424
2015	820	676	558	463	386

Even moderate inflation can eat away at wealth. After studying economic growth in nearly 100 countries over several decades, economist Robert Barro found that significant inflation is almost always associated with slower growth in real GDP.

The United States experienced hyperinflation just after the Revolutionary War, when prices doubled in a single year. Even lower inflation can be costly. In 1979, consumer prices rose at a rate of about 13 percent a year. At that rate, the cost of living would double every five years. By 1982, the rate of inflation had been cut by two-thirds but was still high enough that the cost of living would double every 15 years.

Government Policies

By the late 1990s, the rate of inflation in the United States dropped to about 2.2 percent a year—the lowest rise in prices since 1965. Inflation declined because the federal government took steps to control the rise in prices.

Governments have developed a variety of strategies to deal with inflation. Some are more effective than others. One approach focuses on efforts to stop inflation by influencing the nation's money supply.

As you learned in Chapter 15, the **Federal Reserve System** is the central banking system in the United States. It is responsible for the nation's monetary policy. As part of that responsibility, it controls the amount of money in circulation by controlling the amount of interest banks pay for their loans. In the 1980s, the Federal Reserve tried to control inflation by keeping interest rates high. The Federal Reserve sets the interest rate at which it lends money to banks and other financial institutions. That interest rate affects the interest rates banks offer their customers. It also affects the price of bonds and shares.

> **recall**
>
> The Federal Reserve carries out the nation's **monetary policies**—strategies for controlling the size of the money supply and the price of credit.

High interest rates make saving more attractive and borrowing less so. High rates also discourage spending and therefore decrease the amount of money in circulation. Low rates have the opposite effect.

Some of these strategies affect the economy more quickly than others. In general, it takes time before changes in interest rates affect spending and saving decisions. It takes even longer before interest rates affect consumer prices. As a result, the Federal Reserve sets interest rates based on judgments about what inflation might be like in the next few years, not what it is today.

Putting It All Together

Inflation can have harmful effects on a nation's economy. In your notebook, list or describe at least four bad effects of inflation.

Unemployment

Thinking on Your Own

This lesson describes four types of unemployment. In your notebook, define each type and identify its causes and effects. The goal of every presidential administration is to reach "full employment." Is that a realistic goal?

Every month, the U.S. Bureau of Labor Statistics releases the latest unemployment statistics, including the **unemployment rate**—the percentage of individuals in the civilian labor force who actively looked for a job that month but could not find one. Unemployment statistics are among the most closely watched numbers in the country. High unemployment is a signal that the economy is not working efficiently and that resources are being wasted. Low unemployment signals an efficient economy.

Measuring Unemployment

Figure 17.3, on page 281, shows the unemployment rate over a period of over 35 years. Notice that it tends to increase dramatically during recessions and then fall slowly as the economy begins to recover. The rate of unemployment, however, is more than a set of numbers on a graph. Those numbers represent millions of Americans. In June 2005, the unemployment rate was about 5 percent—a relatively low number. This meant that 7.5 million people were unemployed in a labor force of more than 149 million. That number—7.5 million—is roughly equal to the combined populations of three of the nation's ten largest cities—Los Angeles, California; Chicago, Illinois; and San José, California.

focus your reading

How does the government determine the unemployment rate?

Name at least two automatic stabilizers.

What is full employment?

vocabulary

unemployment rate

frictional unemployment

structural unemployment

cyclical unemployment

seasonal unemployment

full employment

automatic stabilizers

unemployment insurance

Yet the real rate of unemployment is higher. The Bureau of Labor Statistics does not count people who are too discouraged to continue to look for a job. These dropouts from the labor force may include as many as one million Americans. The number is misleading for another reason as well. The government considers people employed even if the only work they can find is a part-time job that pays very little. Therefore, someone who works a few hours a week would be considered employed.

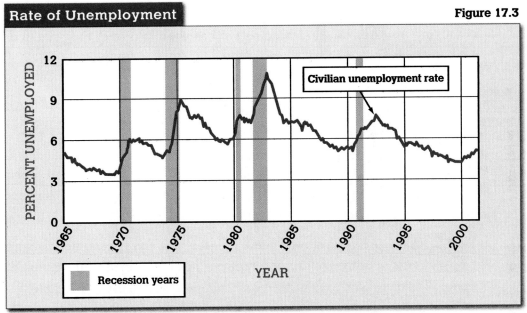

Rate of Unemployment

Figure 17.3

Civilian unemployment rate

PERCENT UNEMPLOYED

YEAR

Recession years

Source: Bureau of Labor Statistics, United States Department of Commerce

Types of Unemployment

Economists have identified four major types of unemployment. Each reveals some of the strengths and weaknesses of a market economy.

Frictional unemployment Some unemployment will always exist in a market economy. This kind of unemployment is known as **frictional unemployment**. It occurs whenever people leave their old jobs and before they have found new jobs. The rate of frictional unemployment tends to rise every spring as high school and college graduates search for their first job. Frictional unemployment is usually brief. The frictionally unemployed have the skills for the jobs available in the economy. It is a matter of finding the right job at the right salary.

Structural unemployment A more serious cause of unemployment is a change in the economy that reduces the demand for a particular group of workers and their skills. Technological innovations and changes in consumer demand can result in **structural unemployment**.

For example, the decision to build automobiles from lightweight materials in the 1980s reduced the demand for steel. As a result, more than 300,000 steelworkers lost their jobs. There were jobs available at the time in computers and biotechnology, but the steelworkers did not have the skills needed for those jobs. They were structurally unemployed. To find another job that paid as well as their old one, they needed to be retrained.

Find a Summer Job

How do you go about getting a summer job if you have never looked for one before? There are many different ways to find summer employment. Here are useful guidelines that can help you in your job search.

1. Decide on the job you want or need. Think about any special needs you have—transportation, hours, salary. You may not be able to find a job that meets all your needs, but you should try to find one that meets as many as possible.

2. Take a close look at your interests and your skills. What do you have to offer an employer? What kinds of work have you done? What have you learned at school that might be useful in a summer job?

3. Prepare a résumé that outlines your education, work experiences, and skills. You can find guides to writing a résumé online or at the public library.

4. Contact people who may be able to help you find a job. Talk about summer jobs with your parents, relatives, your friends' parents, teachers, and any other adults you know. Give them copies of your résumé.

5. Read newspaper want ads and check for jobs online. Apply only for those jobs that interest you and for which you have the necessary qualifications.

6. If you are asked to come in for an interview, dress appropriately. Make sure you know something about the company. Think of questions you are likely to be asked, and practice your answers.

7. If you are planning to attend college, you may want to apply for jobs that will enhance your résumé for the application process.

A change in demand led to the loss of jobs in the steel industry. Sometimes an invention or innovation can have a similar effect. In the late 1900s, automated teller machines (ATMs) reduced the demand for bank tellers. More recently, automated checkout lines in supermarkets and discount stores have had a similar effect on the demand for sales clerks.

Anthony Principi (left), the chairman of the Defense Base Realignment and Closure Commission, speaks with General Counsel David Hague during the August 2005 hearings.

Decisions by businesses or a government can also result in structural unemployment. In the late 1900s, car manufacturers built plants outside the United States to save money on labor. As a result of those decisions, thousands of automobile workers in the United States lost their jobs. A government decision can have a similar effect. In 1993 and 1995, the U.S. Defense Department closed a number of navy shipyards. The workers in those shipyards had to find new jobs or move to other regions where their skills were still in demand.

Cyclical unemployment Some unemployment is directly related to fluctuations in the business cycle. **Cyclical unemployment** means there are not enough jobs to go around. During a recession, for example, many people are laid off because there is no longer a demand for the goods and services they provide. Once the economy recovers and demand increases, these workers will generally be rehired.

stop and think

In your notebook, create a Venn diagram that compares and contrasts two of the types of unemployment. Compare your diagram with that of a partner.

The Great Depression of the 1930s is a dramatic example of cyclical unemployment. At its height in 1933, one in four Americans who wanted to work was unable to find a job. It was not until 1941, when World War II was under way, that the official unemployment rate finally fell below 10 percent.

Seasonal unemployment Seasonal changes in the weather or in the demand for certain products can cause **seasonal unemployment**. There is little or no demand for mall Santa Clauses before Thanksgiving and after Christmas. Construction workers in cold climates, people who work in hotels and resorts, and farmers have a similar problem. They often have more work than they can handle in the spring and summer months. In late fall and early winter, there is little or no work to be done.

One example of seasonal unemployment is a ski resort that closes during the warmer months of the year.

The Limits of Full Employment

Most nations seek **full employment**. However, full employment does not mean zero unemployment. It means the lowest possible unemployment rate in a growing economy with all factors of production used as efficiently as possible.

What is the lowest rate of unemployment? Economists disagree on this issue. Many believe it is reached when the

unemployment rate drops below 4.5 percent. In 2000, the rate reached a record low of 3.9 percent and remained there for two months before rising again. A low unemployment rate is difficult to maintain because of the business cycle. A downturn in the economy will push the unemployment rate back up again. During the recession of 1981–1982, the unemployment rate reached 10.8 percent—more than one out of every ten workers in the United States was out of a job.

Government Policies

A high unemployment rate affects almost every part of the economy, and it places economic hardship on those who can least afford it. The market provides no easy solutions for unemployment, so people look to the government for help.

Most governments offer a number of **automatic stabilizers** to keep the economy going by stabilizing demand (that is, keeping demand constant) and helping the unemployed. These are programs that automatically provide benefits if the economy threatens the income of individual workers. For example, workers who lose their jobs because of the fluctuations of the business cycle, structural changes, or seasonal shifts in demand can collect unemployment insurance. **Unemployment insurance** is a federal program that provides cash benefits for a specific period of time to workers who have lost their jobs through no fault of their own. The money is paid out of a fund to which the employer, the employee, and the government have contributed.

Federal welfare and Social Security programs also are automatic stabilizers. While Medicare, Medicaid, and Social Security primarily help families meet their basic needs, they also serve an economic purpose. The payments ensure that consumer demand will not fall below a certain level.

Putting It All Together

In a sentence or two each in your notebook, describe the four types of unemployment introduced in this lesson. Then review your answer to the question asked in Thinking on Your Own. Is full employment a realistic goal?

Outsourcing: Is It Bad?

Many American companies are outsourcing jobs to other countries. Kathleen Madigan, the editor of *Business Outlook*, believes Americans should be concerned.

The extent to which industries are moving a wide array of mid-level professional jobs offshore is troubling. We're talking about computers and other high tech, business services, and finance. Add those industries up, along with factory jobs, and you find that one out of three private-sector jobs is now at risk of being outsourced. And that doesn't count back-office functions such as accounts payable, marketing and sales, and human resources. . . . All of them could be shipped overseas in the name of cost cutting. . . .

Another reason for the speed and size of this shift is the nature of service work, especially in our Internet world. Manufacturers must spend years and billions of dollars erecting plants overseas and setting up distribution chains for supply and shipments before moving work offshore. But service jobs need much less infrastructure. Many need only a desk, computer, and Net access. . . .

The only way the U.S. will keep one rung ahead of the rest of the world is to ensure that we have a broadly educated workforce that keeps learning.

"Commentary: Outsourcing Jobs: Is It Bad?"
BusinessWeek, August 25, 2003.

Americans should not fear, writes Michael J. Mandel, *BusinessWeek's* chief economist.

Think of the world economy as a ladder. On the bottom rungs are the countries producing mainly textiles and other low-tech goods. Toward the top are the U.S. and other leading economies, which make sophisticated electronics, software, and pharmaceuticals. Up and down the middle rungs are all the other nations, manufacturing everything from steel to autos to memory chips.

Viewed in this way, economic development is simple: Everyone tries to climb to the next rung. This works well if the topmost countries can create new industries and products. Such invention allows older industries to move overseas while fresh jobs are generated at home. But if innovation stalls at the highest rung—well, that's bad news for Americans, who must compete with lower-wage workers elsewhere. . . .

The biggest danger to U.S. workers isn't overseas competition. It's that we worry too much about other countries climbing up the ladder and not enough about finding the next higher rung for ourselves. ■

reading for understanding

Explain the subject of the debate.

On what issues do the two economists agree? On what issues do they disagree?

What is your opinion? Should Americans be concerned about outsourcing?

Poverty

Thinking on Your Own

Choose three of the vocabulary terms. In your notebook, write one or more sentences that use the three terms.

The United States is the richest of the world's industrialized nations. Yet it also has the highest poverty rate in the industrialized world. What is poverty? **Poverty** is usually defined as not having enough income to buy the essentials—food, shelter, clothing, and other basic needs. At what point does poverty begin? The answer depends on where in the world you live. Those considered poor in the United States would be considered well off in many countries.

The Distribution of Income

Poverty in the United States is defined in relation to other information. Economists rank families by size and income from highest to lowest. Those rankings are then grouped into fifths— each fifth represents 20 percent of all families in the nation. From this perspective, a family is poor if its income falls within the lowest fifth in the nation. Figure 17.4 A, on page 288, shows that in 1980, the 20 percent of families with the lowest incomes received just 5.3 percent of the total income earned by all families in the nation that year. In 2000, those households received even less of the nation's total income—just 4.3 percent. On the other hand, the highest 20 percent received 41.1 percent of all income in 1980 and 47.5 percent in 2000.

Figure 17.4 B, on page 288, places the data presented in the table on a **Lorenz curve**—a graph that illustrates how real income

focus your reading

How do economists measure the distribution of income?

Give at least three reasons for inequality in income.

How do governments try to reduce inequalities?

vocabulary

poverty

Lorenz curve

poverty thresholds

poverty guidelines

welfare

food stamps

Earned Income Tax Credit (EITC)

distribution varies from equal distribution. If all families had exactly the same income, 50 percent of the families in the nation would earn 50 percent of total income. The line labeled "Equality of Income" shows how that distribution would look on a graph. Notice that it is a diagonal line that runs from one corner of the graph to the other. Unlike the curves that show how income is actually distributed, equal distribution is a straight line.

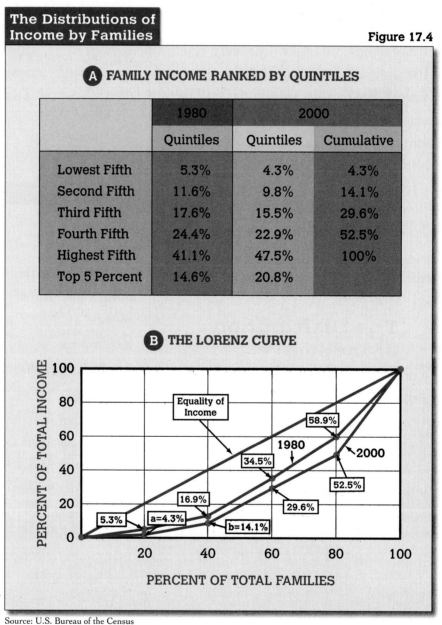

The Distributions of Income by Families

Figure 17.4

A FAMILY INCOME RANKED BY QUINTILES

	1980	2000	
	Quintiles	Quintiles	Cumulative
Lowest Fifth	5.3%	4.3%	4.3%
Second Fifth	11.6%	9.8%	14.1%
Third Fifth	17.6%	15.5%	29.6%
Fourth Fifth	24.4%	22.9%	52.5%
Highest Fifth	41.1%	47.5%	100%
Top 5 Percent	14.6%	20.8%	

B THE LORENZ CURVE

Source: U.S. Bureau of the Census

Measuring Poverty

How many people in the United States live in poverty? The government uses poverty thresholds to answer such questions.

Poverty thresholds are dollar estimates of the amount of annual income needed to support families of various sizes. Those whose income falls below those thresholds are considered poor. The estimates are based on pre-tax income and adjusted for inflation.

Poverty guidelines are a simplified version of poverty thresholds. They are issued by the Department of Health and Human Services to determine who is eligible for various federal programs designed to help families in need. Unlike poverty thresholds, the guidelines are adjusted for regional differences.

In 2000, the nation's poverty rate was 11.3 percent. It rose to 11.7 percent in 2001, 12.1 percent in 2002, and 12.5 percent in 2003. Today, nearly 33 million men, women, and children in the United States live in poverty. About 40 percent of the nation's poor over the age of sixteen work either part-time or full-time but cannot earn enough to adequately support a family. For example, if a single parent with two children worked full-time at a job that paid minimum wage, his or her income would be $10,712 before taxes—about $4,507 below the poverty threshold for a family of three.

The percentage of families living in poverty is not fixed. People move in and out of poverty. During a recession, the poverty rate increases. When the economy improves, the poverty rate drops. Poverty is also not evenly distributed across the population. For example, children make up about 26 percent of the total population but 39 percent of the nation's poor. In 2001, 11.7 million children, or 16.3 percent of the population, were poor. Children who lived in households headed by single women were particularly vulnerable. Nearly 49 percent of children under eighteen whose families were headed by single women were poor.

In 2003, 24.4 percent of African Americans and 25.5 percent of Hispanics lived in poverty compared to 12.5 percent of the total population. Poverty rates were highest for families headed by single women, particularly if they were African-American or Hispanic. In 2001, for example, each group had a poverty rate greater than 35 percent.

Causes and Effects of Poverty

Economic principles cannot explain why there is more poverty among some groups than others. The answer lies in past patterns of social behavior—particularly in the history of discrimination. The direct and indirect causes of poverty in the United States include unfavorable economic conditions, unstable home environments, illness or disability, substance abuse, and inadequate education.

stop and think

Poverty rates fluctuate over time and can be higher for one group than for another. Explain these differences in the poverty rate in a paragraph in your notebook. As you continue to read, list what governments can do to cushion the effects of poverty.

What is clear is that people who are poor are often caught in a vicious cycle. They are poor because they do not have the skills to be productive, but because they are poor, they don't have the money to acquire the skills necessary to get a good job. To make matters worse, they also lack the money to provide their children with the kind of education that will help them find good-paying jobs in the future.

One cause of poverty is discrimination. The differences in income along racial and ethnic lines have led many to believe that historic and ongoing racism is responsible for much of the poverty in the United States today. They point to limited job opportunities for some races and ethnic groups. They also note that 21 percent of all children in the United States live in poverty, but 46 percent of African-American children and 40 percent of Hispanic children live in poverty. Those children are at risk of continuing the cycle of poverty.

The Government and Anti-poverty Programs

Local, state, and federal governments have created a number of programs to help the poor. Most of those programs are collectively known as **welfare** programs. These are social and economic programs that provide regular assistance to individuals and families based on need.

Federal job training programs and welfare-to-work programs help people learn the skills that are needed to find good employment.

Some welfare programs provide income assistance to needy families. For example, Temporary Aid to Needy Families (TANF) is a monthly cash assistance program for poor families with children under the age of eighteen. A family of three (a parent and two children) may qualify for TANF if their income before taxes is under $806 a month and they have less than $1,000 in assets. The family is eligible for cash assistance for just five years. To qualify, an adult with a child over the age of one is required to participate in a work activity. These activities help adults gain the experience needed to find a good job and become self-sufficient.

Other programs provide assistance to poor families but do not make direct cash payments. The **food stamp** program allows needy individuals to exchange stamps for food products at authorized stores. In some places, the Electronic Benefits Transfer (EBT) has replaced actual food stamps with a debit card. The federal government pays for the benefit, and individual states pay the costs of determining eligibility and distributing the stamps. Individuals who work for low wages, are unemployed or work part-time, receive public assistance, are elderly or disabled and have a small income, or are homeless are among those eligible for food stamps.

In some areas, food stamps are being replaced with a debit card as part of the Electronic Benefits Transfer program.

The food stamp program is not the only government-supported food program, but it is the most significant. Other programs include the Child and Adult Care Food Program (CACFP), which provides federal grants of money and food to nonprofit elementary and secondary schools and child-care institutions so that they can serve milk, well-balanced meals, and snacks to children. In addition, the Special Supplemental Food Program for Women, Infants, and Children (WIC) provides food for pregnant and nursing women, as well as for infants and children under the age of five.

Individual states have also developed a variety of social service programs to help people in need. These programs provide services that range from job training to programs designed to prevent child abuse.

Some working families are also eligible for the **Earned Income Tax Credit** (EITC). It is a reduction in the amount of income tax a worker owes. If the EITC is greater than the amount of taxes withheld from his or her salary, the individual receives a refund. Who qualifies? In 2005, individuals and families qualified if they had earned incomes under

- $11,490 ($12,490 if married) with no child in the household

- $30,338 ($31,338 if married) with one child in the household

- $34,458 ($35,458 if married filing jointly) with more than one child in the household

How successful are these programs? The answer is complicated. When compared to 19 other wealthy, industrialized nations, the record is mixed. According to *The State of Working America 2004/2005*, the United States ranked highest in per capita income, but had greater inequalities in income than the other nations. The U.S. also had the highest overall poverty rate and the highest child poverty rate. More disturbing, the U.S. had the highest rate of permanent poverty among the 20 countries surveyed. That means that it was harder for Americans to get out of poverty than it was for people in other countries.

Putting It All Together

What are some actions you think the United States should take to reduce its rate of permanent poverty? Write a persuasive paragraph expressing your opinion. Be sure to give facts from the lesson and use logic to support your views.

Chapter Summary

- Types of inflation include **demand-pull inflation** and **cost-push** (or supply-shock) **inflation**. The most severe form of inflation is **hyperinflation**.

- The **Federal Reserve System** directs the monetary policy of the United States.

- The **unemployment rate** is calculated monthly by the Bureau of Labor Statistics. **Structural unemployment** is considered less serious than **frictional unemployment**. **Seasonal unemployment** and **cyclical unemployment** signal a temporary rather than a permanent change.

- An economy reaches **full employment** when its unemployment rate is less than 5 percent.

- **Unemployment insurance** is an example of an **automatic stabilizer**.

- **Poverty** is measured by the size of a family's income.

- A **Lorenz curve** shows income distribution in a country.

- The government uses **poverty thresholds** to determine the poverty rate and **poverty guidelines** to decide who is eligible for government programs that fight poverty.

- The government **welfare** programs for individuals and families are based on need. Some provide money assistance, while others, like the **food stamp** program, do not make cash payments. The **Earned Income Tax Credit** reduces the amount of income taxed by a qualifying worker.

Chapter Review

1 Use your notes to compare inflation, unemployment, and poverty. What similarities do you notice in both causes and effects? How do you account for differences?

2 Review the business cycle (see Chapter 16). At what points in the cycle are inflation, unemployment, and poverty most likely to increase? At what points in the cycle are they least likely to grow? What do your answers suggest about the way the three are related to one another and to the business cycle?

Skill Builder

Read Special-Purpose Maps

Special-purpose maps use lines, color, and symbols to provide information about a particular place. The following steps will help you read a special-purpose map:

- Read the title to determine what the map is trying to show.

- Read the legend to find out what the symbols stand for.

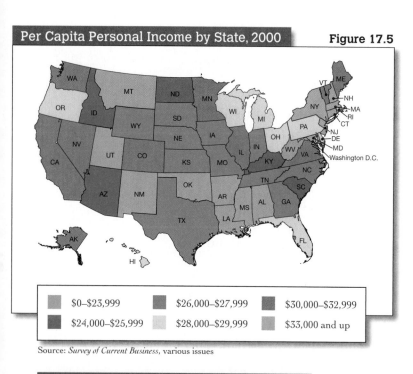

Figure 17.5

Per Capita Personal Income by State, 2000

▨ $0–$23,999	▨ $26,000–$27,999	▨ $30,000–$32,999
▨ $24,000–$25,999	▨ $28,000–$29,999	▨ $33,000 and up

Source: *Survey of Current Business*, various issues

Average Annual Percentage Growth of Real Per Capita Personal Income, 1990–2000

Figure 17.6

▨ Negative growth	▨ 1.0%–1.24%	▨ 1.50%–1.74%
▨ 0%–0.99%	▨ 1.25%–1.49%	▨ 1.75%–1.99%
		▨ 2.0+%

Source: *Survey of Current Business*, various issues

The government calculates a state's per capita personal income by dividing the total state income by its population. It uses that information to make comparisons with other states and with growth in previous years.

Study both maps carefully and then use them to answer the following questions.

1 Which map would you use to find your state's per capita income?

2 Which map would you use to find out how quickly your state's per capita income grew between 1990 and 2000?

3 Which map's information takes inflation into account?

4 Write a sentence that sums up what you learned about your state from the two maps.

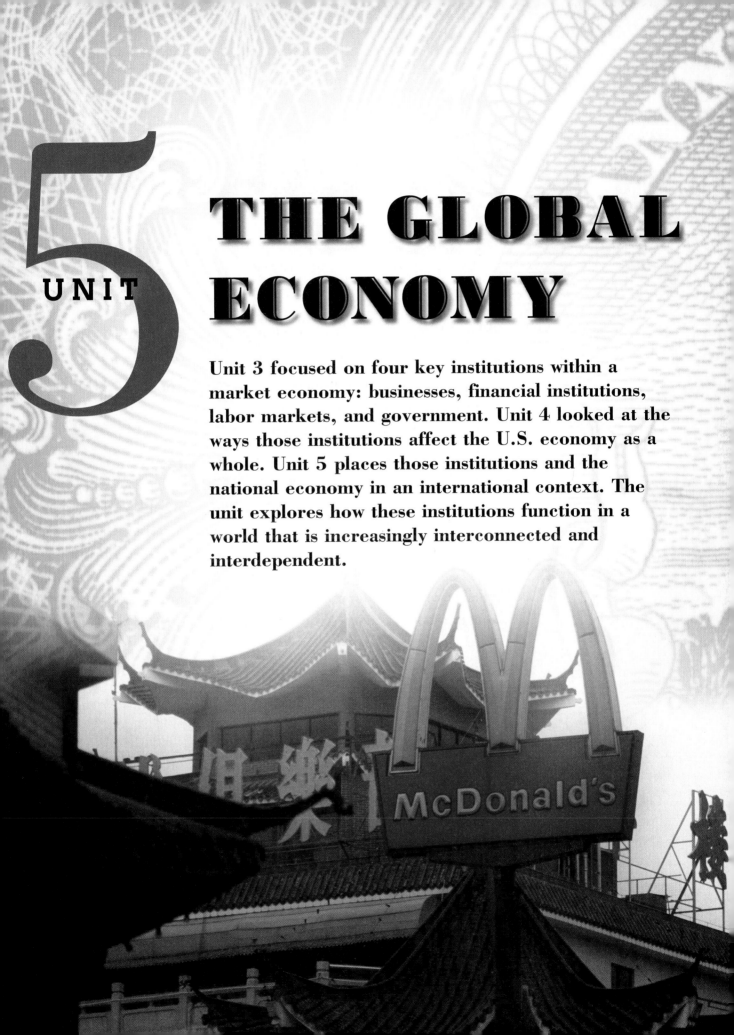

5 UNIT

THE GLOBAL ECONOMY

Unit 3 focused on four key institutions within a market economy: businesses, financial institutions, labor markets, and government. Unit 4 looked at the ways those institutions affect the U.S. economy as a whole. Unit 5 places those institutions and the national economy in an international context. The unit explores how these institutions function in a world that is increasingly interconnected and interdependent.

Chapter

18 INTERNATIONAL TRADE

Getting Focused

Skim this chapter to predict what you will be learning.

- Read the lesson titles and subheadings.
- Look at the illustrations and read the captions.
- Examine the graphs and charts.
- Review the vocabulary words and terms.

In this chapter, you will learn about international trade—trade among the nations of the world. Think about what you know about trade in general and international trade in particular. How does trade with other nations affect the things you and your family buy? How does it affect jobs in your community and your chances for a successful future? What questions do you have about international trade? In your notebook, record your ideas and your questions.

Hamburg, Germany, is a center for international shipping. Trade between nations has been occurring for thousands of years. However, with advances in technology, nations are better able to import and export goods and services.

20

Globalization and Trade

Thinking on Your Own

Select five terms from the vocabulary list. Write them in your notebook. Under each term, write what you think it means. As you encounter each term, correct or add to your definition.

People in distant lands have been trading with one another for thousands of years. Long ago, the goods that were sold in world markets were rare and therefore very valuable. Many of these goods—items like salt, gold, jewels, spices, iron, or cotton—were valuable because they were in great demand but were produced in only a few places in the world.

In recent years, trade has grown dramatically. The volume today, for example, is 20 times greater than it was just 50 years ago. This growth led to a dramatic increase in per capita GDP in many nations, including the United States.

focus your reading

Explain the two main influences on globalization.

List five ways nations have tried to limit international trade.

Describe how nations encourage international trade.

vocabulary

globalization	protectionist
integration	tariff
policy	quota
export	intellectual property
import	

Globalization

Globalization is the **integration** of economic activities through a market and across borders. Economists use the word *integration* to describe the creation of a single world market through the free flow of goods, services, labor, and capital. Two important forces influence the integration of national economies: technology and government policies.

Technological advances The ability to transport resources and other goods safely and cheaply is important in all markets. Buyers and sellers also need accurate and timely information.

That is one reason why the Europeans who settled in North America in the 1600s and 1700s made their homes along the Atlantic coast or a navigable river.

In the mid-1800s, railroads created regional markets—and later, national markets—by cutting the cost and increasing the speed with which goods were transported from place to place. The development of clipper ships in the 1840s had a similar effect on international trade.

Clipper ships were designed to carry small but profitable cargo over long distances at high speeds. At a time when most ships sailed 150 miles in one day, clippers traveled about 250 miles per day. Some covered more than 400 miles in a single day. They carried not only gold from California and tea from China but also ice from the ponds and rivers of New England. Boston, Massachusetts, was the center of an international ice trade. In 1846, Boston shipped 65,000 tons of ice to ports in countries as far away as India, Australia, and China. Ten years later, clippers carried more than twice as much ice to Asia and beyond. Speed was essential to the trade. If a ship took too long to reach harbor, its profits literally melted away.

The masts on clipper ships could reach as high as a 20-story building. The crew controlled those sails with a complicated web of rigging.

Clipper ships—and later, steamships—also carried the mail. As a result, information moved more quickly than ever before. By the mid-1800s, the news also traveled by telegraph. This invention could bring information to distant places almost

Timing the Spread of Technologies

Figure 18.1

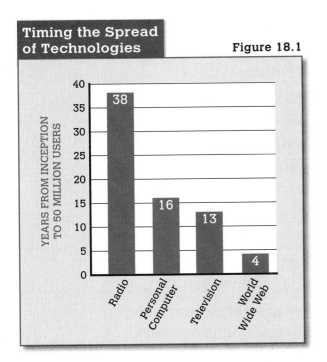

instantaneously. At first, telegraph lines linked only large cities within the nation, but gradually they crossed national borders. In 1866, workers completed the first transatlantic telegraph cable. Americans could now exchange information with Europeans in a matter of minutes. The telegraph also linked stock exchanges, such as those in Philadelphia and New York.

By the 1900s, such inventions as the automobile, airplane, telephone, radio, television, and computer were having similar effects. New technologies are also taking hold more quickly than ever before. Figure 18.1 shows how long it took for four twentieth-century inventions to reach large numbers of people. Notice that 38 years passed before 50 million people had easy access to a radio. It took just four years for the World Wide Web to acquire the same number of users.

Today, letters and packages can reach almost anywhere in the world within 24 hours. News and other information travel even faster at little or no cost.

stop and think

Look carefully at Figure 18.1. Why do you think the World Wide Web spread more quickly than the three earlier inventions? How does the Web encourage global connections? Share your ideas with a partner.

Governments and Trade

Improvements in transportation and communication encourage global connections. However, those improvements are just one part of the process. Government policies also make a difference. A **policy** is a plan of action on an issue—in this case, international trade.

Over the years, governments have both discouraged and encouraged trade with other nations. At times, some have taken both positions at the same time. That is, they encouraged **exports**—sales to other countries—even as they discouraged **imports**—purchases from other countries.

Barriers to trade Government policies that seek to limit imports are often called **protectionist**. Their goal is to protect local businesses from foreign competition. Some protectionists see restrictions as a way of helping a few industries for a limited amount of time—just long enough to allow a new industry to gain enough strength to compete with foreign-made products. Others see restrictions as a way to protect workers and their jobs. They consider the production of goods by foreign, low-wage workers to be unfair competition.

To limit or stop imports, governments rely on tariffs, quotas, and subsidies. **Tariffs** are taxes on imports. In the 1800s, the government got most of its revenue from tariffs. Those taxes were not only a source of government funds but also a way of protecting local businesses. Tariffs make imported goods more expensive than locally made products, because the tax is passed on to consumers in the form of higher prices.

Among other things, the International Tribunal for the Law of the Sea enforces quotas placed on bluefin tuna, shown here at a Tokyo fish market.

Quotas limit how much of a particular good can be brought into a country during a specific period of time. These goods are limited to protect local businesses. In the past, the United States has placed quotas on milk, cream, brooms, ethyl alcohol, anchovies, tuna, and olives. The nation has also placed quotas on peanuts, cotton, tobacco, sugar, and syrup.

Subsidies are government payments to the producers or consumers of a good or service. Subsidies are intended to encourage local production of a product. They can also reduce the cost of that product to consumers. As recently as 2002, Congress passed a law that increased subsidies for soybeans, wheat, and corn. The law also contained subsidies to dairy farmers, as well as to those who plant peanuts, lentils, and chickpeas.

The United States and a number of other nations also place limits on the sale of technology and other capital resources to other countries. In addition,

many limit the movement of workers from one country to another. A nation's immigration laws are often written to protect the jobs of citizens. The United States is no exception.

Other countries have limited not only who may enter the country but also who may leave. In the years after World War II, for example, Communist countries like the former Soviet Union, China, and Cuba placed strict limits on the freedom of their people not only to move to another country but also to travel freely.

Toward Freer Trade

Those who favor freer trade believe that protective tariffs do more harm than good. For example, some economists point out that during the 1980s and early 1990s, the United States tried to limit steel imports to protect American steelworkers. As a result, the price of everything made from steel—including automobiles—went up. The high price of steel hurt American manufacturers who used steel. Unable to compete with products made abroad with cheaper steel, some firms had to lay off workers. Others built factories abroad to take advantage of the less expensive foreign steel. As a result, the nation lost some manufacturing jobs in order to "save" jobs in the steel industry. People who support free trade argue that retraining programs would have been an easier and more effective solution to the problems in the steel industry.

When a steel mill in Farrell, Pennsylvania, closed its doors, local residents lost jobs, businesses closed, and the population of the community declined.

Protectionist policies have other unintended consequences, as well. In 1930, the United States was in a serious recession. Congress insisted that international trade was responsible for the loss of jobs. Too many Americans were buying foreign goods. Lawmakers decided to raise tariffs on a wide variety of goods. They increased some tariffs by as much as 50 percent.

Free trade economists around the world protested the new tariffs. So did 36 nations. Despite these efforts, Congress

recall

A **recession** is a period of little or no economic growth and widespread unemployment.

passed the law. It had an immediate effect. Fewer imports entered the nation. At the same time, other nations retaliated by raising their own tariffs. World trade dropped by two-thirds. Many economists believe that those tariffs helped bring about the Great Depression of the 1930s. After World War II, many people were determined to knock down such barriers to free trade.

In 1944, the United States and other nations agreed to rebuild a global economy on the basis of freer trade. Each nation would also create a "safety net" of worker protections to reduce unemployment and poverty. To achieve those goals, the countries that founded the United Nations also formed the International Monetary Fund (IMF) and the World Bank. These financial institutions loan money to help nations develop their economies and participate more fully in international trade. The IMF works to foster global monetary cooperation, secure financial stability, facilitate international trade, promote high employment and sustainable economic growth, and reduce poverty. The World Bank provides assistance to developing countries around the world in order to reduce global poverty and improve standards of living. Those same countries also created the General Agreement on Tariffs and Trade (GATT) to set rules for trade agreements. The aim was to reduce tariffs and ban quotas on imports.

By the 1990s, 117 nations were trading under GATT agreements. In 1995, those countries updated the GATT by creating a new group called the World Trade Organization (WTO). The WTO enforces the old GATT agreements. In addition, it has expanded those agreements to include trade not only in goods but also in services. By the 1990s, people in distant places no longer traded only in merchandise. They also exchanged services. New trade agreements now cover the work of banks, insurance firms, hotel chains, telecommunications companies, tour operators, and transport companies that do business abroad. The

In 2005, Paul Wolfowitz, head of the World Bank, visited Nigeria—a country that benefits from the Bank's programs.

Protestors demonstrated against the WTO in Seattle in 2002.

WTO also protects **intellectual property**—ideas, designs, and other creative ventures. Rules now govern how countries handle copyrights, patents, trademarks, and industrial designs.

A number of nations have created regional agreements that promote trade within smaller areas. The most important such agreement is the European Union (EU). The EU is made of 25 independent nations (as of 2005) that trade freely with one another. The goal of the EU is to build a single European market. To achieve that goal, the EU has its own currency—the euro.

In 1993, the United States, Mexico, and Canada also formed a regional trade agreement—the North American Free Trade Agreement (NAFTA). It is designed to reduce barriers to trade among the three nations. By 2002, Mexico and Canada accounted for 36 percent of total U.S. exports. Figure 18.2 shows the large increase in U.S. exports of processed foods and beverages.

In 2005, the United States also joined the Central American-Dominican Republic Free Trade Agreement (CAFTA-DR), a comprehensive trade agreement that includes Costa Rica, the Dominican Republic, El Salvador, Guatemala, Honduras, and Nicaragua. Some people regard CAFTA-DR as a first step toward a Free Trade Area of the Americas (FTAA). Such an agreement would include 34 nations.

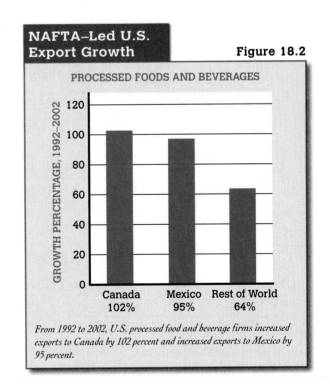

NAFTA–Led U.S. Export Growth

Figure 18.2

PROCESSED FOODS AND BEVERAGES

GROWTH PERCENTAGE, 1992–2002

Canada 102% Mexico 95% Rest of World 64%

From 1992 to 2002, U.S. processed food and beverage firms increased exports to Canada by 102 percent and increased exports to Mexico by 95 percent.

Putting It All Together

Make a two-column chart in your notebook. Title one column "Barriers to Trade" and the other column "Promoting Freer Trade." In each column, list at least three policies or organizations designed to bring about that outcome. Share your work with a partner.

Multinational Corporations and Competition

Thinking on Your Own

You may have heard the term *multinational corporation*. In your notebook, write a one-sentence definition of this term and list three corporations that you think are multinational. As you read, check to see if your definition and list are correct.

A multinational corporation (MNC) is a firm that has factories, offices, or branch plants in two or more countries. It is, in effect, a citizen of more than one country at one time—it is subject to laws of several nations, as well as to international laws. Microsoft, Ford, Sony, and Wal-Mart are all multinationals. As the global economy has expanded, so has the number of MNCs. Multinationals are responsible for much of the world's **cross-border**, or international, investments.

Characteristics of Multinationals

In 1969, there were about 7,300 multinationals. By the year 2000, the number had grown to more than 63,000 firms with about 690,000 foreign affiliates. A **foreign affiliate** is a firm that is owned wholly or in part by a multinational.

Multinationals often participate in cross-border trading through their foreign affiliates. That is, multinationals and their affiliates purchase and sell one another a wide variety of services. These include financial services, management and

consulting aid, research and development, computer support, and payments of royalties and license fees. Such exchanges are known as **intra-firm trades**. The prefix *intra-* means "within" — in this case, "within a firm." Intra-firm trade may allow an MNC to keep down the cost of distributing goods abroad or acquiring resources. It may also help the firm integrate the production process on a global scale. Some economists think intra-firm trades protect an MNC from competitive forces in certain markets. As Figure 18.3 shows, both intra-firm sales

Figure 18.3 A

U.S. Sales of Services to Foreigners

	Total private services	Transportation	Royalties and license fees	Other private services								
				Total	Financial services	Business, professional, and technical services						Film and television tape rentals
						Total business, professional, and technical services	Computer and information services	Management and consulting services	Research and development and testing services	Operational leasing	Other business, professional, and technical services	
Total receipts:												
1997	52.0	0.4	24.5	27.1	2.3	22.4	1.6	N/A	N/A	1.5	19.3	2.4
1998	54.9	0.4	26.3	28.2	2.7	22.9	1.3	N/A	N/A	1.7	20.0	2.5
1999	62.6	0.5	29.3	32.8	4.0	26.4	1.2	N/A	N/A	2.3	22.9	2.4
2000	66.9	0.5	30.5	35.9	3.8	29.8	1.1	N/A	N/A	2.1	26.6	2.2
2001	69.0	0.6	29.2	39.3	4.1	33.0	1.3	2.1	5.5	2.2	22.0	2.2
2002	76.7	0.7	32.7	43.3	4.1	36.5	1.7	2.4	6.1	2.5	23.8	2.7
2003	85.1	0.7	35.9	48.5	5.1	40.6	2.1	2.4	5.5	2.6	27.9	2.7

* Less than $50 million   N/A Not Available

Figure 18.3 B

U.S. Purchases of Services from Foreigners

	Total private services	Transportation	Royalties and license fees	Other private services								
				Total	Financial services	Business, professional, and technical services						Film and television tape rentals
						Total business, professional, and technical services	Computer and information services	Management and consulting services	Research and development and testing services	Operational leasing	Other business, professional, and technical services	
Total payments:												
1997	24.8	0.4	6.7	17.6	2.8	14.8	0.8	N/A	N/A	0.9	13.1	(*)
1998	28.4	0.4	8.5	19.4	4.2	15.3	0.9	N/A	N/A	0.9	13.5	(*)
1999	36.6	0.4	10.4	25.8	5.9	19.8	3.0	N/A	N/A	1.1	15.8	0.1
2000	41.7	0.4	12.5	28.8	7.1	21.7	2.6	N/A	N/A	1.0	18.0	(*)
2001	43.6	0.5	13.2	29.8	6.7	23.2	2.8	1.8	1.7	1.0	15.9	(*)
2002	47.4	0.5	15.1	31.8	5.3	26.6	2.9	2.2	1.5	0.8	19.1	(*)
2003	52.5	0.6	16.4	35.5	5.6	29.9	3.3	2.5	1.6	0.7	21.7	(*)

* Less than $50 million   N/A Not Available

and purchases of services by firms in the United States are growing faster than U.S. cross-border trades.

Multinationals directly employ more than 90 million workers worldwide. Those workers produce about one-fourth of the world's gross product. The 1,000 largest companies account for 80 percent of the world's industrial output. Within the United States alone, American multinationals and their foreign affiliates employ about 30 million people, or more than 20 percent of the civilian workforce. U.S.-based multinationals account for 21.8 million workers, and their foreign affiliates account for the additional 5.2 million. U.S. affiliates of foreign MNCs employed 5.2 million people in the United States—about 5 percent of the civilian workforce.

Top 25 Multinationals in 2001

Figure 18.4

Corporation (Home Economy)	Industry	Foreign Assets	Assets	Total Sales	Employees
Vodafone (UK)	Telecommunications	187,792	207,458	32,744	67,178
General Electric (US)	Electrical and electronic equipment	180,031	495,210	125,913	310,000
BP (UK)	Petroleum expl./ref./distr.	111,207	141,158	175,389	110,150
Vivendi Universal (FR)	Diversified	91,120	123,156	51,423	381,504
Deutsche Telekom AG (GE)	Telecommunications	90,657	145,802	43,309	257,058
ExxonMobil Corporation (US)	Petroleum expl./ref./distr.	89,426	143,174	209,417	97,300
Ford Motor Company (US)	Motor vehicles	81,169	276,543	162,412	354,431
General Motors (US)	Motor vehicles	75,379	323,969	177,260	365,000
Royal Dutch/Shell Group (UK/NL)	Petroleum expl./ref./distr.	73,492	111,543	135,711	89,939
Total Fina Elf (FR)	Petroleum expl./ref./distr.	70,030	78,500	94,418	122,025
Suez (FR)	Electricity, gas, and water	69,345	79,280	37,975	188,050
Toyota Motor Corporation (JP)	Motor vehicles	68,400	144,793	108,808	246,702
Fiat Spa (ITA)	Motor vehicles	48,749	89,264	52,002	198,764
Telefonica SA (SP)	Telecommunications	48,122	77,011	27,775	161,527
Volkswagen Group (GE)	Motor vehicles	47,480	92,520	79,376	324,413
ChevronTexaco Corp. (US)	Petroleum expl./ref./distr.	44,943	77,572	104,409	67,569
Hutchinson Whampoa Ltd. (HK)	Diversified	40,989	55,281	11,415	77,253
News Corporation (AUS)	Media	35,650	40,007	15,087	33,800
Honda Motor Co., Ltd. (JP)	Motor vehicles	35,257	52,056	55,955	120,600
E.On (GE)	Electricity, gas, and water	33,990	87,755	71,419	151,953
Nestle SA (CH)	Food and beverages	33,065	55,821	50,717	229,765
RWE Group (GE)	Electricity, gas, and water	32,809	81,024	58,039	155,634
IBM (US)	Electrical and electronic equipment	32,800	88,313	85,866	319,876
ABB (CH)	Machinery and equipment	30,588	32,305	19,382	156,865
Unilever (UK/NL)	Diversified	30,529	46,922	46,803	279,000

Those numbers can be misleading. Most multinational companies employ fewer than 250 workers, and some companies are even smaller. Most of these relatively small multinationals are located in Europe and East Asia. Denmark, for example, is headquarters for nearly 9,400 multinationals, and South Korea is home to 7,460 MNCs.

By comparison, only about 3,380 MNCs have their main offices in the United States. However, the largest multinationals are based in the United States and other nations with large economies. American, European, and Japanese firms account for 93 of the top 100 multinationals.

A Global Supply Chain

A **supply chain** consists of a firm and the various companies that supply it with key natural, human, and capital resources. Each supplies a step in the process of providing a good or service. Most firms rely on local companies, but multinationals

The Ford Motor Company manufactures the popular European Ka at a factory in Spain.

have global supply chains that include both intra-firm and cross-border investment and trade.

How does the chain work? Automobile manufacturers are good examples. Almost all are multinationals. Ford Motor Company, for example, has assembly plants and parts-making operations not only in the U.S., Canada, and Mexico, but also in Thailand, the Philippines, Russia, Colombia, India, Turkey, China, Brazil, and Argentina. The same is true of foreign automakers. They, too, rely on a mix of domestic and imported components. As a result, a car made by an American company includes parts manufactured by firms not only in the United States but also in Japan, Canada, and other countries. The car itself may be assembled in Mexico.

In every country, an automaker has to adapt its cars to local demand. Ford and other U.S. automakers produced small cars for the European market long before they made or sold such cars in the United States. Why? In Europe, gas prices have always been high and space limited. So small, economical cars made sense. In the U.S., gas was relatively inexpensive for many years. As a result, Americans were more interested in size and comfort than economy.

The choices that multinationals make are similar to those that other firms make. They also want to make a profit. They, too, deal with the problem of scarcity by maximizing their resources. As a result, they, too, make trade-offs. The laws of supply and demand and diminishing returns apply to them just as they apply to other firms. The difference is in scale. Multinationals make their choices in world markets. The opportunities are greater, but so are the risks. A war, a labor dispute, or a natural disaster in a remote part of the world can affect every part of a multinational's supply chain.

Putting It All Together

Review the notes you took about corporations when you read Chapter 8. How is a multinational corporation similar to other corporations? How does it differ from other corporations? Write a paragraph explaining those similarities and differences.

Finance and Trade

Thinking on Your Own

As you read this lesson, turn the subheadings into questions and then read to find answers to those questions.

When you buy a movie ticket or a bag of popcorn, you pay for your purchase in dollars. How do you pay for services or goods when you have dollars and the seller wants euros or pesos or yuan?

Foreign Exchanges

To change dollars into pesos, you will need to consult the **foreign exchange** market. It is the place where currency—money or other units of exchange issued by a nation or group of nations—is bought and sold. The **foreign exchange rate** is the price of one country's currency in terms of another country's currency. The rate is reported in two ways. Suppose you have a dollar and you want to know how much that dollar is worth in pesos. You determine that one dollar is equal to 10.8 pesos. Later that same day, a peso is equal to about nine cents (0.09 US dollar). If you checked the exchange rate the following week or even the next day, the rate might be higher or lower.

focus your reading

How do the laws of supply and demand affect the foreign exchange rate?

Describe the relationship between the foreign exchange rate and the balance of trade.

How do the intra-firm trades of multinationals affect the balance of trade?

vocabulary

foreign exchange

foreign exchange rate

fixed rate of exchange

devalue

flexible exchange rate

depreciate

balance of trade

trade surplus

trade deficit

Before 1971, exchange rates were fixed. They did not change daily. The foreign exchange market had a **fixed rate of exchange**. Under this system, governments set the value of their currency in relation to the amount of gold each nation held in reserve. With a fixed rate of exchange, governments, importers, exporters, and travelers knew exactly how much their own money was worth. The system also allowed the

Federal Reserve and other central banks to **devalue**, or lower, the worth of the nation's currency in relation to other currencies.

Today, most nations use a **flexible exchange rate** system—one in which the prices of various currencies are based on the supply and demand for goods that can be purchased with that currency. For example, if the quantity of American dollars demanded by European sellers is greater than the quantity supplied by American consumers, the dollar will be more expensive in relation to the euro.

On the other hand, if the quantity supplied is greater than the quantity demanded, the price of a dollar will fall in relation to the euro. Whenever the price of a dollar or other currency falls, that currency **depreciates**, or goes down in value, in comparison with other currencies.

EXCHANGE RATES

		WE BUY AT	WE SELL AT
AUSTRIA	ATS	146	0
BELGIUM	BFR	0	0
CANADA	CAD	13	12
UNITED KINGDOM	GBP	6	8
FRANCE	FRF	6.9	
GERMANY	DEM	4	0
EURO		11	12
ITALY	ITL	0	0
JAPAN	JPY	11	10
MEXICO	PESO	0	0
SPAIN	PTS	17	
SWITZERLAND	CHF	3	3

Exchange rates are listed daily in newspapers and airports around the world.

stop and think

Assume that you are about to take a trip abroad. Would you prefer a fixed rate of exchange for your currency or a flexible exchange rate? What would be the advantages of each? As you read ahead, think about the effect that the exchange rate has on international trade.

Balance of Trade

A currency's exchange rate affects the **balance of trade**—the difference between the value of a nation's exports and imports. If a nation's currency depreciates, the nation is likely to export more goods, because its products will be less expensive for other nations to buy. If a nation's currency increases in value, its exports will be more expensive.

When the value of goods leaving a nation is greater than the value of those entering, the balance of trade is positive. The nation has a **trade surplus**. This means that the value of

exported goods is greater than the value of imported goods. If the value of goods entering a nation is greater than the value of those leaving, the balance of trade is negative. The nation has a **trade deficit**. This means that the value of imported goods is greater than the value of exported goods.

A trade deficit is not necessarily bad for a country's economy. A trade deficit allows foreign businesses to invest in the economy of the United States. This investment supports industry and creates jobs for U.S. citizens.

Figure 18.5, on page 312, shows the U.S. balance of trade in goods and services from 1975 to 2005. Notice that the nation has not had a trade surplus since 1975. A nation's

Applying for a U.S. Passport

To travel to another country, you need a passport. It allows you to leave and later reenter the country freely.

1. Apply in Person If

- you are applying for a U.S. passport for the first time.
- your previous passport was lost, stolen, or damaged.
- your previous passport has expired or was issued more than 15 years ago.
- your previous passport has expired and it was issued when you were under age sixteen.
- your name has changed since your passport was issued and you do not have a legal document formally changing your name.

For All Minors Age Fourteen to Seventeen:

- You must appear in person.
- For security reasons, parental consent may be requested.
- If you do not have identification of your own, your parent or guardian must accompany you and present identification.

2. To Apply in Person for a U.S. Passport, You MUST

- complete an application form available online or at a passport agency. Do **NOT** sign the form until the Passport Acceptance Agent instructs you to do so.
- present proof of U.S. citizenship by presenting a previous U.S. passport or a certified birth certificate issued by the city, county, or state; a consular report of a birth abroad or certification of birth, a naturalization certificate, or a certificate of citizenship.

Checklist

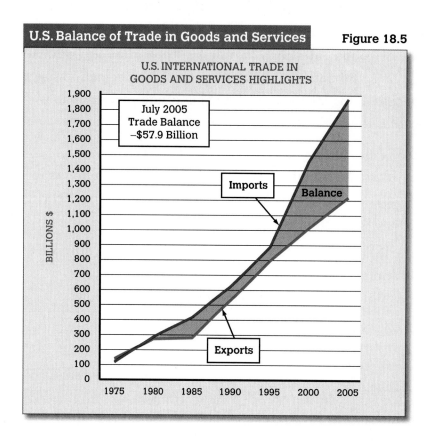

U.S. Balance of Trade in Goods and Services **Figure 18.5**

U.S. INTERNATIONAL TRADE IN
GOODS AND SERVICES HIGHLIGHTS

July 2005
Trade Balance
–$57.9 Billion

Imports

Balance

Exports

BILLIONS $

currency exchange rate can have a powerful effect on the balance of trade. If a country's currency increases in value, that currency is considered strong. A strong currency means that people in other nations are likely to find the country's exports expensive and trade tends to decline. If the currency depreciates in value, it is considered weak. A weak currency means people in other nations are likely to find the country's exports inexpensive and trade tends to increase.

The trade deficit is limited to imports and exports of goods. The nation has a trade surplus in imports and exports of services. Many economists believe that the value of those exports is much higher than Figure 18.5 shows. Why? Governments do not count the intra-firm trades of multinationals. Those trades are mainly service exchanges.

Putting It All Together

Draw two diagrams. The first should show how supply and demand affect a nation's currency exchange rate. The second should show how the nation's currency exchange rate affects balance of trade. Compare your diagrams with those of a partner.

Musical Chairs in the Job Market

Amey Stone writes that globalization is causing lots of layoffs, but hiring is rising, too.

A U.S. labor market that's becoming more like a game of musical chairs is one of the byproducts of globalization, say economists and analysts. As whole classes of jobs— including higher-paid, white-collar professions—move overseas, it's becoming more important than ever for American workers to be able to reinvent themselves, says Nick Colas, director of research at Rochdale Securities, who says he has reinvented his own career on Wall Street several times in the past 10 years. "The average American worker isn't going to have one career for his or her lifetime," he says. "Think about what your key skills are. You're going to have to change careers." . . .

Tim Lewis, a managing director at turnaround consulting firm TRG, is on the front lines of these changes. The struggling companies he works with usually have little choice but to outsource non-core parts of their business or close their doors entirely. That means job cuts for lots of employees.

And while low-wage workers can usually find another job easily (in fact, he says, one of the hardest parts of his job is convincing them to stay when a plant closing is imminent), midlevel workers often have a tough time landing a new spot. For them, the only way to find a job that pays as well as the one they lost may be to relocate, something many are reluctant to do, he notes. . . .

"In my experience, there's always a job out there for a great employee," says Lewis, "but it might not be a great job." The key question for the U.S. labor market going forward, he says, is: "Are we as a country giving people the skills they need so they can be flexible and move from one role to another role?" ■

"Musical Chairs in the Job Market" by Amey Stone. *BusinessWeek Online*, July 28, 2005.

reading for understanding

Why does the writer compare the U.S. job market to a game of musical chairs?

Why are some jobs disappearing?

What advice do the experts have for American workers?

How might that advice apply to you as you prepare for a career?

Chapter Summary

- Through **globalization**, economic activities are **integrated** through markets and across borders.

- Advances in technology and government **policies** influence both **imports** and **exports**.

- **Protectionists** use **tariffs**, **quotas**, and subsidies to limit trade.

- The World Trade Organization sets international rules for trade in goods and services and provides protection for **intellectual property**.

- **Multinational corporations** are responsible for much of the world's **cross-border** investments.

- Multinationals and their **foreign affiliates** exchange services through **intra-firm trades**. As a result of those exchanges, their **supply chain** is global.

- People exchange their own currency for the currency of another country on the **foreign exchange** market.

- The **foreign exchange rate** today is no longer a **fixed rate of exchange**; it is a **flexible exchange rate**.

- Banks can **devalue** the worth of a nation's currency.

- Whenever the price of a dollar or other currency falls, that currency **depreciates** in value.

- A nation's **balance of trade** is determined by whether it has a **trade surplus** or a **trade deficit**.

Chapter Review

1 How do organizations and policies like the World Trade Organization, the European Union, and the North American Free Trade Agreement promote globalization?

2 How do restrictions on trade affect producers of goods and services? Consumers? Workers? The economy as a whole? Give reasons for your answers.

Skill Builder

Analyze a Table

Tables and charts are often used to show comparisons between similar categories of information. Tables usually show numbers in columns or rows. To understand a table, read

- the title, to learn what content is being presented.

- the headings in the top row. They explain how the information is organized.

Figure 18.4, on page 306, is titled "Top 25 Multinationals in 2001." The title raises some questions. In what sense are these companies the top 25? If you read the top row, the numbers show foreign assets, total assets, total sales, and total number of employees. Notice that Vodafone is number one in the world only in terms of its foreign assets.

Figure 18.4

Top 25 Multinationals in 2001					
Corporation (Home Economy)	Industry	Foreign Assets	Assets	Total Sales	Employees
Vodafone (UK)	Telecommunications	187,792	207,458	32,744	67,178
General Electric (US)	Electrical and electronic equipment	180,031	495,210	125,913	310,000
BP (UK)	Petroleum expl./ref./distr.	111,207	141,158	175,389	110,150
Vivendi Universal (FR)	Diversified	91,120	123,156	51,423	381,504
Deutsche Telekom AG (GE)	Telecommunications	90,657	145,802	43,309	257,058
ExxonMobil Corporation (US)	Petroleum expl./ref./distr.	89,426	143,174	209,417	97,300
Ford Motor Company (US)	Motor vehicles	81,169	276,543	162,412	354,431
General Motors (US)	Motor vehicles	75,379	323,969	177,260	365,000
Royal Dutch/Shell Group (UK/NL)	Petroleum expl./ref./distr.	73,492	111,543	135,711	89,939

1 Which company is number one in total assets?

2 Which company is number one in total sales?

3 Which company is number one in total employees?

4 Create two new tables from Figure 18.4. The first should show the top five multinationals in the petroleum industry. The second table should show the top five multinationals in the motor vehicle industry.

Chapter

19 ECONOMIC DEVELOPMENT

Getting Focused

Skim this chapter to predict what you will be learning.

- Read the lesson titles and subheadings.
- Look at the illustrations and read the captions.
- Examine the maps and graphs.
- Review the vocabulary words and terms.

Economic development consists of all of the activities that help a nation produce more goods and services. Examine the headings and subheadings in this chapter. What do they suggest about the ways nations develop their economies? What do they suggest about the effects of little or no economic development? What do the illustrations and graphs suggest? Record your ideas in your notebook.

Open-air markets help fuel the economies of many developing nations, including that of Nigeria.

Industrialized Nations and Developing Nations

Thinking on Your Own

The quality of life in industrialized nations differs greatly from the quality of life in developing nations. Think of three ways in which a person living in an industrialized nation is likely to live a better life than someone living in a developing nation. List these in your notebook.

Wealth is relative. That is, a person's wealth is always measured in relation to the wealth of other people. Suppose, for example, you earn $5 per hour and are struggling to buy the things you need. Someone who earns $20 per hour may seem rich to you, but probably not to someone who earns $100 an hour. A nation's wealth is also relative. It, too, is measured in relation to the wealth of other nations.

Measuring Economic Development

Economists assess how rich a nation is by its ability to produce the goods and services its people want and need. Using a variety of measures, including gross national product (GNP) per capita, economists roughly divide the world into two large groups: industrialized nations and developing nations.

An **industrialized nation** is a high-income nation—one with an annual GNP per capita, or per person, of $9,206 or more in 2003. Most industrialized nations have economies based on manufacturing and trade. Many people in high-income countries also work in service industries, such as

focus your reading

Explain what distinguishes low-income nations from other nations.

How does poverty affect life in developing nations?

Describe what is meant by the vicious cycle of poverty.

vocabulary

industrialized nation

developing nation

life expectancy

malnutrition

refugees

education, banking, transportation, and communications. In the United States, more than one-half of all workers are employed in service industries.

Japan is an example of an industrialized nation.

The World Bank ranks 29 nations with populations of one million people or more as industrialized, or high-income, nations. Among them are the United States, Canada, Japan, the United Kingdom, France, and Germany. The combined population of the industrialized nations is just under one billion, less than one-sixth of the world's population. Yet those nations control 80 percent of the world's resources.

Economists categorize a low- or middle-income nation as a **developing nation**. People in developing nations have a lower standard of living and access to fewer goods and services than

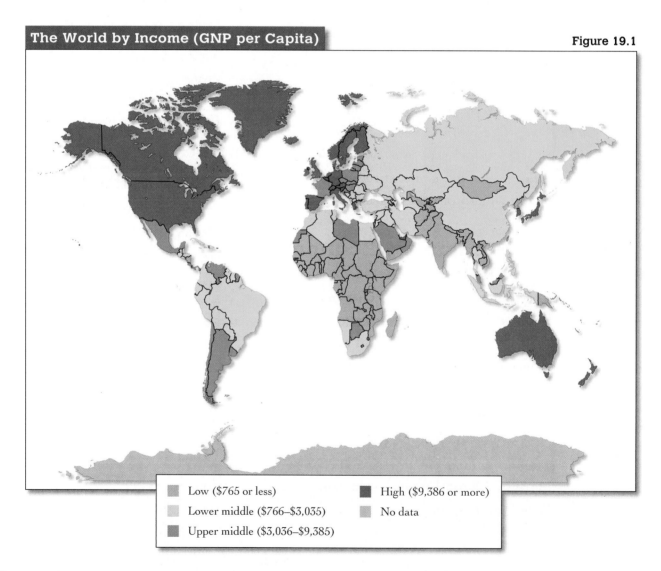

The World by Income (GNP per Capita)

Figure 19.1

■ Low ($765 or less)	■ High ($9,386 or more)
Lower middle ($766–$3,035)	No data
■ Upper middle ($3,036–$9,385)	

do most people in industrialized nations. There are currently about 126 developing nations with populations over one million. Their total population is more than five billion—over five-sixths of the world's population. Those nations control 20 percent of the world's resources.

What is the main difference between a low-income nation and a middle-income nation? In 2003, middle-income nations had an annual GNP per capita of more than $745 but less than $9,206. At that time, there were about 65 middle-income countries with populations of one million or more. Their combined population was approximately 2.7 billion. Figure 19.1, on page 318, shows the countries of the world according to their GNP per capita. Middle-income nations include Mexico, Brazil, China, and Russia.

A country that had an annual GNP per capita in 2003 of $745 or less was considered a low-income nation. In a low-income nation, many people are unable to meet basic needs.

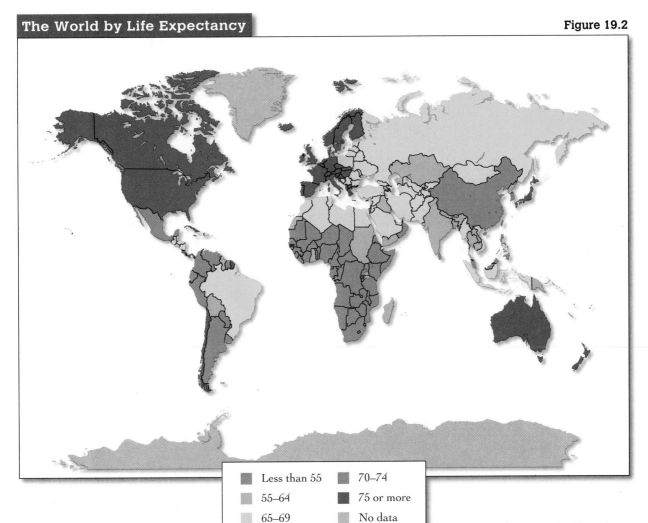

The World by Life Expectancy　　　　Figure 19.2

	Less than 55		70–74
	55–64		75 or more
	65–69		No data

In 2003, the world had about 61 low-income countries in the world with a combined population of about 2.5 billion. Among those nations were India, Indonesia, Haiti, and Sudan.

In most developing nations, poverty is widespread. Definitions of poverty vary from place to place. Like wealth, poverty is relative. However, people worldwide generally agree that absolute poverty means that an individual or family lacks the income to maintain a minimum diet. Figure 19.2, on page 319, shows one result of absolute poverty—a shorter life span. The map shows the life expectancy of babies born in 2000 in both industrialized and developing nations. **Life expectancy** is an estimate of how long a baby born in a particular year can expect to live. As Figure 19.2 shows, people in developing nations have a significantly shorter life span than those in industrialized nations.

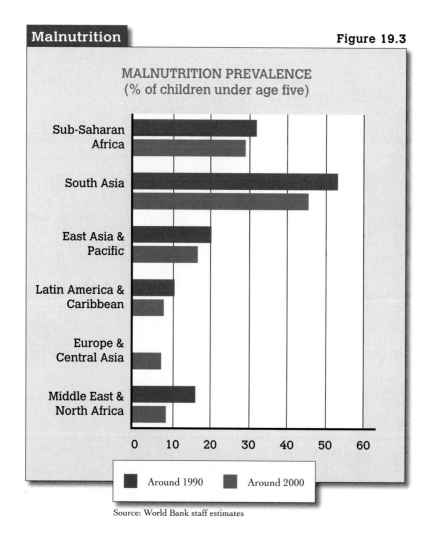

Malnutrition **Figure 19.3**

Source: World Bank staff estimates

People who are very poor do not have a long life span because they do not always get enough food or medical care. Figure 19.3, on page 320, shows **malnutrition** as a serious problem in developing countries. In 2000, about 30 percent of all children in sub-Saharan African nations—African nations south of the Sahara Desert—and more than 45 percent in South Asia were malnourished. Because those children do not get enough to eat, they are physically smaller than other children. They also develop more slowly, enter school later, and do not perform as well when they are in school.

stop and think

Using Figure 19.1, on page 318, as your source of information, write a sentence summarizing the relative wealth of nations on each continent. Which continents are home to mostly industrialized nations? Which continents are home to mostly developing nations? Which continents have the highest GNP per capita? Which have the lowest GNP per capita?

Poverty in a Rich World

Of the six billion people in the world at the end of the twentieth century, almost one-half—about 2.8 billion people—lived on less than the equivalent of US$2 a day, and about 1.2 billion of them lived on less than US$1 a day.

Most of the world's poor live in South Asia (more than 40 percent), sub-Saharan Africa (nearly 25 percent), and East Asia (about 23 percent). Almost one-half live in just two nations—China and India. The highest rate of poverty is in sub-Saharan Africa, which has almost half of its population living on less than US$1 a day.

The existence of widespread poverty in much of the world has consequences. In a world in which every country is linked to other nations, a problem in one place inevitably affects the rest of the world. The problems associated with poverty—including crime, disease, and violence—spread across borders and affect even the most distant places. The spread of diseases like AIDS is one example of the problem. Another is the number of **refugees** in the world—people who flee their homeland to escape hunger, political unrest, or persecution.

Many economists speak of poverty as a vicious cycle. They argue that developing nations are poor because the people in those nations are unable to save and invest. Without investment, countries are unable to develop their economies and improve their welfare, causing more poverty, more dissatisfaction, and more political instability. Can the cycle be broken?

Most economists believe it can. Poverty is not inevitable. It can be reduced, and even ended, through economic development. For example, in the 1990s, the countries of East Asia used not only their own savings, but also foreign loans and investments, to build factories, roads, hospitals, and schools. Through that process, they reduced the percentage of people living below US$2 a day from 29 percent in 1990 to about 15 percent in 2000. In China alone, nearly 150 million people were able to raise their incomes above the poverty line.

Poverty affects people the world over, including residents of Tirana, Albania.

Yet in other parts of the world, poverty increased in the 1990s. In sub-Saharan Africa, the rate of poverty and the number of poor people increased from 47 percent to 49 percent, or by 74 million. In relative terms, poverty grew even more quickly in eastern Europe and central Asia. The countries in this part of the world were in the process of reforming their economies from Communist state-run systems to market-oriented systems. As a result of those changes, poverty increased from 0.2 percent to 5.1 percent, and the number of poor people rose from one million to 24 million.

Putting It All Together

Look again at the list of differences between industrialized and developing nations that you made at the beginning of this lesson. What differences presented in this lesson did you not include in your list? Add to the list based on what you now know. Then write a paragraph to summarize the differences between industrialized and developing nations.

Toward Economic Development

Thinking on Your Own

Imagine that you are a citizen of a very poor developing nation. In your notebook, write a letter to your nation's president listing three basic steps your nation must take to get economic development under way.

No one knows a simple formula for making poor countries richer. People used to think that wealth required an abundance of natural resources. Today, some of the world's richest nations, such as the United States and Canada, have an abundance of natural resources. However, there are also a number of poorer nations that are equally rich in resources. Russia is a good example. Switzerland and Japan—both relatively small nations with few resources—are far better off than Russia. What are the factors that make countries like Switzerland or Japan rich?

Trade, private property, profit, and competition are central to a market economy. These elements are also important to economic development. Each requires a government that has one set of rules for everyone in the country. People have to feel confident that the laws are fair and enforced without special favors, and that the courts judge every citizen fairly.

Government also plays a key role in promoting trade. A strong currency, or system of money, is part of that effort. So is building and maintaining an infrastructure. A nation's **infrastructure** consists of the basic services and systems needed for the nation to function—including transportation and communications systems, water and power lines, and

focus your reading

What effect do natural resources have on economic development?

How do governments promote economic growth?

Explain how governments get in the way of economic growth.

vocabulary

infrastructure

famine

infant mortality

external debt

default

China's infrastructure is expanding quickly, as demonstrated by road construction projects near Guangzhou.

such public institutions as schools, post offices, and prisons.

Some people think that only wealthy countries benefit from trade. In fact, everyone who participates in an exchange of goods and services benefits. Trade opens new jobs in developing nations. It also gives poor countries access to markets in industrialized nations, which is where most of the consumers with money to spend live. In 2000, for example, Congress passed the African Growth and Opportunity Act. It allows Africa's poorest nations to export textiles to the United States with little or no tariff. Within one year, exports from Madagascar to the U.S. had increased 120 percent. Exports from Malawi and Nigeria were up 1,000 percent!

Amartya Sen, an economist who won the Nobel Prize in Economics in 1998, has studied famines in India and China. A **famine** is an extreme, widespread shortage of food. He found that the world's worst famines were not the result of crop failures but of government actions. Relatively small agricultural setbacks became catastrophes because the government did not allow imports, tried to keep prices low, or interfered in some other way with a market's normal ability to correct itself.

In 2005, the medical staff at a Doctors Without Borders clinic in Maradi, Niger, worked to combat a devastating famine that struck the country.

Sen found that famines rarely occur in countries with regular elections or political parties that can freely criticize government policies. India experienced many famines in the 1800s and early 1900s but has not had one since it won its independence from Britain in 1947. One reason that India has avoided famines is that the government has created a system to prevent them. The country has a food distribution system that stabilizes prices and a triggering mechanism—a way of alerting the nation to the danger and setting into motion protections for the most vulnerable people.

China has a similar system for responding to famines. Yet, from 1958 to 1961, the nation experienced the largest famine in recorded history. Sen estimates that between 16.5 million and 29.5 million people died in the famine. Why didn't the Chinese system work as well as the system developed in India? The answer lies in the Chinese political system, in which one party—the Communist Party—makes all decisions. The famine raged for three years without the government ever admitting the famine existed or taking steps to end it. Much of the world, including much of China, was simply unaware of the extent of the tragedy. India, on the other hand, has a relatively free press and a wide variety of political parties. Journalists and politicians would have made it impossible for the government to get away with failing to minimize the danger or not acting at the first sign of a famine.

Education

Economists point out that before a nation experiences significant economic growth, it has significant increases in education. Education allows workers to increase their productivity. In the 1970s, for example, the Daewoo Corporation of South Korea was a major producer of textiles. When Americans and Europeans placed import quotas on South Korean textiles, Daewoo decided to move its operations to Bangladesh, which had no import quotas. In 1979, Daewoo and a Bangladeshi textile company signed an agreement. Daewoo then made an important decision: it brought 130 workers from Bangladesh to South Korea for training. The company invested in their education.

Years later, Daewoo moved its business elsewhere, but it left behind the start of a major export industry. About 115 of the 130 workers that Daewoo trained would go on to start their own garment-exporting companies. By 2000, that investment in education had helped create a $3 billion industry.

Education set into motion a process that made a very poor country more productive and, therefore, richer. Education has other benefits, too. For example, it often leads to improvements in public health. Higher rates of education for women in developing countries are associated with lower

stop and think

How might education help end the cycle of poverty? What kind of education would have the greatest impact? Share your opinions with a partner. Be sure to give reasons in support of your opinion.

rates of **infant mortality**—the number of babies out of every 1,000 born that die before the age of one.

A Matter of Money

To build a new business or expand an existing one, money is needed to purchase capital and other resources. In industrialized nations, that money comes from savings. In poor countries, savings tend to be small and those who do save are often unwilling to invest their savings in their own economy. They prefer to send their money abroad.

As a result, almost every developing nation has large **external debts**—debts to foreign banks and governments. For example, a number of countries, including Ethiopia, Syria, Jordan, and Sudan, have debts two and even three times larger than their gross domestic product (GDP). Some may never be able to repay their loans. At best, they pay only the interest. At worst, they default on their loans. A nation that **defaults** fails to pay off its debts. It is therefore likely to have trouble borrowing in the future.

A Fragile Economic Balance

Many developing nations exist close to financial ruin. Any natural or human-made disaster can result in an overwhelming setback. For example, in December 2004, many nations in

Catastrophes such as the 2004 tsunami that stuck many Indian Ocean nations, including Sri Lanka, can have devastating effects on a nation's economy.

South and Southeast Asia were making considerable progress in reducing poverty when an underwater earthquake suddenly erupted in the Indian Ocean. It generated a tsunami that killed about 175,000 people in the region.

For the developing nations of South and Southeast Asia, the tsunami was an economic disaster, as well as a natural one. It ruined much of the region's infrastructure by wiping out roads and railways. The huge mass of water broke sewage and water pipes, contaminating water and food sources. Power and communication lines were disrupted.

Economic losses from disasters affect industrialized nations, as well as developing ones. In 2005, Hurricanes Katrina and Rita devastated New Orleans and much of southern Louisiana, Mississippi, and Alabama. The difference between the tsunami and Hurricanes Katrina and Rita is that a natural disaster in an industrialized nation—even a disaster as powerful as the hurricanes—affects only a very small percentage of the economy. In a developing nation, the cost of the disaster may be identical, but it is likely to affect a huge percentage of the economy.

Hurricane Mitch, for example, devastated Central America in 1998. The damages were estimated at between $5 billion and $7 billion—an amount almost equal to the annual combined economic activity of the two hardest-hit nations, Honduras and Nicaragua. Their economies were very slow to recover.

Human-made disasters also have devastating effects. The wars in Afghanistan and Iraq are not the only wars in recent years. East Timor, Sierra Leone, and Bosnia have also been war zones. Over the last 40 years, nearly 20 African countries have experienced at least one civil war. The region is also home to many smaller conflicts.

The destruction caused by many years of war is tremendous. War always increases poverty. Many people are injured or killed. Homes and business are destroyed. Jobs are hard to find. Almost everything that allows a city or a nation to function efficiently—electricity, running water, sewage systems, roads, and buildings—is ruined and needs repair. Food is scarce because farm fields are used as battlegrounds. During a war, the enemy often hides land mines in those fields.

These buried mines make it dangerous to use the fields for many years to come. For example, it is estimated that between five million and ten million land mines remain in Cambodia, even though the Khmer Rouge conflict officially ended in 1979.

Refugees who fled the conflict in Rwanda in the 1990s eventually returned home from exile in Tanzania.

It takes money and effort to rebuild a nation after fighting stops. Once a conflict has ended, nearly everything has to be rebuilt. Roads, bridges and other parts of a nations's infrastructure often require extensive repair. Adding to the challenge is that all these things must be done at the same time because everything is interconnected.

Putting It All Together

In your notebook, make a two-column chart. Title the first column "Obstacles to Economic Development." In that column, list obstacles that developing nations face. Title the second column "Ways to Overcome." In that column, write a sentence or two about what nations must do to overcome each obstacle. Discuss your list with a partner. Revise it on the basis of your discussion.

LESSON 3

Financing Economic Development

Thinking on Your Own

At the beginning of Lesson 2, you wrote a letter giving advice about economic development. Imagine that you received a letter in response explaining that the government is too poor to finance any of your proposals. In your notebook, write a follow-up letter that explains at least one way the nation can get the funds needed for economic development.

Poor nations cannot break the cycle of poverty without economic development. However, economic development is expensive and poor nations have very little money to invest. Most countries look to outside sources for assistance. Two major sources of assistance are foreign businesses and foreign aid from industrialized nations. Yet, a number of countries are also encouraging local investments.

In Patria, Bangladesh, Laili Begum demonstrates the use of a cell phone that was purchased through a loan from the Grameen Bank.

Microcredit and Economic Development

Many people often think that it takes large sums of money to make a difference in an economy. Economist Muhammad Yunus of Bangladesh takes a different view. During a famine in 1974, he discovered that very small loans could make a significant difference in a person's ability to survive. He loaned $27 to a woman who made bamboo furniture. She sold the furniture to support herself and her family. With Yunus's loan, the woman was able to expand her business.

Traditional banks are not interested in **microcredit**—tiny loans to poor people, who are considered poor repayment risks. After all, they have no **collateral**, or assets, to secure a loan. Yunus disagreed with that approach to loaning money. He founded his own bank, the Grameen Bank, in 1976. Since then, the Grameen Bank has issued more than $5 billion in loans to some four million borrowers. To the surprise of many bankers, more than 95 percent of those loans have been repaid.

The success of the Grameen Bank has inspired similar efforts in other developing nations and even some industrialized nations, including the United States. What kinds of businesses do these people start? One of the most popular in Bangladesh is the Grameen Village Phone. Local entrepreneurs—usually women—purchase or lease a cellular phone with borrowed money and then sell phone services to customers by the call. An average of 70 customers a month use each phone.

In poor villages with no other access to telephones, the service is extraordinarily popular. The "Grameen phone ladies" can pay off their loans and still make a profit. In a nation where the average annual income is $380, these villagers can expect to earn more than $1,000 a year—enough to send their children to school and provide medical care for the family.

Foreign Investment

Muhammad Yunus looks at development from the bottom up. His efforts empower ordinary people to improve their lives. The process is slow and changes are gradual. Many developing nations want more rapid change, and many of them look to foreign investors as a quicker way of bringing about change.

Almost every country in the world attracts some foreign investment. Investors put their money into businesses in someone else's nation for the same reasons they invest in their own country. They see opportunities to make a profit. For example, large nations like China and India have millions of potential consumers. Many foreign businesses are eager to tap those markets. Countries with low wages and abundant resources also attract investors. So does a stable government.

Political instability scares away investment. Without investment, however, countries are unable to develop their economies and improve welfare, causing more dissatisfaction and increasing political instability. How, then, can the cycle be broken? One way is through foreign aid.

Foreign Aid

Foreign aid consists of the money, goods, and services that the government of one nation gives to help the government of another nation. In 1970, industrialized nations agreed to spend a minimum of 0.7 percent of their gross national product (GNP) on official development assistance (ODA) to developing nations.

That aid was designed to provide economic and technical assistance. **Economic assistance** consists of loans or outright grants of money or equipment to build and improve a nation's infrastructure—improving harbors, building schools, creating dams, and maintaining highways. **Technical assistance** is education. Teachers, engineers, and technicians from industrialized nations share their knowledge and skills.

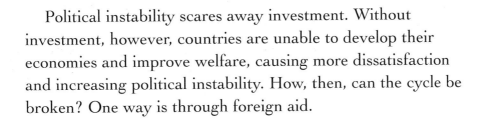

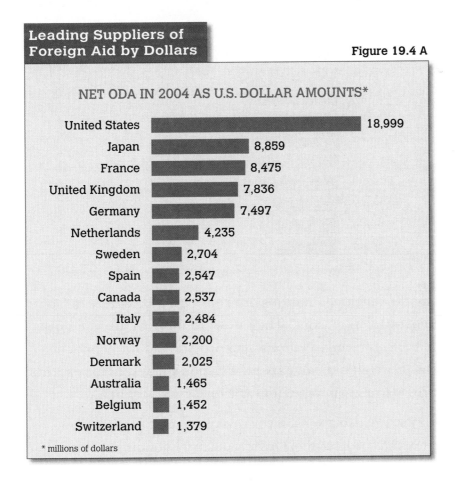

Leading Suppliers of Foreign Aid by Dollars

Figure 19.4 A

NET ODA IN 2004 AS U.S. DOLLAR AMOUNTS*

United States	18,999
Japan	8,859
France	8,475
United Kingdom	7,836
Germany	7,497
Netherlands	4,235
Sweden	2,704
Spain	2,547
Canada	2,537
Italy	2,484
Norway	2,200
Denmark	2,025
Australia	1,465
Belgium	1,452
Switzerland	1,379

* millions of dollars

Figure 19.4 A, on page 331, shows the amount of development assistance that 15 industrialized nations provided in 2004 in dollars, and Figure 19.4 B shows those dollars as a percent of gross national income (GNI). (After 2000, gross national income is used in place of GNP; it is a similar measure but includes a trade adjustment.) Both graphs focus on economic and technical assistance. Neither includes military assistance to developing nations. **Military assistance** involves help in the form of training and military equipment—including guns, tanks, and airplanes. The graphs also do not show **humanitarian aid**—emergency assistance of food, clothing, and medical supplies to victims of natural or human-made disasters.

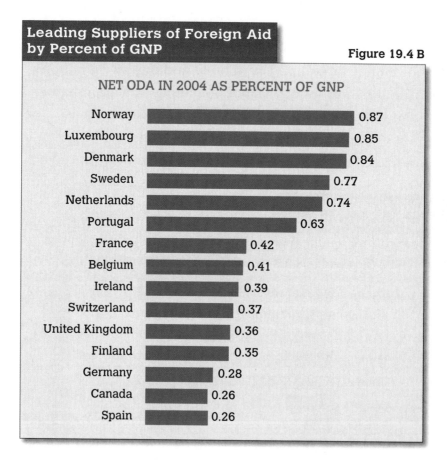

Leading Suppliers of Foreign Aid by Percent of GNP

Figure 19.4 B

NET ODA IN 2004 AS PERCENT OF GNP

Country	Percent
Norway	0.87
Luxembourg	0.85
Denmark	0.84
Sweden	0.77
Netherlands	0.74
Portugal	0.63
France	0.42
Belgium	0.41
Ireland	0.39
Switzerland	0.37
United Kingdom	0.36
Finland	0.35
Germany	0.28
Canada	0.26
Spain	0.26

Why do developed nations offer foreign aid? Many do so for humanitarian reasons. They want to improve people's lives and reduce suffering. Nations also provide aid for economic reasons. Foreign aid can expand a nation's markets for exports and provide new opportunities for foreign investment.

Politics are also a reason for providing aid. Nations use foreign aid to protect their own security. Economic aid is often

a part of a military alliance with a developing nation. Through such alliances, the United States has gained overseas military bases. The United States has also used foreign aid to win allies in the United Nations and other international groups.

The United States and other industrialized countries also give some aid indirectly to other nations. The U.S., for example, channels much of its foreign aid through the Agency for International Development (AID). Funds are also channeled through the World Bank, which makes loans to developing nations at low interest rates. The International Monetary Fund also provides loans to countries that are unable to obtain financing elsewhere.

stop and think

Study Figure 19.4 A. Write a sentence that tells what the graph shows. Then study Figure 19.4 B. Write a sentence that tells what that graph shows. Write a final sentence that explains the two graphs.

Muhammad Yunus: Banker to the Poor

In 2004, the Grameen Bank was awarded a prize for its Village Phone Project. In his acceptance speech, Muhammad Yunus explained the bank's philosophy.

"When we [first] presented the Village Phone Project to the professional people, they expressed serious doubt about the capacity of the illiterate women to understand this state-of-the-art telecommunication technology. We remained thoroughly convinced that while people may be poor and illiterate, they are not stupid. Potentially, they are as smart as anybody else in the world.

"As soon as we launched the project, we were struck by its success.... Telephone ladies quickly learned.... all the ropes of the telephone business. Today there are 60,000 telephone ladies providing telephone service in 80 percent of the villages of Bangladesh. In villages where grid electricity does not exist, solar energy powers the phones." In 2006, Muhammad Yumas and the Grameen Bank were awarded the Nobel Peace Prize.

reading for understanding

How does Yunus regard the people who borrow from his bank?

Explain how projects like the Grameen Phone Project can reduce poverty.

What does Yunus want people in other countries to know about poor people?

Biography

The International Federation of Red Cross and Red Crescent Societies provide aid to many parts of the developing world.

Private Aid

Governments send aid to other governments. A number of private citizens and organizations also give aid to developing nations. They make loans, provide grants, offer training to individuals and groups, and supply medical assistance. There are no complete figures on private aid, but one economic estimate is that Americans privately gave at least $34 billion to developing nations in 2002—more than twice the $15 billion the U.S. officially offered in foreign aid that year. That figure included approximately

- $1.5 billion in international giving by U.S. foundations

- $2.8 billion in charitable giving

- $6.6 billion in grants, goods, and volunteers supplied by American nongovernmental organizations (NGOs)

- $3.4 billion in health care, education, relief, and development by religious groups

- $1.3 billion in scholarships to foreign students by U.S. colleges and universities

The largest amount of money, however, came not from groups but from individuals—particularly, immigrants and foreign workers. Each year, they send about $18 billion in **remittances**, or payments, to relatives and friends abroad. That money is used mainly to help families meet basic needs. Although that money is rarely invested, it does fuel local economies.

Putting It All Together

Complete the following sentences.

- Microcredit can result in . . .

- Foreign investment can lead to . . .

- Foreign aid can help to . . .

- Remittances can result in . . .

Which form of aid do you think has the greatest impact in the short run? Which has the greatest impact in the long run? Write a persuasive paragraph to support your opinion.

A Major Swipe at Sweatshops

A sweatshop is a factory where people work for very low wages, producing consumer goods. Many people claim that multinational corporations are creating sweatshops in poor nations. Aaron Bernstein writes of a new project to address the concerns of both human rights groups and manufacturers.

Remember sweatshop exposés? They haven't hit the headlines much in the past few years. In part that's because high-profile companies such as Nike Inc. and Gap Inc. now work regularly with labor rights groups to monitor their vast global networks of supplier factories. Still, only about 100 U.S. and European multinationals participate in such efforts. . . . The vast majority of Western companies haven't followed suit. . . .

Now global labor monitoring may get a big leg up. Nike, Patagonia, Gap, and five other companies have joined forces with six leading anti-sweatshop groups to devise a single set of labor standards with a common factory-inspection system. The goal: to replace today's overlapping hodgepodge of approaches with something that's easier and cheaper to use. . . . After two years of debate, the parties quietly signed an agreement in late April [2005] to run a pilot project in several dozen Turkish factories that produce garments and other products for the eight companies.

If it works, the 30-month experiment would create the first commonly accepted global labor standards—and a way to live up to them. . . .

More broadly, the Turkey experiment will shed light on a fundamental conflict between multinationals' desire for decent factories and their constant search for the cheapest suppliers. Typically, Western companies monitor supplier factories, then work with them to fix the problems they find. Usually, that costs money. But companies also switch suppliers frequently as they bid out production to the cheapest and most efficient plants. "We hope the initiative will test this relationship, since a factory that can lose the next order to the guy across the street will always feel pressure to cut corners on labor standards," says Scott Nova, executive director of Worker Rights Consortium (WRC), a group founded by U.S. students. ∎

"A Major Swipe at Sweatshops" by Aaron Bernstein. *BusinessWeek Online*, May 23, 2005.

reading for understanding

What is the goal of the project the author describes?

What seems to be the central issue?

How do you think global labor standards might affect American consumers? How might they affect American workers?

Chapter Summary

- People in **developing nations** have a lower standard of living and access to fewer goods and services than do most people in **industrialized nations.**

- People living in poverty have a shorter **life expectancy** and are more likely to suffer from **malnutrition.**

- Poverty can lead to crime, disease, violence, and an increase in the number of **refugees.**

- Governments in developing nations are often responsible for building and maintaining the nation's **infrastructure** and preventing **famines.**

- Higher rates of education for women in developing countries are associated with lower rates of **infant mortality.**

- A developing nation often has large **external debts** that can sometimes lead it to **default** on loans.

- **Microcredit** allows people in developing nations to secure small business loans without **collateral.**

- **Foreign aid** often includes **economic assistance, technical assistance, military assistance,** and **humanitarian aid.**

- **Remittances** sent by immigrants and foreign workers to their homelands help to fuel local economies.

Chapter Review

1 Which of the following do you consider most essential to economic development: a democratic government, education, or foreign investments? Give reasons in support of your answer.

2 Economists sometimes define development as "meeting the needs of the present without compromising the ability of future generations to meet their own needs." What does the statement mean? What happens when present needs conflict with future needs? For example, what happens when a company's need for cheap labor conflicts with workers' needs for livable wages? Or when a family's need to have every family member work conflicts with a child's right to an education? What are the trade-offs? What are the opportunity costs?

Skill Builder

Draw Inferences from Graphs

To *infer* means to evaluate information and arrive at a conclusion. When you make an inference, you are reading between the lines. Sometimes statistics or numbers tell only a part of the story. To make inferences, you should:

- Identify the stated facts.
- Summarize the information.
- Apply any related information.
- Use your knowledge and the facts to reach a conclusion.

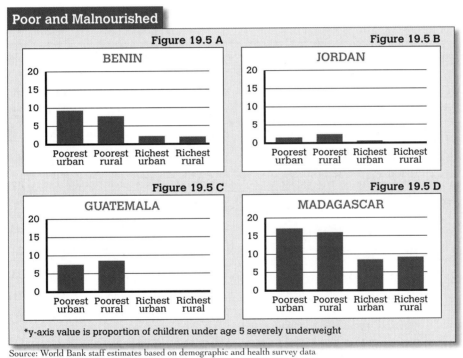

Source: World Bank staff estimates based on demographic and health survey data

Use the graphs to answer the following questions.

1 Which of the four countries seems to be the poorest?

2 Which of the countries has the least malnutrition?

3 In which country or countries are urban dwellers more likely to be poor than people who live in rural areas?

4 Jordan and Guatemala have a similar annual income per capita. How do you explain differences in the rates of malnutrition between the two nations?

5 Write a sentence that summarizes the four graphs.

Chapter 20

Globalization of National Economies: Opportunities and Challenges

Getting Focused

Globalization is the integration of economic activities throughout a market and across borders. The end result is a single world market with a free flow of goods, services, labor, and capital.

However, there are many bumps and detours on the road to globalization. For one thing, not all nations start with the same resources. Some lack natural resources such as gold, silver, oil, and coal. Others lack human resources such as an educated and skilled workforce. Still others lack the capital to create infrastructure by building schools, roads, hospitals, and similar facilities. They may also lack the capital to build factories and modernize farming.

Because of the differences among nations, the efforts to achieve a global market are uneven. So are the effects of globalization. For a wealthy nation such as the United States, globalization has many advantages. It means cheaper foreign goods and the chance for U.S. companies to do business in other countries. For developing nations with few resources, globalization is very different. For some nations, their efforts to join the global market have made their poverty worse.

Globalization presents many challenges as well as opportunities for the world's governments and people.

Emerging Economic Powerhouses

Outsourcing and Developing Nations

The Environment and Energy Issues

Regional Economic Blocs

e-commerce

Case Studies 339

Case Study 1:

Emerging Economic Powerhouses

> **What is causing the rapid growth of some emerging economies?**
> **What problems still exist despite rapid economic growth?**

An *economic powerhouse* is a nation with a fast-growing economy. A number of developing nations have become economic powerhouses—also known as economic miracles—since the 1970s. Advances in technology and infrastructure have driven their economies.

Supporters of globalization believe that it promises a better life for a nation's citizens. They argue that higher-paying manufacturing jobs replace low-paying farm work. Nations are able to spend more money on education. This enables people to get professional jobs as managers in the new companies. Health care and social programs often improve. Modern transportation networks are built. Unemployment levels are reduced.

Critics believe that globalization benefits only the multinational corporations of the United States and western Europe. These opponents claim that local businesses cannot compete with the money and business tactics of Western companies. They argue that local cultures suffer when young people adopt the clothes, makeup, and values that are portrayed in Western music, movies, and on television shows. Few benefits of globalization, they argue, reach ordinary citizens.

Like most issues, there is some truth to both sides. Although the benefits of globalization have not reached every citizen, nations realize that globalization is here to stay. As a result, they are working together through the United Nations and regional groups to find solutions.

NAMES IN THE NEWS

Nongovernmental Organization (NGO): An NGO is a private organization that usually does not receive any government funding. NGOs work to achieve specific goals. Labor unions, conservation groups, and women and children's rights organizations are examples of NGOs.

Civil Society Organization (CSO): A CSO is any nongovernment group that works to express the interests of social groups and raise awareness of key issues. These groups work closely with local populations. CSOs include NGOs, Indigenous Peoples' organizations, charitable organizations, and other grassroots organizations.

Food and Agriculture Organization of the United Nations (FAO): The FAO is an agency of the United Nations that works with NGOs, CSOs, and other organizations to reduce hunger and poverty in the world.

Lifting Everyone Up

High-tech jobs go to educated workers. However, almost three-fourths of India's one billion people live in farming villages. Beginning high-tech workers earn from $6,000 to $18,000 a year. This is low compared to U.S. wages, but about 200 million people earn less than a US $1 a day. This is good news, because it is a 6 percent drop from just a few years ago.

The Indian government, along with civil society organizations (CSOs), nongovernmental organizations (NGOs), and villagers themselves, is working to raise the country's standard of living. NGOs and CSOs may receive government funding and help to implement government policies and programs. One project, run by BAIF Development Research Foundation, helps farmers learn to raise fruit and nut trees along with their grain crops. Another project, funded by the government's Tribal Affairs Ministry, helps farmers buy seeds and fertilizer. Government projects also help villagers lay pipes to bring water into their homes.

Wangfujing Street—Beijing, China

"Who's Afraid of China, Inc.?"

Wal-Mart—Shanghai, China

The above was the headline of a recent newspaper article on China's fast-growing economy. China did not enter the global race for goods, services, and capital until the late 1980s when the Communist government eased controls on business. Since then, China's economy has been growing at the rate of 9.1 percent a year. In contrast, the U.S. economy grows around 2 percent a year. Economists speculate that China will be able to keep up an amazing growth rate of 7 to 8 percent for years to come.

How does China do it? Manufacturing is the key to China's economic success. In 2004, it exported close to $500 billion worth of goods. By 2006, exports reached $900 billion. Economists estimate that by 2010, China will be exporting close to double that amount. Chinese factories manufacture clothing, consumer electronics, home appliances, cell phones, cars, and steel. Chinese companies also produce and distribute oil and mine mineral resources. China's major exports are machinery and equipment, textiles, and clothing.

About 200 of China's largest businesses are partially owned by the Chinese government. The government gives these companies preferred treatment. When China began to industrialize in the early 1990s, these companies received big contracts and good terms from banks for loans. The government cut tariffs to make the products from these companies less expensive on the world market.

China also attracts tens of billion of dollars in foreign investment. The money is used to build factories, transportation and communication networks, and other businesses.

China sells much of its goods as exports. However, China has a population of more than 1.3 billion. Many Chinese are spending the money they make from the new supply of jobs. China is the third-largest market for passenger cars in the world. It has 350 million cell-phone users, the most in the world. With a market of 1.3 billion people, Western companies rushed in to sell everything from soap and shampoo to washing machines and cars. However, they are finding tough competition from Chinese companies.

Barriers to Continued Growth

Many developing nations, including China and India, have problems that could slow their economic growth:

- lack of health care
- large numbers of people with HIV/AIDS
- water and air pollution
- growing lack of clean water
- debt and poor banking systems

India's conflict with Pakistan and China's conflict with Taiwan also impact the ability of the government to grow national economies.

Field workers—Dunhuang, China

Fast Facts

The Organization for Economic Co-operation and Development (OECD), based in Paris, France, consists of 30 member countries that share a commitment to democratic government and the market economy. These nations work with some 70 other countries, NGOs, and civil society to form a global reach that focuses on economic and social issues including trade, education, development, science, and innovation.

Economic Profile of Brazil

Brazil has one of the fastest-growing economies of Latin America. Like many other developing nations, Brazil has a history of rule by the military. By the 1990s, the nation had a stable civilian government. This attracted new investment capital. Because of the new businesses, Brazil has a growing middle class of educated workers. These are the men and women who manage the new factories and offices.

However, agricultural products still account for a large part of Brazil's exports. Orange juice, soybeans, and bran are among the nation's major exports. The majority of farmland is owned by a small number of wealthy families. Most Brazilians still live on less than US $2 a day.

Income	$140.6 billion
Expenses	$172.4 billion
GDP	$1.49 trillion
Per capita income	$8,100
Major industries	textiles, consumer goods, machinery, chemicals
Labor force	79 million out of 186 million 66% service industry 20% agriculture 14% industry
Unemployment	11.5%
Exports	$95 billion
Imports	$91 billion

—Statistics from *CIA World Factbook*

Unequal Benefits: Chile

In the 1970s and 1980s, Chile was called "an economic miracle." The government reduced tariffs and welcomed foreign investors. The economy grew rapidly. Unemployment dropped, and the poverty rate was cut to 18 percent. However, economic growth has slowed greatly since the 1990s.

Chileans believe that much work still needs to be done. The poverty rate remains at 18 percent. Unemployment is at 8.6 percent. One problem is the lack of spending on education. Chile wants to attract high-tech companies to build factories. However, without a large educated workforce, this has been difficult. Some Chileans believe the problem is the nation's dependence on natural resources for export. Its major exports are copper, wine, and fish.

Spreading Chile's Wealth

What Has Been Done

- Economy has grown on average 5.7 percent a year for the last 15 years.
- Poverty has been cut in half as a result of social programs.
- College enrollment has doubled since 1990.

What Needs to Be Done

- New investment is needed to end dependence on natural resources for export.
- The gap between rich and poor needs to be reduced. Income tax reform could aid in this goal.
- The 24 percent unemployment rate among young people needs to be reduced. Reforming labor laws could assist in achieving this goal.

VIEWPOINT

The Perils of Unskilled Labor

"The developed nations look increasingly to the Third World to provide them with ever-cheaper items to maintain high living standards. . . . But too-rapid wage inflation in developing countries puts that symbiotic relationship at risk.

"The real problem for [developing nations] isn't a lack of workers. . . . Instead, . . . the ability to train new workers can't keep pace with [a] . . . rapidly expanding economy's demand for manpower. . . .

"The lesson here is that education, training, and development of intellectual infrastructure are every bit as important as low wages for today's global trading powers. . . . Interestingly, that same message also offers hope for the more mature economies (and expensive workforces) of the U.S. and Europe. Continued investment in human capital may be their best hope to remain truly competitive in a world full of faster-growing, low-wage competitors."

—*Editorial*, BusinessWeek, *November 7, 2005*

Taiwan's Economic Success

Communist and Nationalist forces had been fighting for control of China since the 1920s. In 1949, the Communist forces gained control under the leadership of Mao Zedong. The Nationalists fled to the nearby island of Taiwan and set up their own government. More than one million mainland Chinese followed them. They joined the Chinese already living on the island. By the 1990s, Taiwan had been turned into an economic miracle. Foreign aid began the process of economic growth and government policies encouraged continued development. Foreign investment was welcomed.

Taiwan went from an economy based on farming to an industrial economy. By the early twenty-first century, it was exporting $143 billion worth of goods a year. Most of these items are machinery and electronics. About 3.5 million people work in Taiwan's industries, making and selling goods.

Taiwan's Global Industries

Taiwanese companies make thousands of items needed for the global economy. Most appear under the name of another company and most are put together in China.

- #1 provider of chip manufacturing services— 70% of the market worth $8.9 billion

- #1 producer of notebook PCs— 72% of the market worth $22 billion

- #1 provider of LCD monitors— 68% of the market worth $14 billion

- #1 producer of PDAs—79% of the market worth $1.8 billion

- #2 providers of servers—33% of the market worth $1.8 billion

- #2 producer of digital cameras— 34% of the market worth $2 billion

Fast Facts: Korea's Emerging Economy

- More than 200 foreign-owned companies have auto parts factories in South Korea.

- South Korean companies sold $36.4 billion worth of auto parts in 2005.

- South Korean carmakers sold 2.4 million of their cars in other countries.

South Africa's Two Economies

South Africa was a colony of the Dutch during the 1600s. In the 1700s, the British took control and ruled until 1934. In that year, the colony became self-governing. In 1948, white South Africans passed a series of apartheid, or segregation, laws. These laws ensured that whites would remain in control. However, by the late 1980s, black South Africans were demanding an end to apartheid. In 1993, apartheid came to an end, and Nelson Mandela was elected the first black president of South Africa. The government inherited a dual economy with many problems.

Whites controlled an economy that was similar to the economy of developed nations. It was based on mining, manufacturing, services, and farming. Most black South Africans, however, either worked in cities in low-paid service positions or practiced subsistence farming—producing only enough food to meet a family's needs. This was especially a problem in rural areas. Mandela's government developed programs to address the fundamental inequalities of the apartheid system. New industries have created a small black middle class. However, most employed blacks are miners or low-paid factory or service workers.

The government has adopted policies to make South Africa more competitive in world markets. It has cut its tariffs by half. Inflation has been brought under control. Foreign investment is encouraged and so is new business development by its own citizens.

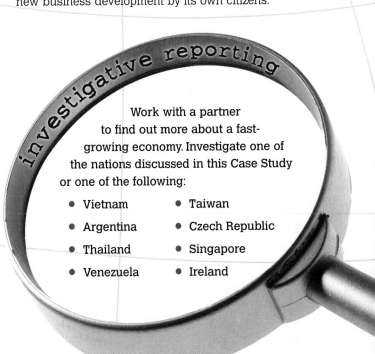

investigative reporting

Work with a partner to find out more about a fast-growing economy. Investigate one of the nations discussed in this Case Study or one of the following:

- Vietnam
- Taiwan
- Argentina
- Czech Republic
- Thailand
- Singapore
- Venezuela
- Ireland

Case Study 2:

Outsourcing and Developing Nations

▶ **What are some of the issues facing developing nations?**

▶ **How are developing and developed nations working together to solve these problems?**

▶ **What effects does outsourcing have on developing and developed nations?**

Beginning in the mid-twentieth century, a number of Asian and African nations won their independence from colonial rulers. Most of them lacked industries. A number of them lacked infrastructure. Many also suffered from lack of schools, clean water, medical care, and similar services for their citizens. The economies of these nations depended on agriculture. Because colonial governments were mostly interested in raw materials, these countries had few factories. The processing of raw materials was done by businesses in the ruling country.

Nations in Latin America had been independent much longer. However, they had similar problems. In each country, a small number of wealthy families owned most of the land. The majority of people were hired farm workers. To keep their power and wealth, the wealthy also controlled the governments of these nations. Slowly, through the last half of the twentieth century, the control of the wealthy families ended. In some nations, it took civil war. In other nations, democratic elections changed those in power.

The goals of many newly formed Asian, African, and Latin American nations were similar. Many wanted to industrialize their economies and improve the standard of living of their people. To achieve their goals, government leaders borrowed huge sums of money from developed nations and from the World Bank and

International Monetary Fund (IMF). By the 1990s, many nations were so far in debt that some would never be able to pay it off. Even paying the interest on loans became a problem for various countries.

In 1999, the World Bank and the IMF started a new policy for loans to developing nations. They required that countries develop a plan to reduce poverty before they asked for new loans. The Poverty Reduction Strategy Paper is now the basis for loans by these two international groups. The Asian Development Bank (ADB) also requires a poverty reduction plan prior to granting loans.

Outsourcing is when an organization contracts some of its work out to another individual or company. It has come to mean much more to workers in all parts of the world, however. Over the past several years, many organizations have moved jobs from developed countries, such as the United States and England, to developing countries, such as India and the Philippines.

Some economists argue that outsourcing encourages developed nations to increase productivity and to innovate. Others argue that governments should enact laws to protect domestic workers.

The final issue this case study examines is farm subsidies. Developed nations pay subsidies to their farmers for their crops. These subsidies keep prices low for consumers. At the same time, subsidies enable farmers to earn more than the market price for their crops. These agricultural subsidies harm farmers in developing nations.

The subsidies keep the price of farm goods lower than where free market forces would set them. As a result, farmers in developing nations earn less. Their nations also take in less revenue. In 2000, the World Trade Organization set a goal of reducing farm subsidies. Farmers in developed nations put pressure on their governments to resist.

Rice field—Asia

MDG: 2005 Progress Chart

Goals and Targets	Africa		Asia				Oceania	Latin America & Caribbean	Commonwealth of Independent States	
	Northern	Sub-Saharan	Eastern	South-eastern	Southern	Western			Europe	Asia

Goal 1–Eradicate extreme poverty and hunger

Reduce extreme poverty by half	low poverty	very high poverty	moderate poverty	moderate poverty	high poverty	low poverty	—	moderate poverty	low poverty	low poverty
Reduce hunger by half	very low hunger	very high hunger	moderate hunger	moderate hunger	high hunger	moderate hunger	moderate hunger	moderate hunger	very low hunger	high hunger

Goal 2–Achieve universal primary education

Universal primary schooling	high enrollment	low enrollment	high enrollment	high enrollment	moderate enrollment	moderate enrollment	moderate enrollment	high enrollment	moderate enrollment	high enrollment

Key:

The progress chart operates on two levels. The words in each box tell what the current rate of compliance with each target is. The colors show the trend toward meeting the target by 2015 or not. See legend below:

- ■ Target already met or very close to being met.
- ■ Target is expected to be met by 2015 if prevailing trends persist, or the problem that this target is designed to address is not a serious concern in the region.
- ■ Target is not expected to be met by 2015, if prevailing trends persist.
- ■ No progress, or a deterioration or reversal.
- ■ Insufficient data

✷The available data for maternal mortality and malaria do not allow a trend analysis. Progress in the chart has been assessed by the responsible agencies on the basis of proxy indicators.

Developed Nations Support MDGs

The Group of 8 (G8) is made up Canada, France, Germany, Italy, Japan, Russia, the United Kingdom, and the United States. The leaders of these nations meet at an annual economic and political summit. The presidency of the group rotates among member nations. The head of each government is president for a year.

The G8 holds a yearly summit of the heads of government of the eight nations. These top officials discuss issues and reach agreements on actions to take. Between summits, top officials from each government continue to meet and work on the G8's programs.

In 2005, Tony Blair, the prime minister of the United Kingdom, was the G8's president. At the 2005 summit, Blair asked his fellow leaders to agree to a package of aid for poor nations. Included in this package was loan forgiveness for 18 of the world's poorest nations. The G8 leaders agreed to forgive $40 billion in loans to these African nations. The G8 leaders also agreed to make drugs available to more of the world's HIV/AIDS patients and to fund the effort to end polio in the world.

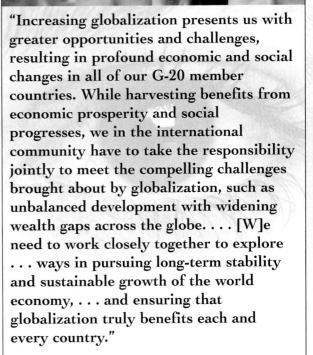

VIEWPOINT

"Increasing globalization presents us with greater opportunities and challenges, resulting in profound economic and social changes in all of our G-20 member countries. While harvesting benefits from economic prosperity and social progresses, we in the international community have to take the responsibility jointly to meet the compelling challenges brought about by globalization, such as unbalanced development with widening wealth gaps across the globe. . . . [W]e need to work closely together to explore . . . ways in pursuing long-term stability and sustainable growth of the world economy, . . . and ensuring that globalization truly benefits each and every country."

—*Zhou Xiaochuan, Finance Minister of China, President of G-20 for 2005*

India: A Leader in Technology and Outsourcing

Telephone call center— Bangalore, India

India's economy has grown 6 percent each year for the last 20 years. Economists estimate that it will continue to grow at this rate, or even increase a point or two, for many years to come. India's growth is based on high-tech businesses. Its companies are leaders in designing software and selling the services to support it.

Indian companies also sell a range of services related to business processing. For example, a company in the United States or France will outsource operations such as accounting to companies in India. Other services that are outsourced to India include processing insurance claims and loan applications, and reading medical X-rays. Computers and the Internet make this kind of long-distance rapid transfer of information possible—and cheap.

Many of these high-tech companies are Indian-owned and operated. However, U.S. businesses such as IBM, Hewlett-Packard, and Electronic Data Systems have their own branches in India. They employ thousands of Indians to work on information technology service projects.

The Effects of Outsourcing on the United States

Many people believed that outsourcing would have a negative effect on the U.S. economy. Workers were especially worried that their jobs would be lost overseas. However, a 2004 study done by Global Insight, a company that specializes in economic research and analysis, showed that worldwide outsourcing is actually increasing employment in the United States—257,042 net new U.S. jobs in 2005. The study also found that outsourcing is leading to higher real wages for U.S. workers.

Where Do the Jobs Go?

Manufacturing jobs remain the largest category of jobs lost to outsourcing. Many companies also contract overseas workers for software and programming services, information technology services, and customer service call centers.

The following countries receive most of the outsourcing jobs: India, Canada, China, Ireland, Hungary, the Philippines, Poland, Russia, and South Africa. Many other nations are trying to benefit from outsourcing as well. Up-and-comers include Panama, Romania, Costa Rica, Colombia, Egypt, Estonia, and Venezuela.

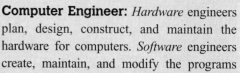

JOBS IN THE NEWS

Jobs that can be outsourced to other countries:

Information Technology Analyst: People in this job research, review, develop, and test information technology systems for businesses, medical facilities, schools, and stores.

Computer Engineer: *Hardware* engineers plan, design, construct, and maintain the hardware for computers. *Software* engineers create, maintain, and modify the programs that computers use, such as Microsoft Word, Filemaker, and custom-designed systems for large corporations.

Customer Support Representative: People in this job answer questions from people who are using a product and are having problems with it. These people use both telephones and the Internet to do the work.

Customer Sales Representative: These people take orders for goods and services over the telephone and on the Internet.

Millennium Development Goals

The Millennium Development Goals (MDGs) were developed by the United Nations as a blueprint for aiding the world's poorest people. The MDGs were adopted by most of the world's nations and leading development organizations such as the World Bank, the IMF, and the ADB. There are eight goals:

Goal 1   Eradicate extreme poverty and hunger.
Goal 2   Achieve universal primary education.
Goal 3   Promote gender equality and empower women.
Goal 4   Reduce child mortality.
Goal 5   Improve maternal health.
Goal 6   Combat HIV/AIDS, malaria, and other diseases.
Goal 7   Ensure environmental sustainability.
Goal 8   Develop a global partnership for development.

Nations agreed to the year 2015 as the deadline for achieving the goals. The UN oversees country-by-country monitoring to assess how well the goals are being met. However, there are nations that have failed to adopt the MDGs or allow for their implementation.

Doha Accords on Agriculture

The Doha Accords were reached at a meeting of top officials of World Trade Organization (WTO) nations in 2001. The accords set up a program of negotiations among member nations for 21 areas of concern to members. The accords also set up a program for implementing agreements once they are reached. Finally, they provide for analysis and monitoring of implementation. The accords cover such topics as

- agriculture
- trade and competition
- trade and investment
- trade and the environment
- subsidies
- sales of electronic equipment
- trade, debt, and finance

Negotiations on the various issues were supposed to be completed by January 1, 2005. However, nations could not agree about issues related to agriculture. Developing and developed nations have different views about tariffs and subsidies. An informal deadline for solving these problems was set for the end of 2006.

Group of 20

In 2003, a group of 20 developing nations joined in what has become known as the Group of 20 (G-20). Their goal was to pressure developed nations to live up to the Doha Accords. The G-20 is primarily interested in easing trade barriers established by developed nations on agricultural imports.

The economies of the G-20 nations depend largely on agricultural exports. The G-20 accounts for 26 percent of the world's agricultural exports. These 20 nations have close to 60 percent of the world's population. This represents 70 percent of the world's farmers.

The G-20 has become an important force in the negotiations set up by the Doha Accords. The group has been able to coordinate members' interests and present them as concrete proposals to the other members of the WTO.

Argentina
Bolivia
Brazil
Chile
China
Cuba
Egypt
Guatemala
India
Indonesia
Mexico
Nigeria
Pakistan
Paraguay
Philippines
South Africa
Tanzania
Thailand
Venezuela
Zimbabwe

NAMES IN THE NEWS

The following international organizations work with developing nations on economic growth:

World Bank—The UN founded the World Bank in 1944 to lend money to member nations for investment, foreign trade, and repayment of foreign debts. Today, it serves almost all of the world's nations. The full name of the bank is the International Bank for Development and Reconstruction. The World Bank provides about 10 percent of the world's foreign aid.

International Monetary Fund (IMF)—The IMF, founded in 1945, is an agency of the UN. Its purpose is to promote economic cooperation among its member nations. Almost all world nations belong. The IMF works with nations to set exchange rates for their money and to expand foreign trade.

World Trade Organization (WTO)—The WTO was created in 1995. It oversees compliance with international trade agreements and rules on violations by member nations. It has more than 148 members, including all major industrialized nations of the world.

investigative reporting

With a partner, research the status of achieving the Millennium Development Goals. The UN Web site posts a report card each year on progress for each of the eight goals. This Web site also contains current information, background, news reports, Webcasts, documents, and much more. Use the information to write a three-page report about progress on the MDGs.

Case Study 3:

Regional Economic Blocs

▶ **What are the goals of regional economic blocs?**

▶ **What are some issues facing these groups?**

A *bloc* is a group of nations acting together in support of one another. A number of nations in the mid- and late twentieth century joined together in regional blocs. Most groups focus on trade and other economic issues. Their economic goals generally include

- reducing or ending tariffs and quotas among member nations
- promoting international trade for member nations
- encouraging international investment in member nations

Some regional blocs such as the Caribbean Community and Common Market (CARICOM) and the Common Market for Eastern and Southern Africa (COMESA) also cooperate for social and political goals. Member nations of CARICOM support joint education, health, and labor policies for their citizens. COMESA tries to promote peace and stable governments among its members. Some of its members, such as Rwanda and Sudan, however, have suffered civil wars in recent years.

The Asia Pacific Economic Cooperation (APEC) unites nations in Asia with those in North America and South America. Its main goal is to promote trade and investment among member nations. Developing nations such as Indonesia, Malaysia, and Peru hope to benefit from good trade relations with wealthier nations such as the United States and Australia.

Some nations belong to several regional groups. The United States, for example, belongs to APEC and both the North American Free Trade (NAFTA) and Central American Free Trade (CAFTA) groups. Several Central American and South American nations belong to regional groups within their local area and also to APEC. Multiple membership means that a nation has the benefit of reduced trade barriers with many nations.

Regional economic blocs have made great progress for member nations. However, these regional groups have not been able to erase all barriers to economic growth. This is especially true for developing nations. These nations still face problems. Among them are debt and unstable governments. Both make attracting foreign investment difficult. With limited foreign investment, economic development becomes more difficult to achieve. As a result, these nations cannot take full advantage of the benefits of regional groups.

Major Regional Economic Groups

1957	European Union (EU): 25 nations
1961	Central American Common Market (CACM): 5 nations
1967	Association of South East Asian Nations (ASEAN): 10 nations
1973	Caribbean Community and Common Market (CARICOM): 15 nations
1975	Economic Community of West African States (ECOWAS): 15 nations
1989	Asia Pacific Economic Cooperation (APEC): 21 nations
1991	Mercado Comun del Cono Sur (MERCOSUR): 4 nations
1992	Southern African Development Community (SADC): 13 nations
1994	Common Market for Eastern and Southern Africa (COMESA): 20 nations North American Free Trade Agreement (NAFTA): 3 nations
2005	Central American Free Trade Agreement (CAFTA): 7 nations

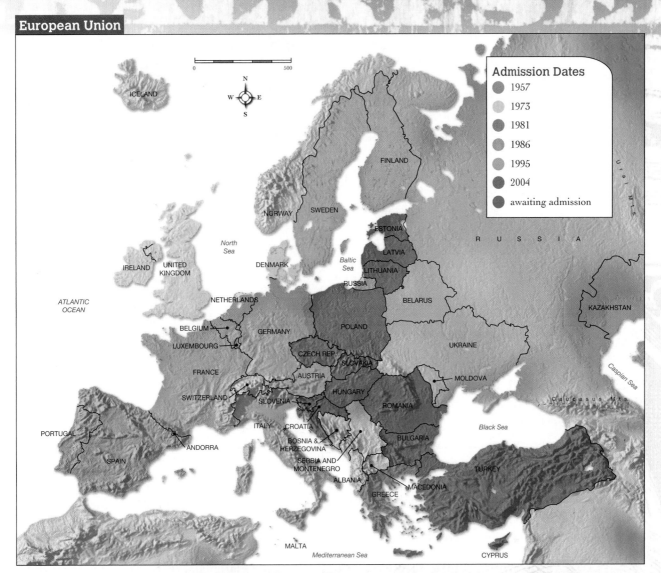

Admission Dates
- 1957
- 1973
- 1981
- 1986
- 1995
- 2004
- awaiting admission

Spotlight on the European Union

The European Union (EU) began as a regional trade group. However, over the years, the EU has become a major force in shaping social and cultural policies across Europe. It even influences political issues within member nations.

At the end of World War II, much of Western Europe lay in ruins. Slowly, with billions of dollars in aid from the United States as part of the Marshall Plan, these nations were rebuilt. As early as 1948, the Netherlands, Luxembourg, and Belgium joined in an economic union to reduce tariffs.

In 1952, Belgium, France, West Germany, Italy, Luxembourg, and the Netherlands created the European Coal and Steel Community (ECSC) to regulate their coal and steel industries. In 1957, the six created the European Economic Community (EEC). Its first goal was to do away with all tariffs on trade among member nations. They worked to reduce competition among the six member nations. They agreed to apply a single set of tariff rates on exports to nonmember nations. The EEC also made it easier for workers to move between countries for jobs and for investors to do business in member nations.

In 1973, the EEC was transformed into the European Community (EC). Three more nations including the United Kingdom, Denmark, and the Republic of Ireland joined. Over the next 20 years, six more western European nations joined.

In 1993, the EC became the European Union (EU)—its present name. In addition to economic unity, the EU works for political unity. On January 1, 2002, the euro—a single currency that uses the symbol €—was introduced in 12 of the 15 EU nations. In 2004, the EU expanded once again. Eight former Communist nations from eastern Europe joined. The EU now totals about 450 million people. Its economy rivals that of the United States.

The Impact of CAFTA

Regional economic blocs are set up to slowly reduce and finally end tariffs. However, some economists believe that the real benefit from CAFTA for Central American nations will be foreign investment. Central American nations have a history of political unrest. El Salvador, Guatemala, Nicaragua, and the Dominican Republic all suffered civil wars in the last part of the twentieth century.

The trade agreement signals that these nations are committed to making economic progress. Economists expect to see increased investment from the United States and industrialized countries in Europe and Asia.

Cargo ship—Ho Chi Minh City, Vietnam

ASEAN's Goals

The Association represents the collective will of the nations to bind themselves together in friendship and cooperation and, through joint efforts and sacrifices, secure for their peoples and for posterity the blessings of peace, freedom, and prosperity.

—ASEAN Declaration
Bangkok, Thailand, August 8, 1967

VIEWPOINT

U.S. Trade Pact Divides Central Americans, with Farmers and Others Fearful

The Central America Free Trade Agreement, known as CAFTA, was barely passed by [the U.S.] Congress in late July…It has become a toxic political issue here in [Costa Rica], Central America's richest economy as well as in several others, including countries where the pact has already passed the legislatures.

A high-ranking Costa Rican official, speaking on the condition of anonymity for fear of offending his American counterparts, said the implicit threat was that temporary trade preferences enjoyed under old agreements would not be renewed. Central American countries had to get on board with the new pact or risk watching their exports dwindle.

United States trade officials say they argued that a permanent agreement was a better deal for smaller countries than the two-decade-old, one-way trade preferences that could disappear at the whim of Congress. But they did not dispute that reluctance to extend the preferences past 2008 might have spurred countries to join the new pact.

As such, the treaty has divided Costa Ricans and others in the region, with people both for and against it now warning of impending doom if they do not get their way.

If the pact is approved, small farmers like Mr. Elizondo say they will be wiped out. If it is not, Costa Rican manufacturers like Luis Gamboa, whose factory produces stoves and refrigerators, say they may move to another country.

Labor leaders threaten strikes and scream that the treaty will force public-sector layoffs and drive up health care costs. Flower growers say they will go out of business without it.

Even in Guatemala, where the legislature did approve the agreement, there were violent demonstrations against it. In El Salvador, one of the United States' closest allies, health care workers marched to protest the pact before it passed.

Critics across the region, mostly laborite or leftist in their views, see the pact as a one-way street, benefiting United States multinational corporations at the expense of Central America's small businesses and farmers.

Opponents…point to the experience of Mexico, whose 10-year experiment in free trade with the United States has depopulated much of the countryside and sent waves of migration north of the border.

—*James C. McKinley, Jr.*, New York Times,
August 21, 2005

Common Market of Eastern and Southern Africa (COMESA)

COMESA was formed in 1994 in Africa to replace an earlier trade agreement called the Preferential Trade Area. The new organization was established "as an organization of free independent sovereign states which have agreed to cooperate in developing their natural and human resources for the good of all their people." Today, COMESA has 20 member nations with a total population of over 374 million people.

The following infrastructure gives the organization policy and direction:

- The Authority, made up of the 20 heads of state and government, is responsible for general policy, direction, and achievement of aims and objectives.
- The Council of Ministers, made up of 20 ministers (one from each member nation), is responsible for making sure that COMESA follows the provisions of the agreement.
- The COMESA Court of Justice ensures the proper interpretation and application of the provisions of the treaty. It hears cases regarding disputes among the members.
- The Committee of Governors of Central Banks determines the maximum debt and credit lines.

Several other institutions have been created within the organization.

- The COMESA Trade and Development Bank in Kenya
- The COMESA Clearing House in Zimbabwe
- The COMESA Association of Commercial Banks in Zimbabwe
- The COMESA Leather Institute in Ethiopia
- The COMESA Re-Insurance Company in Kenya

According to the COMESA Web site, it offers its members

- a wider, harmonized, and more competitive market
- greater industrial productivity and competitiveness
- increased agricultural production and food security
- more rational exploitation of natural resources
- more harmonized monetary, banking, and financial policies
- more reliable transport and communications infrastructure

Nations belonging to COMESA in 2005 were Angola, Burundi, Comoros, D.R. Congo, Djibouti, Egypt, Eritrea, Ethiopia, Kenya, Libya, Madagascar, Malawi, Mauritius, Rwanda, Seychelles, the Sudan, Swaziland, Uganda, Zambia, and Zimbabwe.

SADC's Vision for Its Future

The SADC vision is one of a common future. It is a future in a regional community that will ensure economic well-being, improvement of the standards of living and quality of life, freedom and social justice, and peace and security for the peoples of Southern Africa. This shared vision is anchored in the common values and principles and the historical and cultural affinities that exist between the peoples of Southern Africa.

—Regional Strategic Development Plan, Southern African Development Community

Classroom—Camacupa, Angola

investigative reporting

With a partner, research one of the regional economic blocs listed on pages 348–349. Create a poster listing the group's

- member nations
- goals
- headquarters' city
- three major projects
- achievements

Case Study 4:

The Environment and Energy Issues

> ▶ **What environment and energy issues do developing nations face?**
> ▶ **How are developing nations dealing with these problems?**

The environment is the air, water, land, and natural resources of Earth. Every day, nations pollute the environment and use up resources that cannot be replaced. Coal, oil, and natural gas are some of these nonrenewable natural resources. They are also the major sources of energy to power homes, businesses, factories, cars—anything that requires energy.

Factories and cars are the major polluters of the environment. A number of industrialized nations have laws to regulate pollution. They set standards for factories and fuel-efficiency and emissions controls for cars. However, not all industrialized nations have tough laws.

Controlling pollution is expensive. It requires changes in how companies do business. New engines for cars need to be designed and new machines built to make the new engines. Factories have to be outfitted with new equipment to control pollution. Water treatment and sewage treatment plants have to be built. Better methods of farming need to be taught to farmers.

Many developing nations recognize the importance of preserving the environment. In its list of objectives, the Southern African Development Community states that the group will work to "achieve sustainable utilization of natural resources and effective protection of the environment." This is an economic model known as sustainable development.

However, it is not easy for nations to balance the need for economic development and protection of the environment. In 1997, more than 150 countries took part in a meeting in Kyoto, Japan, to discuss the issue of global warming. Global warming is the increase in the surface temperature of Earth because of the buildup of greenhouse gases. These are caused by things like car emissions and the smoke from factories.

The result of the meeting was the Kyoto Protocol. A protocol is a set of rules. Industrialized nations agreed

to reduce greenhouse gases by 2010. The target was a reduction of about 5.2 percent below 1990 levels. Developing nations were not required to observe the treaty. The goal is that these nations will spend money on development rather than on the costly equipment to cut air pollution.

It is not only developing nations that claim cutting greenhouse gases is too costly. President George W. Bush rejected the Kyoto Protocol. He said that meeting the terms of the treaty would have a negative impact on the U.S. economy. Instead, the United States, China, and India are working together on a separate plan to deal with climate issues.

Good for the Environment, Good for the Economy

In 1977, Wangari Maathai began the Green Belt Movement (GBM) in Kenya. The government of Kenya had allowed developers and loggers to cut down much of its forestland. Maathai's group set out to reforest the countryside. Since then, the GBM has planted more than 30 million trees.

Besides repairing the environment, the GBM has given jobs to more than 100,000 people. Most of these workers are women. They plant and then take care of the young trees. In Kenya, as in other developing nations, women have few opportunities to work for pay.

In 2004, Maathai was awarded the Nobel Peace Prize for her work as an environmentalist.

NEWS FLASH

The U.S. Environmental Protection Agency (EPA) claims that 25 percent of the air pollution over Los Angeles, California, floats across the Pacific Ocean from China. Unless China tightens its pollution laws, air polution levels will only get worse.

Kyoto Protocol

"The Kyoto Protocol is a legal agreement under which industrialized countries will reduce their collective emissions of greenhouse gases by 5.2 % compared to the year 1990."

—Press release from the United Nations Environment Programme, 1997

The purpose of the Kyoto Protocol is to lower the worldwide emissions of six greenhouse gases that contribute to global warming. These gases include carbon dioxide, methane, nitrous oxide, sulfur hexafluoride, HFCs,

Environmental activists—
Tokyo, Japan

and PFCs. The treaty is actually an amendment to the United Nations Framework Convention on Climate Change (UNFCCC). It was adopted after a meeting in Kyoto, Japan, in 1997. Fifty-five nations that accounted for 55 percent of carbon dioxide emissions needed to sign the treaty before it could be enforced. Russia was the 55th nation to sign it in 2004. As of September 2005, 156 nations had signed.

The United States and Australia are two major industrialized nations that have not signed the treaty. Opponents cite as reasons for not signing the possible impact on economic growth, nongovernmental scientific studies about global warming, and that the treaty is not strict enough.

NGOs and the Environment

There are a number of nongovernmental organizations (NGOs) worldwide that work to save the environment. Among the well-known international conservation and environmental NGOs are the World Wildlife Fund, the World Conservation Union, the Nature Conservancy, and UNESCO World Heritage Center.

Earth Day

Earth Day is organized by the Earth Day Network. Its goal is to encourage people, governments, and corporations to work for a clean and healthy environment. Nations on every continent participate each year. For example, in 2000, a group of Ghanian journalists organized a series of workshops to familiarize reporters with the issues their country faces.

Land Use Issues in African Nations

Environmental issues in African nations focus on land use rather than air pollution. The destruction of forests, mining, and increased farming all result in damage to the land.

The Democratic Republic of Congo (DRC) faces serious deforestation, or the cutting down of forests without planting new trees. The nation has close to one-half of Africa's tropical rain forest. The government of the DRC has granted the right to log 33 million hectares of its rain forest. This amounts to 15 percent of the nation.

Some African nations also have valuable mineral deposits such as gold, diamonds, and bauxite. Aluminum is made from bauxite. Mining can be as destructive to the land as logging. In Ghana, for example, 250 companies operate mines. Most of the mines are surface mines, which scar the countryside. Machines dig out large sections of earth to get at the minerals. When the mine is exhausted, the mining company moves on without replacing the soil or replanting trees.

Farming can also damage the land and water resources. An example is in Zambia. Zambian farmers began using chemical fertilizers and new crops in the 1970s. The new farming methods resulted in soil erosion, or the wearing away of topsoil. Farms no longer produced harvests as large as they once had. In Cote d'Ivoire, farmers had the opposite problem. Cote d'Ivoire's cocoa crop is very profitable. It is so profitable that farmers have been cutting down the rain forest to plant crops. Officials estimate about half a million farmers operate illegal farms in the nation's rain forest.

Wherever chemical fertilizers are used, there is danger to the water supply. The runoff of water from the chemical fertilizers can pollute a community's wells. It contaminates, or poisons, the water that villagers use for drinking and cooking.

Deforestation—Liberia

Coal-fired power plant—Indiana, U.S.A.

Environmental Damage in China

Air, water, and land pollution harm the quality of life for citizens of a nation. All these cost money and take away from a nation's economic growth. China provides an example of how damage to the environment can harm the economy.

Acid rain is pollution caused when industrial smoke and car-exhaust fumes in the air dissolve in water vapor and fall as rain or snow. It is a type of air pollution. In 2005, an official of the Chinese government predicted that the nation's pollution could quadruple by 2020.

Fast Facts

- The United States is the number one producer of greenhouse gases.
- China is the second-biggest producer of greenhouse gases.
- One million people per year die in China and India from the effects of air pollution.
- Japan is the world leader in solar power and the use of hybrid cars.
- Six of the world's ten most polluted cities are in China.
- Acid rain falls on one-third of China.
- 80 percent of China's sewage flows untreated into its waterways.
- Contaminated water kills more than 30,000 children annually.
- Pollution costs China more than $54 billion a year.

TERM IN THE NEWS

Pollution trading is the process that allows a polluter to gain a credit against future pollution, or to sell rights to pollute by polluting less. The idea is that developing nations will sell their credits to developed nations and use the money to clean up their own pollution. Pollution trading has helped China pay for some of its environmental clean-up.

Making Progress in China

Reducing pollution is an enormous issue because China is an enormous country, but the nation is making progress. Both foreign-owned and local Chinese companies are helping factories and cities clean up their pollution.

Equipment called scrubbers are used to clean dangerous ingredients from smoke that comes from factories. Experts estimate that Chinese factories will buy $1 billion worth of scrubbers each year. China is also buying engines powered by wind and natural gas. The latter

Pollution—Beijing, China

is cleaner than oil or coal. Beijing, the capital of China, recently bought 2,500 buses powered by natural gas. A number of cities have built water treatment plants to ensure clean water for their residents.

Polluted water source—Shanghai, China

The Future of Alternative Energy

"Residential energy use in the United States will increase 25 percent by the year 2025," according to U.S. Department of Energy (DOE) forecasts. A small but increasing share of that extra power will trickle in from renewable sources like wind, sunlight, water, and heat in the ground. Last year alternative energy sources provided 6 percent of the nation's energy supply, according to the DOE.

"While renewable energy is generally more expensive, . . . alternative power helps to reduce pollution and to conserve fossil fuels. Below, a look at some recent developments in renewable-energy technology:

Solar Power

"Photovoltaic, or solar-electric, systems capture light energy from the sun's rays and convert it into electricity. Today these solar units power everything from small homes to large office buildings.

"Technological improvements have made solar-electric modules more cost-effective. Today the average [price of photovoltaic energy] has dropped to around 20 cents per kilowatt-hour, according to Brad Collins, the executive director of the American Solar Energy Society, a Boulder, Colorado–based nonprofit.

"The cheaper rate is still more expensive than the average national price of electricity, which in 2003 was a little over 8 cents per kilowatt-hour, according to the U.S. Department of Energy's Annual Energy Review.

"In the last two decades solar-thermal panels (units used to warm household hot water, pools, and spas) have become highly efficient. Energy costs have decreased from 60 cents to 8 cents per kilowatt-hour since the 1980s, Collins said.

Wind Power

"Compared to other renewable energy sources, wind power competes with conventional energy at a price less than 4 cents per kilowatt-hour, Collins said.

Wind energy projects around the world now generate enough energy to power nine million typical U.S. homes, according to the American Wind Energy Association, a Washington, D.C.–based trade group.

"Europe now has 17 wind farms spinning offshore. The Arklow Bank Offshore Wind Park, 8 miles (13 kilometers) off the eastern coast of Ireland, is one such project. Its seven turbines generate enough electricity to power 16,000 homes.

Ground Heat

"Tapping into the ground offers another option to regulate household heating and cooling. In most areas of the United States, the ground below the frost line maintains an average temperature between 50 and 54 degrees Fahrenheit (10 to 12 degrees Celsius). Ground-source heat pumps, also called geo-exchange systems, use this relatively constant temperature to keep homes at comfortable temperatures.

"A U.S. Environmental Protection Agency study found that geo-exchange systems can save up to 70 percent of home-heating costs."

—*Cameron Walker*, National Geographic News, *October 28, 2004*

investigative reporting

With a partner, research one of the alternative sources of energy listed below. Find out how it works, and what its advantages and disadvantages are. Create a poster with your information.

- wind power
- solar power
- nuclear power
- geothermal power
- hybrid cars
- electric power for cars
- hydroelectric power

Case Study 5:

e-commerce

- ▶ **What is e-commerce?**
- ▶ **How is e-commerce contributing to globalization?**

E-commerce is the buying and selling of goods through the Internet. This includes the sales of advertising on Web sites. Advertising often fills the columns on either side of the information you are looking for online. An ad also often fills the banner at the top of the page. Pop-up ads tend to appear just when you find what you are looking for on a site.

Some of the most profitable online ads are search advertising. These are the ads that appear on search engines. Advertising pays for search engines such as Google, Yahoo!, and AskJeeves. Without advertisers, search engines would not be able to operate. They need the money that advertisers pay them to maintain their sites. Other kinds of sites also depend on selling ad space in order to stay on the Web. For example, a newspaper sells space on its Web site to advertisers. A city may sell space on its Web site to local businesses.

Businesses that sell goods and services over the Internet are called e-tailers—rather than retailers. Some businesses, such as Amazon.com, have no stores. You cannot go to the mall and find an Amazon.com. Other e-tailers have what are called "bricks and mortar," meaning traditional stores. If you want to spend an afternoon in a bookstore, you can visit your local Barnes and Noble. If you are in a hurry to find a book,

you can go online to the Web site for Barnes and Noble, Borders, or maybe even your locally owned bookstore, and order a book.

You can buy and sell stocks and bonds online. You can find a new coat or a used car online. You can also sell online through an online auction house such as eBay. If you want to start your own small business, you can sell anything from pet supplies to handmade clothes online. In 2004, U.S. Internet e-tailers sold more than $145 billion worth of goods. That was a jump of 26 percent from 2003. Each year, Internet sales grow dramatically.

E-commerce works in the United States because more than one-half of all Americans are online. Other developed nations such as Great Britain and France also have large numbers of people online. E-commerce in these countries is also big business.

What about the rest of the world? There are nearly 1 billion people online worldwide. That is close to one in six of the world's population. In developing nations, there is little online business now. Less than 10 percent of China's 1.3 billion people are online. However, the possibilities for the future are tremendous.

Buying and Selling Beyond the United States

The nation's most successful online auction house is eBay. In 2005, it had 125 million registered buyers and sellers of goods. However, to continue its success, eBay is looking beyond the United States. The company bought online auction sites in China, India, and South Korea.

Fast Facts

Online U.S. stockbrokers are entering the market in China and are beginning to provide financial services. Chinese investors can open online accounts and buy and sell stocks and bonds through these accounts.

Internet café—Tokyo, Japan

Chinese Search Engine

While U.S. Internet-based companies are entering foreign markets, they are meeting competition. In China, for example, Baidu.com is a Chinese-owned search engine. In 2005, it sold shares of its stock on the U.S. stock market.

At the opening, the shares were priced at $27 a share. By the end of the day, U.S. investors had bid up the price of Baidu.com's stock shares to $122.54. This was a gain in price of 354 percent. Investors were putting their money on Baidu.com's ability to grow with China's market for Internet business. One of its investors was Google, the large U.S. online search company.

Yahoo! co-founder Jerry Yang

Building Customer Loyalty Outside the United States

Google and Yahoo! are among the biggest online search engines in the United States. They have been able to successfully export their businesses to industrialized nations such as France. The question is whether they can export their businesses successfully to developing countries.

Both companies have bought or invested in local companies that operate search engines. However, they also want to establish their own businesses as key players in local economies. From e-mail servers to online shopping to chat rooms, these companies have to learn how to match their online offerings with local ways of doing things.

Blogs Are for Business

Web logs, or blogs, are interactive Web journals. They were begun by ordinary people who wanted to share information with others. Some people write every day about what they do, who they see, or what they think. Others use blogs to share their thoughts on politics, business, celebrities, the best places to shop for things, the best music to buy—whatever interests them. Readers can write back and add their comments.

In the next few years, businesses will figure out a variety of ways to use blogs. Advertising may be moved to blogs from newspapers, television, radio, and even search engines. Blogs might even be used to develop new products by asking consumers what they want. As one executive said of his company's blog, blogs are "a way to concentrate your thoughts, test your ideas, and accept criticism."

International Blogging

Blogging began in the United States, and most bloggers are U.S.-based. However, blogging is catching on in the rest of the world. In 2005, the United States had an estimated 9 million bloggers, or 3 percent of the populaton. France had an estimated 3 million bloggers, which is 4.9 percent of the French population. China had 3 million bloggers. Within two years, experts estimate the number of Chinese bloggers will reach 7 million.

Identify Theft

There is a great deal of talk these days about identity theft. Identity theft is using someone else's personal or financial information to open credit or bank accounts in that person's name. The criminal then uses these accounts to get money or buy things. Personal information includes such things as a person's name and Social Security number.

Most identify theft occurs through the theft of credit cards, or credit card information such as from the receipt from a purchase made by credit card.

There are some ways to be sure that your credit card information is safe when you buy online. First, buy only from well-known sites. These sites have powerful encryption software to safeguard buyers' information. Only the company that owns the Web site can translate the encrypted code.

Second, you can tell if your credit card information is safe when you type it into the Web site. Look at the URL at the top of the page. The *http* should change to *https* or *shttp*. The browser may also signal that your information is safe. Look for a broken key or an open padlock icon. When your information has been received, the broken key will change into a whole key. If the open padlock is used as symbol, it will appear closed.

You should also never send your credit card information in an e-mail. E-mail is not secure and can be seen by other people. Some experts even recommend that you use a separate credit card, with a low limit, for online purchases. This helps to keep your credit safe if the account number is stolen. The Internet is safe if it is used wisely.

Internet Scams: How to Protect Yourself

The Federal Trade Commission, the nation's consumer protection agency, issued the following suggestions for students:

1 **Consider the National Do Not Call Registry.** As hard as it may be for your parents to believe, there may be times when you *don't* want to be on the phone—especially when the caller is a stranger trying to sell you something. Visit www.donotcall.gov and register your phone number with the National Do Not Call Registry.

2 **Stay Away from "Guarantees" to Get Scholarships.** Reputable groups don't charge money for information about scholarships. Steer clear of anyone "guaranteeing" you financial aid for college or vocational school—especially if they insist you pay them for the information first.

3 **Don't Buy Bogus Weight-Loss Products.** Good health isn't about a number on a scale. It's about cultivating a positive attitude, enjoying a variety of foods, and staying fit and active. Take a pass on any product that promises easy weight loss; instead, focus on healthy habits that will last a lifetime.

4 **Keep Your Personal Information to Yourself.** In the past five years, more than 27 million Americans have been victims of identity theft, including many students. Protect your passwords, guard your credit card number, shred sensitive paperwork, and don't leave your mail lying around where it might tempt a potential identity thief.

5 **Understand Credit.** Credit is so much more than just a plastic card. It's your financial future. Before you sign on the dotted line, make sure you "speak credit." Remember that "permanent record" your teachers always warned you about? It's real—and it's called a credit report. Late payments now will come back to haunt you when you try to buy a car, get an apartment, or even land a job.

6 **Practice P2P File Sharing with Care, If at All.** Peer-to-peer file sharing can open the door to unwanted content, spyware, and viruses. You might give strangers access not just to the files you intended to share, but also to other information on your hard drive, like e-mail and personal documents. Remember that sharing copyrighted music or other entertainment via P2P can land you in legal hot water.

7 **Travel Scams Make Busts out of Spring Breaks.** Be aware that shady pitch people target students who are looking for low-cost vacations. Before you show up at the airport with your sunscreen, review the tour package carefully and investigate the operator.

8 **Phishing Scams Reel in Your Personal Information.** We've all seen them—e-mails claiming to be from your bank or ISP asking you to "verify" your credit card or checking account number. It's called phishing, so don't take the bait. Never give out personal information in response to an e-mail. When in doubt, check it out by calling the company directly.

9 **Some Employment Services Are Scams.** There are bona fide job placement services that can help launch you in the career of your dreams. There are also bogus companies whose only business is scamming you out of your money. Before paying anything up front to someone offering to help you land a job, check out who you're doing business with.

10 **Ask Questions. Do Your Homework. Speak Up.** Before spending your hard-earned money, ask questions and do your homework. www.ftc.gov is just one place to go for accurate consumer information. But if something goes wrong and you aren't able to get satisfaction, speak up. Report fraud and deceptive practices to the FTC by filing a complaint online.

Vietnam Targets Bad Internet Connections

HO CHI MINH CITY—"Vietnam is doing everything it can to join the World Trade Organization (WTO) this year, but at the same time its Communist government is doing its best to restrict cyber cafes—the main window to the rest of the world for ordinary citizens.

"No fewer than four ministries have joined hands to 'regulate and standardize the fledgling and troublesome Internet cafes business.' Yet, while conformists and officialdom are one in welcoming new restrictions imposed last month . . . others see in them attempts by the government to put more barriers on free access to cyberspace.

"Since logging into the world wide web in 1997, Vietnam has supervised access to the global information highway . . . But the increasing number of Internet users . . . has made the government's efforts to control access to web content cumbersome.

"Last year, the Vietnam Internet Center reported that the number of Internet subscribers had jumped to more than 2 million from 823,000 in 2003. Alongside, the number of web surfers at Internet cafes has doubled and now represent 7.35% of the country's population of 83 million people.

". . . Internet cafes have become affordable places for young . . . people to communicate with the outside world.

"The latest controls demand that cafe owners register clients' details, including name, age, address, and ID number. . . . They are also asked to close shop before midnight and disallow under-14 children, unless accompanied by adults.

"However, the majority of Internet cafe owners and their clients do not agree. . . . 'We are not policemen,' said Tran Trung, owner of Than Huu Net . . . referring to the obligation for Internet cafe owners to demand to see clients' IDs.

"Trung told IPS that he thought the real reason for the new laws may be political rather than ethical and moral.

". . . Several Vietnamese dissidents and democracy activists living in the country as well as abroad have taken this opportunity to intensify their criticism of the VCP on the Internet.

"Both the United States and the European Union support Vietnam's entry into WTO . . . although the new restrictions on Internet access seem to run counter to the general policy of opening up."

—Tran Dinh Thanh Lam, Inter Press Service

File-Sharing and Music Piracy

The Internet is an amazing tool for sharing information. However, not all information is free for the sharing. Music is copyrighted material. U.S. copyright laws protect the ownership of the words and music. Movies and printed materials such as magazines and books are also copyrighted under U.S. law. This kind of creative work is known as intellectual property.

Unfortunately, not everyone obeys copyright laws. As early as the 1990s, some software programmers had figured out how to download and share music and movies without paying for them. There were at least nine major file-sharing services operating on the Internet by 2005.

The U.S. Supreme Court effectively ended file-sharing services in 2005 with its ruling in *Metro-Goldwyn-Mayer* v. *Grokster*. Grokster was one of the file-sharing businesses. The Court ruled that file-sharing services made illegal activity possible. The result was the shift of at least some of these file-sharing businesses into legal music services.

File-Sharing Continues

File-sharing services may be illegal, but file-sharing continues. People still download and share files. However, the music industry is fighting back. To drive home the point that it is illegal to share downloaded music without paying for it, the music industry is going after violators. In 2005, the industry filed lawsuits against 635 students at 39 colleges. They were charged with "illegally distributing copyrighted music on the Internet."

investigative reporting

Some people think that music, movies, and print material should be free if they are on the Internet. What do you think? With a partner, discuss the issue of free versus purchased online material. Think in economic terms about writing the work, and producing and selling it. Consider also why someone might think that the same album that is sold in stores is free if it is on the Internet. Take notes about your discussion and then write a three-page essay stating your opinion.

Appendix

Databank and Glossary

The Economy and Financial Markets: Slowing Back Down

By David A. Wyss, Ph. D.
Managing Director and Chief Economist, Standard & Poor's

After a strong performance in 2004 with 4.4 percent growth, the economy is slowing down. In the past year, all domestic sectors of the economy were strong, aided by low interest rates and tax cuts. Now household savings are at historic lows, slowing spending. Although business investment is accelerating, it does not fully offset the slower consumer growth.

During the 2001 recession, inflation was low, and the Federal Reserve was able to lower interest rates. In 2003 the core inflation rate (consumer prices excluding food and energy) rose 1.1 percent, the lowest rate in 40 years. However, inflation has since reaccelerated, with core inflation up 2.2 percent over the 12 months ending in April 2005 and the total up 3.5 percent. Although inflation remains low by historical standards, it is rising, and the Fed wants to ensure that it does not rise further. The Fed has been tightening monetary policy since June 2004, raising interest rates at nine consecutive meetings. The Fed does not really want to slow the economy down. It would like to raise interest rates back to a neutral rate that would keep inflation down without restricting economic growth, in part so that if something does go wrong, the Fed has the flexibility to lower rates.

Labor markets are beginning to tighten. The first two years of this expansion saw no employment growth, but in 2004 employment finally began to rise, with payrolls adding 2.2 million jobs during the year. That trend is continuing in early 2005 and is expected to continue. The unemployment rate is down to 5.1 percent, below its 50-year average of 5.6 percent.

Low interest rates have encouraged consumers to borrow and discouraged them from saving. The biggest impact was on the housing market, where home sales hit record highs in 2004. More than 69 percent of all American families— a record high—now own their own home. Many observers, however, worry that the easy money has enticed households to overextend themselves, paying more for their houses than they can really afford, and thus has made housing prices vulnerable to a rise in mortgage rates.

Consumers have largely ignored the rise in gasoline prices, which have reached record levels. Americans bought 16.8 million cars in 2004, the best year since 2001. Households offset the higher oil prices by cutting back on saving; the saving rate hit a record low of 1.2 percent of after-tax income in 2004.

Businesses are supporting economic growth—capital spending is rebounding from the recession drop. Strong cash flow has allowed firms to invest, and the need to improve productivity to compete in the world markets has provided motivation. Spending on capital equipment and software jumped 13.6 percent (corrected for inflation) in 2004.

Growth is likely to remain near 11 percent in 2005. Spending on construction projects has been slower to accelerate, however, because of excess space left over from the late 1990s. The slow rise in employment also has meant that there is little need for new office space.

The federal government has aided the economic expansion by cutting taxes and increasing spending. However, in fiscal 2004 this resulted in a record $413 billion federal deficit. The deficit is expected to shrink to about $350 billion in 2005. Getting it back under control will demand tight spending control and probably tax hikes, especially since federal spending will jump when the baby-boom generation starts to enter retirement in the next few years. The administration's emphasis on Social Security reform is well-placed (although Medicare is an even bigger problem), but the proposed reform is too little and too late to keep the deficit from increasing over the next decade.

The weak global economy is putting downward pressure on U.S. growth by slowing exports. Although the dollar has dropped to a more competitive level against other developed currencies, the weak growth of demand in Europe and Japan has made export sales hard to find. The GDP of both Europe and Japan is expected to slow in 2005. The only strong growth outside the United States has been in developing countries, particularly China and India. Unfortunately U.S. exports tend to go mostly to industrial countries, while U.S. imports come from developing countries, against whose currencies the dollar has not declined.

The widening trade gap has been the major drag on the U.S. economy. The United States is now running a trade deficit of more than 6 percent of GDP. Everyone agrees that this level of deficit cannot continue, but it is unclear how long it will take to correct or how painful the process will be. The normal market reaction to a deficit is a currency decline, but extensive intervention by foreign central banks and the weakness of the euro have limited the dollar's drop.

Last year the foreign central bank intervention, involving the purchase of dollars, offset more than 60 percent of U.S. Treasury issuance. The intervention has thus held bond yields down. In addition, the weak European growth and the worries about the euro have made even the low U.S. bond yields attractive to European investors. This has attracted more money into the United States and has held the dollar up despite the record trade deficit.

The stock market has risen strongly on the back of three consecutive years of double-digit growth in corporate earnings. With profits now at a record high as a share of GDP, further gains will be harder to attain. From 1981 through 1999, the stock market returned an average of 18 percent per year. The market is now down by 25 percent from 2000 (S&P 500). The drop is entirely accounted for by two sectors of the market: high tech and telecommunications. Gains are expected to moderate to the 5 to 10 percent range over the next decade.

Overall the economy seems well-placed for continued moderate growth with low inflation. However, there are substantial risks from another oil price surge or an international reluctance to continue funding U.S. deficits. Either would cause slower growth in the U.S. economy and possibly trigger recession.

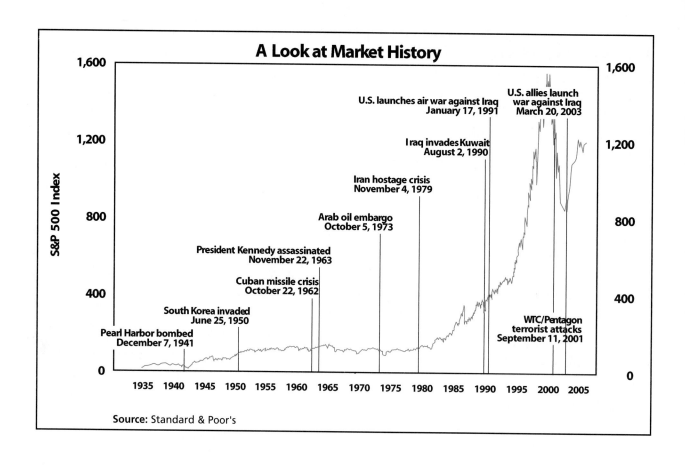

A Look at Market History

S&P 500 Index

1,600

1,200

800

400

0

U.S. launches air war against Iraq
January 17, 1991

U.S. allies launch
war against Iraq
March 20, 2003

Iraq invades Kuwait
August 2, 1990

Iran hostage crisis
November 4, 1979

Arab oil embargo
October 5, 1973

President Kennedy assassinated
November 22, 1963

Cuban missile crisis
October 22, 1962

South Korea invaded
June 25, 1950

Pearl Harbor bombed
December 7, 1941

WTC/Pentagon
terrorist attacks
September 11, 2001

1935 1940 1945 1950 1955 1960 1965 1970 1975 1980 1985 1990 1995 2000 2005

Source: Standard & Poor's

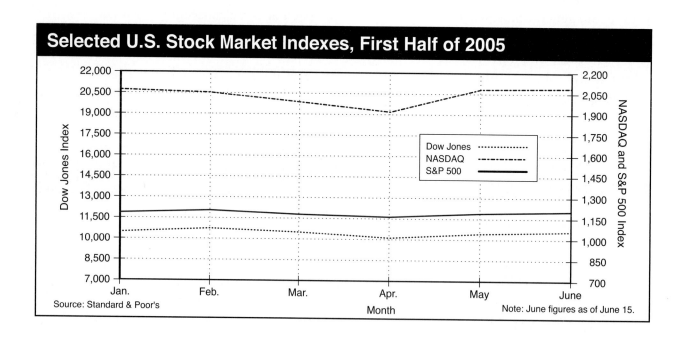

Selected U.S. Stock Market Indexes, First Half of 2005

Dow Jones Index

22,000
20,500
19,000
17,500
16,000
14,500
13,000
11,500
10,000
8,500
7,000

NASDAQ and S&P 500 Index

2,200
2,050
1,900
1,750
1,600
1,450
1,300
1,150
1,000
850
700

Dow Jones ....
NASDAQ — · — · —
S&P 500 ——————

Jan.   Feb.   Mar.   Apr.   May   June

Month

Source: Standard & Poor's

Note: June figures as of June 15.

Selected Foreign Stock Market Indexes, December 2004 to May 2005

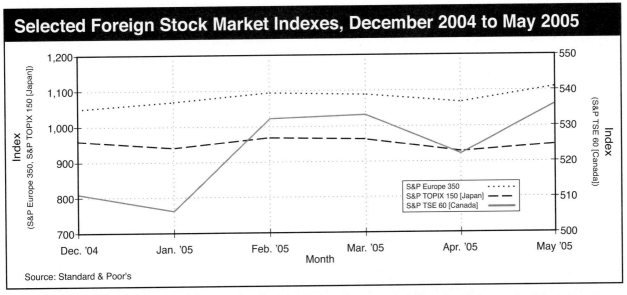

Source: Standard & Poor's

U.S. Markets—Long-Term Performance

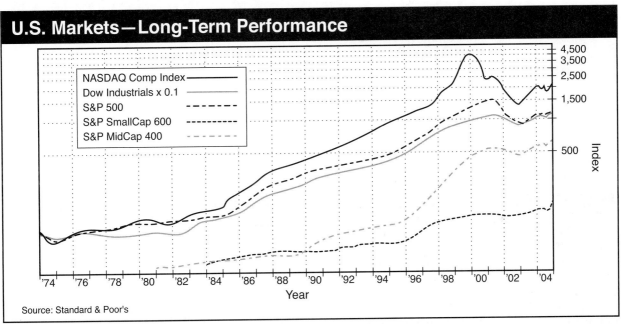

- NASDAQ Comp Index
- Dow Industrials x 0.1
- S&P 500
- S&P SmallCap 600
- S&P MidCap 400

Source: Standard & Poor's

U.S. Exports and Imports of Merchandise, 2003 (in billions of dollars)

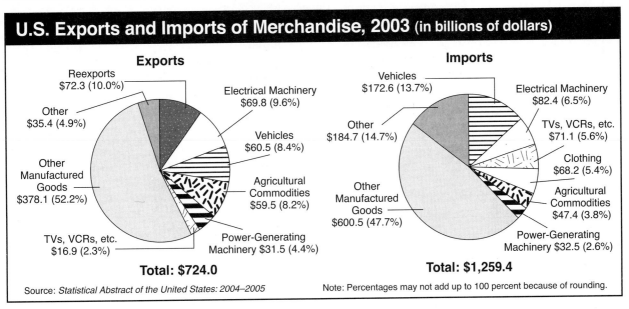

Exports

- Reexports $72.3 (10.0%)
- Other $35.4 (4.9%)
- Other Manufactured Goods $378.1 (52.2%)
- TVs, VCRs, etc. $16.9 (2.3%)
- Electrical Machinery $69.8 (9.6%)
- Vehicles $60.5 (8.4%)
- Agricultural Commodities $59.5 (8.2%)
- Power-Generating Machinery $31.5 (4.4%)

Total: $724.0

Imports

- Vehicles $172.6 (13.7%)
- Other $184.7 (14.7%)
- Other Manufactured Goods $600.5 (47.7%)
- Electrical Machinery $82.4 (6.5%)
- TVs, VCRs, etc. $71.1 (5.6%)
- Clothing $68.2 (5.4%)
- Agricultural Commodities $47.4 (3.8%)
- Power-Generating Machinery $32.5 (2.6%)

Total: $1,259.4

Source: *Statistical Abstract of the United States: 2004–2005*

Note: Percentages may not add up to 100 percent because of rounding.

U.S. Merchandise Trade by Region, 2003 (in billions of dollars)

$52.1 →
← *$118.0*

$24.1 →
← *$37.0*

Canada
$224.2
$169.8

United States

$138.1 $97.5

Mexico

$6.9 →
← *$12.8*
$2.7 →
← *$1.1*
$1.5 →
← *$2.3*

Israel
Kuwait
Egypt

Japan
South Korea

$2.8 →
← *$4.6*

South Africa

Australia

$13.1 →
← *$6.4*

→ Imports from U.S.
← *Exports to U.S.*

Source: *Statistical Abstract of the United States: 2004–2005*

Leading U.S. Trading Partners, 2003 (in billions of dollars)

U.S. Imports by Country

Canada
China
Mexico
Japan
Germany
United Kingdom
South Korea
Taiwan
France
Ireland
Malaysia

U.S. Exports by Country

250 225 200 175 150 125 100 75 50 25 0   0 25 50 75 100 125 150 175 200 225 250
Billions of Dollars

Source: *Statistical Abstract of the United States: 2004–2005*

Economic and Social Statistics for Selected Countries, 2003

Country	Population (in millions)	GNI per Capita (current U.S. dollars)	Life Expectancy at Birth (in years)	Death Rate (per 1,000 persons)	Birth Rate (per 1,000 persons)	Adult Illiteracy Rate (in percent) (men/women)
Argentina	36.8	3,810	74.5	7.6	17.5	*
Australia	19.9	21,950	79.8	7.3	12.6	*
Bangladesh	138.1	400	62.4	8.6	29.9	50/69
Bolivia	8.8	900	64.1	7.9	25.5	7/20
Canada	31.6	24,470	79.3	7.6	11.0	*
China	1,300.0	1,100	70.8	6.9	13.0	5/13
Colombia	44.6	1,810	71.9	5.6	21.6	6/5
Côte d'Ivoire	16.8	660	45.1	15.2	36.3	40/62
Egypt	67.6	1,390	69.1	5.3	24.4	33/56
Ethiopia	68.6	90	42	15.5	39.9	51/66
France	59.8	24,730	79.3	9.1	12.5	*
Germany	82.5	25,270	78.3	10.3	8.6	*
Ghana	20.7	320	54.4	10.3	32.5	37/54
India	1,100.0	540	63.4	8.5	23.3	27/52
Indonesia	214.7	810	66.9	6.3	21.5	8/17
Israel	6.7	16,240	78.8	6.2	18.7	*
Italy	57.6	21,570	79.8	10.1	9.2	*
Japan	127.6	34,180	81.7	8.6	9.6	*
Mexico	102.3	6,230	73.6	4.7	21.9	8/11
Nigeria	136.5	350	44.9	17.6	41.1	26/41
Philippines	81.5	1,080	69.9	5.6	26.3	8/7
Russia	143.4	2,610	65.7	14.9	9.4	*
Sri Lanka	19.2	930	74.0	6.5	16.1	5/10
Switzerland	7.4	40,680	80.5	8.4	9.9	*
Thailand	62.0	2,190	69.3	6.9	14.2	5/9
Ukraine	48.4	970	68.3	15.9	8.3	*
United Kingdom	59.3	28,320	77.6	10.2	11.0	*
United States	290.8	37,870	77.4	8.4	14.1	*
Zambia	10.4	380	36.5	20.9	42.1	24/40

Source: World Bank, *World Development Indicators* database, 2005; UNESCO Institute for Statistics; U.S. Census Bureau, International Database

*Less than 5 percent

Glossary/Index

Glossary terms and locations are shown in bold type. Figures are shown with (fig.).

N

O

P

R

R&D. *See* Research and development (R&D)

Rationing—limiting, **89**–90, 92

Ratios
  capital-to-labor, 266
  reserve ratio, 230, 232, 243–244

Real GDP—GDP in constant dollars, 194–**195**, 257
  aggregate demand increase and, 232
  vs. real GDP per capita, 262 (fig.)

Real GDP per capita—indicates how much output the average person would receive if GDP were divided equally among the entire population, **262**

Real gross domestic product. *See* Real GDP

Real income, 50–51

Real income effect—if prices rise and a person's income stays the same, they are no longer able to buy as much as they once did, **50**

Real per capita personal income, average annual percentage growth of, 294 (fig.)

Real reserve ratio, 232

Real values, 203, 203 (fig.)

Recession—a period of little or no economic growth and widespread unemployment, **196**, 238

Reform, of banking system, 238–239

Refugees—people who flee their homeland to escape hunger, political unrest, or persecution, **321**
  from Rwanda conflict, 328

Regressive tax—a tax that requires everyone to pay the same rate, **212**

Regulate—to control, **109**

Regulation—a rule that controls or directs a business or industry in order to protect consumers or the nation as a whole, **72**
  deregulation and, 112–113
  of industry, 174

Regulatory agencies (federal), 111, 111 (fig.)

Reinvestment, business growth and, 120 (fig.)

Relative scarcity, 5–6

Remittances—payments, **334**

Renewables, tax credits and, 177

Rent control—a limit on how much a landlord can charge for an apartment, **88**–89

Representative money—money backed by a valuable item such as gold or silver, **223**

Research and development (R&D)—scientific research, product

development, innovations in production, and improvements in management, 269

Reserve banks, 239–240

Reserve ratio—the percentage a bank is required to keep on hand, **230**, 243
  Fed and, 243–244
  simple money multiplier and, 232

Reserves—a bank's holdings, which consist of deposits and currency, **143**, 230

Resources—the things people use to produce the things they want or need, **4**. *See also* Choice; specific resources
  allocation of, 17, 88
  capital, 8
  firms and, 119
  human, 8
  natural, 7–8

Retirement accounts, as M3, 229

Retirement benefits, from Social Security, 208

Revenue, governmental, 209–210, 210 (fig.)

Rights
  to private property, 170
  protection of, 171–172

Risk, finance company loans and, 144–145

Robinson-Patman Act (1936), 108

Roosevelt, Franklin D., 200

S

SADC. *See* Southern African Development Community (SADC)

Salaries, 222. *See also* Wages

Sales tax—a tax on purchases, **210**, 213 (fig.)

Sam's Club, 161

S&P 500. *See* Standard & Poor's 500

Savings—money set aside for future use, **137**, 141 (fig.), 267
  definitions of, 141

Savings account—an account at a bank on which interest is usually paid and from which withdrawals can be made, **137**
  as M2, 229

Savings and loans, 143
  as financial institutions, 136

Savings banks, 143

Scarcity—when people do not have enough resources to satisfy their needs and wants, **3**, 4–5
  resources and, 7
  value and, 5–6
  value of money and, 223

Seasonal unemployment—unemployment caused by seasonal

changes in the weather or in the demand for certain products, 284

Secondary market—a market in which existing financial assets are resold, **147**

Secondhand sales—the sales of used goods, **187**

Sector—section of the economy in which a person is employed, **154**
  inflation and, 276

Securities, government, 245

Securities and Exchange Commission (SEC, 134), 111 (fig.)

Securities exchange—a place where buyers and sellers trade securities, **147**–148

Sellers, 32
  in monopolistically competitive industry, 101
  perfect competition and, 98

Semiskilled—requires more training than unskilled work, **156**

Sen, Amartya, 324

September 11, 2001, terrorist attacks, budget response to, 217

Serrill-Robins, Mira, 201

Service industries, as economic sector, 155

Services—activities that satisfy a want or need, **7**. *See also* Firms; Goods and services
  allocating, 19–20
  businesses and, 118
  factors of production and, 31
  government purchases of, 205–208
  in market basket, 193, 193 (fig.)
  U.S. purchases from foreigners, 305–306, 305 (fig.)
  U.S. sales to foreigners, 305–306, 305 (fig.)

Sherman Antitrust Act (1890), 107, 108

Shortage—when the quantity demanded is greater than the quantity supplied, **80**
  price ceilings and, 89, 91
  rationing and, 89–90

Short run, law of variable proportions and, 67–69

Short term, elasticity of demand and, 58

Silver, money and, 223

Simple money multiplier—measures how much the money supply will increase as a result of bank loans, **232**

Singer, Isaac, 121

Skill, workers grouped by, 156–157

Skill Builder
  Analyze a Table, 315
  Averages: Mean and Median, 168, 168 (fig.)
  Categorize Information, 183
  Comparison and Contrast, 29

Acknowledgements

3 ©Photodisc Green/Getty; 4 ©Photodisc Green (Royalty Free)/Getty; 5 ©Underwood & Underwood/CORBIS; 6 ©Bob Krist/CORBIS; 7 ©Photodisc Red (Royalty Free)/Getty; 8 (t)©McGraw-Hill, (b)©Jeff Christensen/Reuters/CORBIS; 9 ©Jeff Christensen/Reuters/CORBIS; 10 ©Ed Kahi/CORBIS; 12 ©David Buffington/CORBIS; 16 ©McGraw-Hill Images; 18 ©McGraw Hill Images; 19 ©McGraw Hill Images; 20 ©Mark A. Johnson/CORBIS; 21 ©Hask Tom/CORBIS Sygma; 22 ©Bettmann/CORBIS; 23 ©Digital Vision/Getty; 25 ©CORBIS; 26 ©AP; 27 ©ARKO DATA/Reuters/CORBIS; 30 ©Bill Varie/CORBIS; 33 ©Reportage/Getty; 38 ©Charles O'Rear/CORBIS; 43 ©Wolfgang Kaehler/CORBIS; 47 ©Stone/Getty; 48 ©Gene Blevins/LA Daily News/CORBIS; 50 ©1974, The New Yorker Magazine, Inc.; 55 ©Associated Press; 58 (t)©Charles Jean Marc/CORBIS Sygma, (b)©Taxi/Getty Images; 59 ©Time Life Pictures/Getty Images; 62 ©Associated Press; 72 ©Bettmann/CORBIS; 73 ©Associated Press; 75 ©Royalty-Free/CORBIS; 78 ©Najlah Feanny/CORBIS; 80 ©Associated Press; 86 ©Associated Press; 87 ©Associated Press; 90 ©Bettmann/CORBIS; 91 ©Najlah-Feanny/CORBIS; 96 ©Associat Press; 98 ©McGraw-Hill Education Digital Image Library; 99 ©McGraw-Hill Education Digital Image Library; 101 ©AFP/Getty Images; 102 ©McGraw-H Education Digital Image Library; 103 (t)©Tom Wagner/CORBIS, (b)©Associated Press, Hereford Brand; 105 ©Associated Press; 107 ©PictureHistory; 112 ©Brian Berman/Getty Images; 116 ©Stone/Getty; 117 ©Owaki-Kulla/CORBIS; 119 ©JLP/Jose L. Pelaez/CORBIS; 122 ©Reuters/CORBIS; 123 ©Associat Press; 125 ©Taxi/Getty; 126 ©Workbook Stock/Getty; 133 ©Associated Press; 136 ©Photodisc Green/Getty; 138 ©Royalty-Free/CORBIS; 140 ©Stone/Gett Images; 143 ©Jose Luis Pelaez, Inc.; 144 ©Associated Press; 145 ©Photodisc Blue/Getty; 147 ©Reuters/CORBIS; 148 ©John Pritchett; 150 ©Reuters/CORBIS; 153 ©Royalty Free/Photodisc Green/Getty Images; 156 (tl)©Royalty Free/Digital Vision, (tr)©Royalty Free/Photodisc Green, (bl)©Photodisc Red/Getty Images, (br)©Photodisc Red/Getty Images; 159 ©Photodisc Red/Getty Images; 161 ©Photodisc Red/Getty Images; 169 ©Photodis Red/Getty Images; 171 (t)©Photodisc Green/Getty Image, (b)©Photodisc Green/Getty Images; 172 ©Photodisc Red/Getty Images; 175 (t)©Photodisc Green/Getty Images, (b)©Photodisc Red/Getty Images; 177 ©McGraw-Hill Companies; 178 ©Photodisc Red/Getty Images; 179 ©Photodisc Green/Getty Images; 181 ©Photodisc Blue/Getty Images; 184 ©Paul A. Souders/CORBIS; 185 ©AP; 188 (l)©The McGraw-Hill Companies, (b)©Brand X Pictures/Getty (r)©The McGraw-Hill Companies; 191 © Royalty-Free/CORBIS; 198 ©CORBIS; 204 ©The McGraw-Hill Companies; 208 ©The McGraw-Hill Companies; 211 ©Najlah Feanny/CORBIS; 215 ©Shaun Heasley/Reuters/CORBIS; 217 ©Najlah Feanny/CORBIS; 221 ©CORBIS; 223 (t)©The McGraw-Hill Companies, (m)©The McGraw-Hill Companies, (b)©The McGraw-Hill Companies; 224 ©Photodisc Green/Getty/RF; 225 ©Christopher Stevenson/zefa/CORBIS; 226 ©Royalty-Free/CORBIS; 228 ©AP; 232 ©James Leynse/CORBIS; 233 ©The McGraw-Hill Companies; 236 ©Joseph Sohm/ChromoSohm Inc./CORBIS; 238 ©CORBIS; 240 ©Richard Ellis/CORBIS Sygma; 247 ©Harley Schwadron/www.Cartoonstock.com; 250 ©G. Baden/zefa/CORBIS; 251 ©Brooks Kraft/CORBIS; 252 ©Najlah Feanny/CORBIS; 256 ©Photodisc Blue/RF/Getty Images; 263 (l)©L. Janicek/zefa/CORBI (r)©Todd Warshaw/POOL/Reuters/CORBIS, (b)©Photodisc Blue/Getty Images; 264 ©Paul Almasy/CORBIS; 267 ©The McGraw-Hill Companies; 268 ©Jupiter Images Corporation; 269 ©Photographer's Choice/Getty Images; 273 ©Joel Stettenheim/CORBIS; 275 ©Bettmann/CORBIS; 277 ©Rolf Bruderer; 283 ©Keving Lamarque/Reuters/CORBIS; 284 ©W. Wayne Lockwood, M.D./CORBIS; 291 (t)©AP, (b)©Charles O'Rear/CORBIS; 295 ©Michael S. Yamashita/CORBIS; 296 ©AP; 298 ©Peter Harholdt/CORBIS; 300 ©Reuters/CORBIS; 301 ©AP; 302 ©AP; 303 ©Christopher J. Morris/CORBIS; 307 ©Pitchal Frederic/CORBIS Sygma; 310 ©Getty Images; 316 ©Paul Almasy/CORBIS; 318 ©Jose Fuste Raga/CORBIS; 322 ©Peter Turnley/CORBIS; 324 (t)©Andrew Holbrooke/CORBIS, (b)©Dominique Derda/France 2/CORBIS; 326 ©Reuters/CORBIS; 328 ©AP; 329 ©AP; 333 ©Getty Images; 334 ©Karen Kasmauski/CORBIS; 339 (tl)©Haruyoshi Yamaguchi/CORBIS, (tr)©Wolfgang Kaehler/CORBIS, (bl)©CORBIS, (m)©B. Fleumer/zefa/CORBIS, (br)©H& Produktion/CORBIS; 340 ©Macduff Everton/CORBIS; 341 (t)©Ming Ming/Reuters/CORBIS, (b)©Richard Powers/CORBIS; 344 ©Michael S. Yamashita/CORBIS; 346 ©Sherwin Crasto/Reuters/CORBIS; 350 ©Steve Raymer/CORBIS; 351 ©Louise Gubb/CORBIS; 353 (t)©Joel W. Rogers/CORBIS (m)©Guang Niu/Reuters/CORBIS, (b)©Michael Gore/Frank Lane Picture Agency/CORBIS; 354 (t)©Joel W. Rogers/CORBIS,(b)©2004 AFP; 356 ©Tom Wagner/CORBIS Saba; 357 (t)©Reuters/CORBIS, (b)©William Whitehurst/CORBIS

(t) top, (b) bottom, (m) middle, (l) left, (r) righ